The European Union
and
Cyprus

Christopher Brewin

EOTHEN

Huntingdon, Cambridgeshire

British Library Cataloguing-in-Publication Data
A catalogue record for this book is available from the British
Library.

Published 2000.

Published by The Eothen Press, 10 Manor Road, Hemingford Grey,
Huntingdon, Cambs., PE28 9BX.

ISBN   0906719 31 3 hard covers
ISBN   0906719 24 0 paperback

Printed and bound in Great Britain by Biddles Ltd
www.biddles.co.uk

See P 63

Denktash terms for acceptance of

THE EUROPEAN UNION
AND
CYPRUS

a single government
by Cyprus, it means the

(c) Independent (d) non Aligned
(e) by Commonwealth (f) Federal.

A sovereign land in a single
country does even more than
this for it checks division
& sovereignty –
Fed by High level agreement between
Makarios and Denktash

To Peggy

who died while I was in Cyprus

Contents

Preface

and

Acknowledgements

The hospitality that characterises the people I have met on all sides of the Cyprus dispute has been so generous that this book is necessarily an inadequate return. I have tried to understand all points of view, and to avoid the use of apostrophes to enclose the mistaken claims of others. To the extent that I have displeased all who have helped me I am indeed sorry. Please write and tell me my errors.

My first debt is to Professor Haluk Kabaalioğlu. At a Wilton Park conference, he invited me to spend the first of what became a series of Easter vacations teaching at the European Community Institute in Marmara University. He made my wife and children feel welcome whenever they could grab time to join me, and went out of his way to help me to meet interesting policy makers and industrialists. Lecturing at Bilkent, Ankara, Istanbul and Bosphorus Universities followed. It was he who invited me to visit Cyprus for the first time to give some seminars on 'European identity', a public lecture on 'Cyprus and the

European Union' in Lefkoşa/Nicosia, and to lecture at the University of Lefke. Finally, I am grateful to him for introducing me to his aunt and his uncle, captain of the ship that took aid from Istanbul to Athens in 1945.

My second debt is to Professor Clement Dodd. He asked me to write this book after hearing me lecture in Cambridge on the importance of the Cyprus issue to good relations between the European Union and Turkey. He has been quick, helpful and patient in remedying my intellectual and grammatical errors to the enormous benefit of any readers of this book.

My next debt is to Professor Stelios Stavrides of Reading University. He asked me to speak at an international conference in Nicosia jointly organised with Professor Andreas Theophanous, at Inter-college. Thanks to the excellent arrangements made by Evi Stylianou at the request of Mr Sotiris Georgallis, I was able to learn a great deal from interviews at the Cypriot Foreign Office, the Central Bank, the Parliament, and the Delegation of the European Comm`ission. I would like to single out Ms Popi Avraam for the economy and moderation with which she answered my questions, and Mr Tassos Papadopoulos for the insights he gave me.

I owe much to the students from Cyprus, Greece and Turkey who took my courses at Keele and Marmara Universities. They taught me that the testing ground for a Europe worthy of respect will be in the Eastern Mediterranean birthplace of the people of the Book, of Islam, Christianity and classical civilisation. Let me mention only Evniki Efthymiadou, Farid Mirbagheri, and Teberrüken Ulucay, who all made me welcome on my visits to Cyprus.

My colleagues in the Department of International Relations have among them a wide range of interests in the problems of Cyprus. Professor Alan James is an expert on UN peacekeeping in Cyprus, and shares with Dr Lorna Lloyd an interest in British and Commonwealth involvement. Professor Patrick Thornberry is equally informed on the legal problems of every kind of minority, and has a particular interest in the Maronites of Cyprus. Professors Hidemi Suganami and Andrew Linklater have taken the trouble to write me long answers to my queries on the changing meaning of sovereignty and of community in international relations. Dr Bülent Gökay has been equally quick to help me with his knowledge of Turkey and Russia. Dr Iain Ogilvie organised a conference on Cyprus, which had the distinction of being weighted towards speakers from the North of the island.

Then there are the individuals. Zenon Stavrinides would brighten anyone's day with his tales and good humour on the subject of Cyprus. He invited me to talk to his Association of Greek, Turkish and Cypriot Affairs on the comparisons between Cyprus and the Franco-British quarrels satirised in Swift's *Gulliver's Travels.* He introduced me to Alper Riza, QC, who like Mr Saffet speaks Greek as well as Turkish. In Cyprus I was delighted to be able to talk to Dr Joseph Joseph at his home. It was also good to meet the man behind so much of the expatriate activity in America, Professor van Coufoudakis. Mr Ergün Olgun has been most helpful. On every occasion I have met him Mr Necati Münir Ertekün, QC, has both charmed and informed me. Tozun Bahcheli epitomises all that is wonderful about Cyprus experts, and also introduced me to Mehmet Ali Birand. Emine Uşakligil and Firdevs Robinson are two other journalists who display charm and understanding in equal measure. Erdal Camgöz's discretion and knowledge make him a delightful companion. Professors Heinz-Jürgen Axt, Barry Bartmann, and Roderick Pace have all influenced my thinking on Cyprus.

I have learnt a great deal from the contributors to several Wilton Park conferences on the EU, especially one on Cyprus. I have also benefited from seminars organised by the Foreign and Commonwealth Office. The Cyprus Embassy in London briefed me at an early stage in the book, and the Turkish Ambassador Özdem Sanberk was personally most encouraging and informative. The Chatham House Library remains a useful resource on current issues. I have to admit to one serious disappointment. When I began in 1997, Serge Abou responded to my request for access to Commission documents by asking me to wait for a year. At the end of a year, his successor was unforthcoming. His deputy, M. Philippe Combescot, did see me in the Delegation Office in Nicosia, where I also interviewed Antony Newlove.

My biggest debt over a long period is to Charmian, who has shown me unfailing encouragement and forbearance. Frances provided ideas for the cover design. For her a trip to Cyprus was all fun.

Introduction

The European Economic Communities and the Republic of Cyprus were established within two years of each other, in 1958 and 1960. Neither fitted easily into the prevailing dogma that international actors were of two kinds, either international organisations or sovereign states. The powers exercised by the EEC were always less than the attributes of a sovereign state but soon became more than those of an international organisation: the direct applicability of EEC directives, the direct elections to the European Parliament and financing of the budget through its 'own resources' are three examples of its unconventional character. The powers of the new Republic of Cyprus did not permit Cypriots themselves to alter their own Constitution without the agreement of three external Guarantor Powers, Great Britain, Greece and Turkey. Ninety-nine square miles of its geographical area were assigned as sovereign base areas to the erstwhile colonial power. In the UN age of self-determination the sovereign bases are a European anachronism perhaps analogous to the Cold War status of Berlin. The Cold War ensured American backing for European unification and for the anti-communist aspects of the Treaties of Guarantee, Alliance and Establishment with which the Cyprus Constitution was inextricably entwined.

However, the EEC and the Republic of Cyprus were established for different purposes. The Common Market was intended to integrate gradually the economies of France and Germany in order to transcend the all-encompassing nationalism enshrined in the doctrine of 'hereditary enemies' taught in the schools of Western Europe. The primary purpose of the Cypriot Constitution was to preclude strife between the two communities on the island. Its secondary purpose was to prevent a nationalist war between two NATO allies over Cyprus. To preclude the establishment of a Cuban-style Soviet base, Greece and Turkey concluded a 'Gentleman's Agreement' to sponsor Cypriot membership of NATO and to urge Cyprus to outlaw the communist party, AKEL, and related trade unions (James, 1998: 13).

The end of the Cold War brought the dismantling of the Berlin wall in 1989 and the reunification of Germany in 1990. To reassure Germany's many neighbours that its economic dominance did not mean a return to a nationalist agenda, Chancellor Kohl agreed with President Mitterand to embed German reunification in the big pan-European project of uniting all Eastern and Central Europe for the first time with Western Europe. The German Government went against its own public opinion in subsuming the German Deutschmark in the new Euro currency. The Member States in the Treaty of Maastricht laid out a timetable for integrating most of their national currencies in a Monetary Union. They also agreed that Political Union should be established on the inter-governmental basis acceptable to the British Government of Mr John Major. The European Community became one of three 'pillars' of the new European Union. A second pillar on foreign and security policy envisaged a possible common policy on defence to compensate for the withdrawal of most American troops and missiles from Europe. A third pillar was intended to improve police co-operation, not least to control immigration from Eastern Europe and the Southern Mediterranean.

Over the next decade all three pillars were closely involved in the EU's big millennial project of enlargement to the East. Faced with the communal, ethnic, and religious divisions in the Balkans, the powerful and secure states of Western Europe and Scandinavia had to face the wholly new question of whether they were willing to risk the lives of their own nationals in conflicts which did not immediately put their own national security at risk. In 1958 multicultural, internal, and human rights' questions had not been issues for those drafting the Treaty of Rome for the EEC6; in 1997 the EU15 had to include them all in the Treaty of Amsterdam as they prepared for enlargement to Central and Eastern Europe.

On 4 July 1990, the wholly Greek Cypriot Government of the Republic of Cyprus applied for full membership of the European Communities. The purpose was not, in the short run, to unify the island. It had been partitioned by force between its two main communities for three decades. After 1964 the Turkish Cypriots had been concentrated in enclaves covering 3.84 per cent of the island, and with the intervention of the Turkish army in 1974 had then taken control of the Northern third of the island. The Greek Cypriot President, Georgios Vassiliou, had several times resisted Greek Prime Minister Andreas Papandreou's pressure to follow Greece into the EU on the grounds that this would make a UN-brokered settlement with the Turkish Cypriots more difficult (Zervakis in Axt, 1997: 142). The purpose was rather to add the rising power of the EU to the declining UN in negating the threat posed by the Turkish army in Cyprus to Greek Cypriot rule through internationalisation of the problem. The European Member States might have been expected to welcome this application more than they did for three very different reasons.

Firstly, a year after the end of the Berlin wall and of the division of Germany, the end of the 'Green Line' dividing Cyprus and its capital city, Nicosia, would have been another step towards a 'frontier-free' Europe. The inner-Cypriot frontier is in two ways more impenetrable than the inner-German frontier. No legal trade in goods can cross the Cypriot demarcation line. Also, the Cypriots on each side of the Dead Zone are more self-consciously different from each other than the East and West Germans. After a quarter of a century of mutual fear and hostility, only 343 Turkish Cypriots now live in the South and only 486 Greek Cypriots and 187 Maronites in the North (Kyle, 1997: 34). Turkish and Greek Cypriots speak different languages and do not learn in their schools the language of the other community. They affirm allegiance to different flags, religions, histories and motherlands.

However, the EU External Relations Commissioner, Hans van den Broek, knew that his rhetoric lacked substance when he claimed on 2 December 1997 that 'Barbed wire and barricades have no place in a united Europe'. His speech was delivered to an audience of Turkish Cypriots at the UN Headquarters in the Ledra Palace Hotel, right on the frontier line. He knew that within two weeks the Luxembourg Council would confirm Turkey's exclusion from the EU enlargement process. By then it was inevitable that the Turkish Cypriots with Turkish support would in response intensify their restrictive measures at the Ledra Palace checkpoint. So far from removing the frontier, the involvement of the EU in Cyprus had the immediate and predictable effect of reinforcing the alienation of the Turkish Cypriots.

A second reason for welcoming the Cypriot application that might have been expected to have greater support than was the case, relates to balancing Eastern enlargement with a Southern enlargement. Support for greater institutionalisation of EU relations with Mediterranean countries from France, Italy and Spain ought logically to translate into support for Greek sponsorship of the 1990 application alongside what became the Barcelona process of 1995.

A third reason whose absence needs to be explained is the applicability of what is now called the 'Community method' to the resolution of dangerous disputes of the kind exemplified by Cyprus. The Community method has long been understood as the unique approach to making law in the economic and social spheres whereby the Commission has the sole right of initiative, and the Council of Member States has the power of decision. However, Jean Monnet in his Memoirs devotes a chapter to describing the origin of this method in solving the dispute over the Upper Silesian coalfield in 1921. As in Cyprus, this was a dispute between two communities in a territory of comparable size. Poland was prepared to go to war in support of its Polish miners, and Germany similarly in support of its German mineowners and engineers, each of them convinced that their economic security required that the coalfield should be included within their national borders. Poland was supported by France and Germany by Britain. As the League of Nations' mediator, Monnet decided to avoid contact with the diplomats of each motherland. He did not look for a settlement from the leaders of the hostile communities. Instead, he used experts to draw up a treaty longer than that of Versailles, providing for a territorial demarcation line based on a plebiscite while enabling Polish labourers and German engineers to cross it for everyday economic purposes as though it were not there. A Court presided by an outsider was also provided. Both Poland and Germany decided to accept the treaty, albeit with extreme reluctance, and Upper Silesia disappeared from European history books until after 1939 when the coalfield was first purged of Poles by the German army and then purged of Germans by the returning Poles. It is not difficult to see the same approach in Monnet's advocacy of the European Coal and Steel Community and in M. Jacques Delors' Single Market programme. In both cases, political frontiers are accepted and then made not to matter in achieving prosperity and peace through economic integration. In institutional terms, neutral experts make proposals that are more than the lowest common denominator of national interest, and decisions are made by representatives of national states without requiring validation by an elected Parliament or common Government. What is surprising is that this method is no longer regarded as of practical use in settling international and communitarian disputes. Upper Silesia is not mentioned in the European Union's brochures in Cyprus. Neither the Council nor the Commission showed any interest in appointing a mediator either directly or through the United Nations.

Instead, the rhetoric of successive European summits expresses the contrast between the leading states' commitment to Eastern and Central Europe and their lack of interest in adding the divided island of Cyprus to the enlargement process. The Heads of State and Government at Essen in 1994 spoke of enlargement to the East as a 'moral obligation'; at Madrid in 1995 it was a 'historic opportunity'; at Berlin in 1999 it was a 'historic priority'. On Cyprus, the leaders at Corfu during the Greek Presidency in 1993 'noted' that the next phase of enlargement will include Cyprus and Malta, a decision 'confirmed' under the French Presidency at Cannes in June 1995. The Commission took three years to deliver its Opinion on Cyprus, longer than it had taken over Turkey, and then recommended that the Council delay its decision for a further eighteen months to await the outcome of intercommunal talks. The Parliament invited the leaders of Eastern Europe to address it, notably in 1994, the Czech

President, Mr Vaclav Havel. It did not invite Mr Glafcos Clerides, the President of wholly Greek Cypriot Republic of Cyprus or Mr Rauf Denktaş, the equally durable leader of the Turkish Cypriots who since 1983 has been recognised by Turkey as the President of the Turkish Republic of Northern Cyprus.

This self-distancing of West European governments and institutions from taking on the Cyprus problem has a long history since 1960. In this post-imperial age, the doctrine of national interest has been interpreted as precluding putting one's own nationals at risk for the sake of others unless there is an immediate and clear danger to defined interests. For example, the British had been prepared to put 40,000 troops into Cyprus before 1960 to retain it as a colony. After 1960 they continued to maintain the air bases at Akrotiri and Dhekelia and their listening posts in the Troodos mountains as useful to the Western Alliance during the Cold War. However, their military plans now focused on withdrawing their nationals in the event of armed conflict, not on military intervention or counter-intervention to maintain the 1960 Constitution.

After 1989, this longstanding European desire to leave Cyprus as a peripheral problem area to be solved by its local communities under the aegis of the United Nations was strengthened by the collapse of the Cold War framework of international relations. Three different kinds of clashes threatened to replace the ideological divide in which the USA and USSR had each maintained order within its own bloc. One was the return to nationalist rivalries. Another was the cultural clash between Western and Eastern Europe conceived as a 'civilisation' opposed on the one hand to Islam and on the other to the Slavic Orthodox civilisation of the Russian Federation, Serbia and Greece. The third, and most difficult, was the clash within states between communities of different allegiance. All three types of conflict came to a head in Yugoslavia. The European Union countries had not provided unconditional financial aid on the scale of the Marshall Plan to help governments in transition, nor earmarked troops to deter local bully-boys. Only gradually and half-heartedly did the EU come to accept that a Europe worthy of the name meant a collective responsibility for intervention to prevent individuals being killed, or expelled for being of the wrong religion or allegiance. As all three clashes have long been present in Cyprus, and could be either exacerbated or eased by the actions of the EU, it is worth saying a little more on each by way of introduction to the problems to be analysed in this book.

Clash of nations

The Member States of the EU have no wish to get involved in war between Greece and Turkey. Western Europe and Scandinavia regard themselves as security communities, no longer characterised by any expectation of wars between neighbours. In the Eastern Mediterranean, however, every nation has reason to prepare for war against one or more neighbours. After a long period of co-existence after 1923, the Cypriot dispute brought Greece and Turkey close to war in 1963, 1964, 1967 and 1974. It is an open question whether the Cypriot thorn has poisoned Graeco-Turkish relations since the beginning of the Greek campaign for union with Cyprus in 1954, or is just one among many derivatives of an underlying 'natural' enmity. In 1987 to the mutual provocation of fighter aircraft disputing the extent of sovereignty in the Aegean was added a military confrontation over rights to prospect for oil in the seabed. Professor Huntington has articulated the view that 'with the disappearance of the Soviet threat, the "unnatural alliance" between Greece and Turkey becomes essentially meaningless' (Huntington, 1996: 126). After 1989 Greece and Turkey were the only NATO countries to increase their expenditure on arms. The non-aligned Republic of Cyprus also modernised its defences, linking itself with Greece in the united Defence Doctrine enunciated in 1993.

During the negotiations for the Maastricht treaty, the other EU Member States resisted Greek demands to define the boundaries of Europe, effectively categorising Turkey as an Asian, Islamic country rather than a secular European Associate Member on the way to full membership. In the parallel talks on aligning membership of the European Union with membership of the Western European Union, the other Member States could not logically resist the Greek demand to become a full member of the Western European Union. Greece made WEU membership the condition of its signature of the Maastricht treaty. In response, the other Member States reasserted their refusal to commit themselves to a war with Turkey. Their Article V commitment to mutual assistance in the event of war was redrafted to exclude the contingency of war between signatories. Turkey as an Associate Member was a signatory. When the Greek and Turkish fleets sailed against each other in January 1996 over the sovereignty of the rocky islet of Imia/Kardak, the Europeans showed little solidarity with Greece. President Clinton intervened to prevent war 'while Europe slept' (Catsiapis, 1996: 156). In the treaty of Amsterdam, there are new expressions of solidarity but not the military commitment for which Greece pressed. However the explicit reference to solidarity could henceforth be invoked to impose sanctions on Turkey. If Cyprus were a member, the economic or political integration of Northern Cyprus with Turkey would constitute a change of frontiers without the consent of the Member State concerned.

The concern to prevent all changes in European frontiers had become an important aspect of the European Union's policy after 1989. Resurgent nationalism had brought the end of the USSR, Czechoslovakia and reduced the territory of Yugoslavia. It had opened up the possibility of other irredentist claims in Central Europe. The unmentionable sub-text in Western Europe was an anxiety to inhibit German nationalist agitation for the return of Silesia and Prussia; Kant's Königsberg remained in the Russian Federation under its post-war name of Kaliningrad. Respect for existing frontiers was one of the conditions applied in 'Europe Agreements' for trade with the EU, aid from the EU, or negotiations with a view to membership. Stability Pacts, supervised by the Organisation for Security and Co-operation in Europe, and Association Agreements with Balkan countries, had similar intentions. However, the EU also showed itself ready to recognise frontier changes in two kinds of situation, both relevant to Cyprus. The 'velvet divorce' of the Czech and Slovak Republics was acceptable because it met the criterion of consent. The new ethnically based statelets like Republika Serbska were recognised more deniably as the only possible basis of order between warring communities. This recognition was not explicit, ostensibly maintaining the fiction of overarching Bosnian frontiers and a right of return for individuals under international protection.

Clash of civilisations

A second explanation of why most member states did not want to take up the Cypriot application can best be expressed by the reception accorded to Professor Huntington's 1993 article and 1996 book setting out his thesis that the ideological confrontation of the Cold War would be followed by a variant of the earlier divisions between the civilisations of Western Christendom, Eastern Orthodoxy and Islam. The phrase 'clash of civilisations' appears frequently in speeches by Turkish and Greek foreign ministers. The thesis was attacked by Commission President Romano Prodi in his first speech to the European Parliament in September 1999, and also in a 1999 book by Dr Roman Herzog, the German President and constitutional jurist, who took responsibility in 2000 for drafting the EU 'Charter of Fundamental Freedoms'.

Huntington argued that Muslim states are the most serious threat to Western civilisation. They are prone to become involved in 'fault-line' wars, an expressive image implying that the dividing lines between civilisations are as dangerous and natural as the grinding together of geological plates. Cyprus and Bosnia illustrate how 'at the local level fault-line wars, largely between Muslims and non-Muslims, generate 'kin-country rallying', the threat of broader escalation, and hence efforts by core states to halt these wars (Huntington, 1996: 27). However, he also argued that 'Greece is not part of Western civilisation, ...an anomaly, the Orthodox outsider in Western organisations' (Huntington, 1996: 162-3). Thus Greece and Greek Cyprus identified with Serbia and Russia in the Balkans even though, 'unlike Serbs, Roumanians or Bulgarians, their history has been intimately entwined with that of the West' (ibid).

This cultural thesis goes to the heart of the European identity question. The leaders of European Christian Democrat parties in March 1997 had to retract a statement agreed by them all that the European Union is based on Christian civilisation. The statement implied that atheists and the thirteen million Muslims within the EU15 could only be second-class citizens. Outraged Liberals and socialists have their own code for recognisably similar cultural prejudice. They insist that new applicants for membership have to demonstrate a good record on human rights. The virtue of accepting Iberians and Greeks as members was that they were thereby seriously helped to get away from their fascist pasts. European identity is not like German and Italian identity where a cultural identity justified the creation of nation-states. Like a Kantian League, it is justified if it better preserves the liberty of the citizens of willing constituent republics linked by geography. The unforeseen benefit of Huntington's thesis was that it brought a reaction defending the right of the modernising national states of Turkey and Greece to EU membership as equals of the pluralist successor states of Western Christendom and Communism. For example, in March 1996, the Greek Foreign Minister, Mr Theodoros Pangalos responded to the Christian Democrat statement by defending the right of Turkey to be as much a part of European history as Greece.

Clash of communities
The third reason for European reluctance to engage with the Cyprus problem is the most obvious. It is a conflict between communities within the internationally recognised borders of one state:

> In coping with identity crisis, what counts for people are blood and belief, faith and family. People rally to those with similar ancestry, religion, language, values and institutions and distance themselves from those with different ones... Identity issues are, of course, particularly intense in cleft countries that have sizable groups of people from different civilisations (Huntington, 1996: 126).

As in Kosovo, the Cypriot communities each have deeply held grievances, have elected belligerent leaders with access to arms, and are happier to rely on strong external support from their motherlands rather than to seek reconciliation with the other community. The Turkish Cypriots are very afraid of the Greek Cypriot majority on the island. The Greek Cypriots are very afraid of the Turkish army in the North and of Turkish power in the region. Athens is 500 miles distant while the Turkish coast is only forty miles north of the Karpas peninsula.

In terms of power politics, the Cypriot dispute is astonishingly clear-cut. Before 1974 the Greek Cypriot majority on the island used its greater power to oppress the Turkish Cypriots:

> Throughout the 1963-74 period there seemed to have been a feeling on the Greek Cypriot side that it was for the Greek side to dictate terms and that eventually the Turkish Cypriot Community would be forced by its own self-segregation and the economic deprivation that entailed to come to the negotiating table. This was a monumental mistake of basic policy (Polyviou, 1975: 53).

After 1974 the intervention of the Turkish army put the Turkish Cypriots in the more powerful position. They did not take the whole island, as the Turkish Deputy Prime Minister, Mr Necmettin Erbakan, suggested. However they took full control of the most prosperous third of the island. The Greek Cypriots who 'fled' were not allowed to return to their properties.

In terms of law, the Cyprus dispute raises immensely complicated questions of recognition. Wholesale loss of rights has become established fact. The European states, as influential members of the United Nations General Assembly and Security Council and as members of the European Union, have hesitantly taken the Greek Cypriot side in terms of constitutional law, international law (including war crimes), European Union law and European law on human rights. Despite the EU commitment to substitute the rule of law for power politics, the EU Court of Justice is not equipped to adjudicate any of these matters. Reference to the International Court of Justice in the Hague requires the consent of the parties. This is impossible because non-recognition of any separate status with respect to Turkish Cyprus is as important a weapon to the Greek Cypriots as the continued presence of the Turkish army is for the Turkish Cypriots. For each community, justice means recognition by the international community of the moral and legal rightness of their own side, to be discussed in Chapters 4 and 5.

Looking at the problems caused by clashing communities from a Brussels perspective, what has first to be noticed is the historic oddity of the success with which the European Community has avoided involvement in internal and external disputes of this nature. Minority problems, abuses of human rights, external involvement by states on behalf of kith and kin communities were, between the wars, the stuff of European history. Yet the insecure institutions of the EEC managed to interpret the doctrine of sovereignty as precluding their involvement in the internal difficulties of member states. Where communitarian differences, as in Ulster, the Basque country, Gibraltar or Wallonia, were the issue within or between member states, this inhibition was effective.

Despite this bias against seeing disputes between communities as an EC concern, the growth in Western Europe of institutional recognition of human and also group rights is clearly visible well before the spurt induced by the end of the Cold War. It took decades for the Community to turn from being a community of merchants to being one of human rights, but the Court, Parliament and the Council have all now adopted the language of multiculturalism which has been written into the Treaty of Amsterdam. Now that sovereign states no longer have to confront a serious external threat to their very existence, the freedom of historic communities within and across their borders is much easier to acknowledge. In 1957 only the ten länder of defeated Germany and four of the regions of defeated Italy had serious pretensions to sub-state autonomy. Today what was the exception has become the norm. In eight states of the EU15, seventy-four autonomous regions have emerged. Fifteen Italian regions have an ordinary statute of autonomy and one has a special statute. In Belgium, the rights of three autonomous regions to differing representation in the Councils of the EU are recognised. There are twenty-five German and Austrian länder. Iberia has seventeen autonomous regions and three cultural communities. The Danish Faroe islands have a special status, and Greenland since 1985 has enjoyed a loose associated status since it withdrew from the Community while remaining in Denmark after a referendum in 1982. Finland added the Åland islanders, with special privileges of relevance to Cyprus in resisting the Community principles of freedom of movement and of capital, and in continuing to sell duty-free liquor on their cruise ships. The UK has granted political devolution to Scotland and Ulster, and cultural privileges to a Welsh

Assembly, while the Channel Islands and the Isle of Man are somehow part of Her Majesty's dominions but not part of the United Kingdom. In addition, the Committee of the Regions established in the EU by the treaty of Maastricht includes all regions, autonomous or not. European political culture has changed from modernity, understood as characterised by sovereign states with rights for all individuals to a postmodernism more protective of culturally different groups. It remains, however, an open question whether this American multicultural discourse depends on the recognition of a common external boundary and the presence of police sufficiently respected by all communities to be deployed throughout the territory. The European discourse of historic allegiance to a flag in defending a particular territory is not finished in Cyprus. The Turkish Cypriot leadership is more impressed by the advent in the UN context of forty-five sovereign states with under a million citizens. This reinforces in their view the viability of their claim for self-determination either as the Turkish Republic of Northern Cyprus, or as a canton exercising some sovereign rights jointly with Greek Cypriots within a confederation.

Since 1989, the European Union has specifically included the need to protect the rights of minorities as a condition of aid. The Copenhagen Council of 1993 set out the criteria of market and political pluralism by which the acceptability of candidates for the enlargement process are to be judged. The same criteria were applied by the Badinter Commission's report on recognition of new states in the former Yugoslavia. By Article 13 of the Treaty of Amsterdam the EU commits itself to 'combat discrimination based on ...racial or ethnic origin, religion or belief'. The Commission was given the power to propose to the Council the suspension of a member state in serious and persistent breach of the 'principles of liberty, democracy, respect for human rights and fundamental freedoms, and the rule of law'. Other European organisations bang the same drum. The 1990 Copenhagen document of the OSCE demands protection of minorities 'from any attempts at assimilation against their will'. The Council of Europe also supports the rights of communities to resist assimilation. Its 1995 Convention for the Protection of National Minorities asks signatory states to refrain from 'practices aimed at assimilation of persons belonging to national minorities against their will' and, with retrospective relevance to Cyprus, 'measures which alter the proportions of the population in areas belonging to national minorities'. In 1995 the fall of Srbrenica when under the protection of a Dutch force of EU peacekeepers made most European leaders uncomfortable. If a city in which eighty per cent of the population were Muslims could be transformed into a city without Muslims, then the universal condemnation of Hitler's ethnic practices was no better than empty rhetoric. It is true that European governments and peoples still prefer not to get involved. However, in comparison with European indifference to the fate of the Turkish Cypriot population between 1963 and 1974, and the Greek Cypriot population after 1974, there was a marked increase in the number and influence of those who thought inaction wrong.

The 1995 compromise
Despite the reluctance shown by most member states to take on the application from the divided island of Cyprus, in March 1995 the French Presidency carefully constructed a diplomatic compromise which set a date for beginning negotiations six months after the end of an inter-governmental conference itself scheduled to begin in March 1996. This did not mean that the interlinked problems that Cyprus would present had diminished. The decision to add Cyprus to the enlargement process was mainly taken on two pragmatic grounds. The first was the conviction that enlargement to 100 million Central and Eastern Europeans would be compromised if it were linked with the simultaneous accession of 60 million Turks. In order to compensate Turkey for this rebuff, the final stage of the Customs Union with Turkey had to surmount the obstacle of a Greek veto imposed in December 1994. The price for Greece lifting its veto was the setting of a date for opening negotiations with the wholly Greek Cypriot Government of Cyprus without requiring a prior settlement of its dispute with the Turkish Cypriots. The second pragmatic ground was also related to making a success of the unification of Eastern with Western Europe. The Greek Government and Parliament would not agree to any treaty enlarging the EU15 unless Cyprus was included in the process.

The contemporary story of the European Union's relations with Cyprus is therefore pegged on this historic compromise of 6 March 1995, the subject of the first chapter. Establishing the contested significance of this agreement raises the question of when and why the two principal communities in Cyprus came to take diametrically different positions on the political and economic merits of the 1990 application. Chapter 2 therefore moves back over the previous decades of EEC relations with Cyprus, long before there was any suggestion that Cyprus had a European vocation. Chapter 3 goes forward from 1995 to describe how the process of accession was largely separate from, and inimical to, a settlement of the communal dispute so long as Greece and Turkey remained at odds. Chapters 4 and 5 examine the relations of each Community with its motherland in terms of concerting their policy towards the European Union. Chapter 6 examines the EU role in Cyprus in its relations with what, since Bosnia, have been known as the Internationals, namely the Americans, the United Nations, the Non-Aligned Countries, NATO, the Council of Europe, and latterly, the G8 group of the richest industrialised countries. The Commonwealth's support of the Greek Cypriot side and the Organisation of Islamic Countries' tepid support of the Turkish side are discussed. The OSCE Secretariat has the distinction of avoiding involvement in the Cyprus question. Finally, the concluding chapter assesses the implications of EU involvement in Cypriot accession and dispute settlement for the articulation of an enlarged European sense of identity, a greater institutional acceptance of responsibility, and for the political and economic integration of Europe.

| 1 |

The Turning Point
March 1995

'The Council of Ministers...reaffirms the suitability of Cyprus for accession to the European Union and confirms the European Union's will to incorporate Cyprus in the next stage of its development.' Conclusions of the EU Council of Ministers (6 March 1995).

Introduction

On 6 March 1995 the French Presidency secured a package deal (*compromis global*) which transformed the prospects of Cypriot accession to the European Union. The General Affairs Council of Foreign Ministers committed itself to open negotiations with the Republic of Cyprus within six months of the end of the upcoming intergovernmental conference on reforming the EU institutions in preparation for enlargement to Central and Eastern Europe. It was a turning point because the Council dropped the condition that the division of the island be ended before accession negotiations could begin.

At their Essen summit in December 1994, the elected leaders of the EU Member States had repeated the call for a settlement of the Cyprus problem that would respect 'the territorial integrity and unity of the country, in accordance with the relevant UN resolutions and high-level agreements'. This formula was also used at the Corfu summit under the Greek Presidency in June 1994, which is sometimes hailed as 'the first time the question of Cyprus' accession had not been linked to a resolution of the Cyprus problem' (Nugent, 1997: 64). The Corfu Conclusions also referred to similar Council decisions of 18 April 1994 and 4 October 1993. Moreover, following the Council's acceptance on 17 October 1993 of the Commission's Opinions on the 1990 applications from Cyprus and Malta, successive European Councils had 'noted' their applications without giving any commitment, or setting a definite date. At Essen the European Council had gone a little further, noting that the next stage of the enlargement process would involve Cyprus and Malta. However, the accompanying instruction to the General Affairs Council to consider in January 1995 the Commission's reports on the progress of the negotiations between the communities implied that progress was expected before Cypriot accession could be contemplated. Finally, it is significant that the wording refers to Cyprus, not to the Republic of Cyprus. The French Presidency had threatened, and would again threaten, to substitute the words 'Federation of Cyprus', which would have restored the precondition of a prior settlement. Instead the communiqué contents itself with hoping for a settlement, and instructing the Commission to inform the Turkish Cypriots, in consultation with the Government of Cyprus, of the advantages of EU membership.

In return, the Government of Greece agreed to lift its veto on implementing the final stage of the Customs Union with Turkey at a meeting of the EEC-Turkey Association Council to be held on the same day. This was the essence of the package deal adroitly put together by the French Presidency in the aftermath of the imposition of the Greek veto the previous December. It was to prove a brittle compromise. Several member states remained reluctant to take on the problems of a divided island in the absence of a settlement between the Cypriots themselves. Neither Greece nor Turkey would publicly accept that the deal constituted a package. Greece did not want improved relations with a Turkey which it regarded as in military occupation of part of a Hellenic island. Turkey was as adamant that the Greek Cypriot Government had no right to negotiate accession on behalf of the whole island.

A stable relationship with Turkey

For the French Presidency, the larger member states, and the Commission, the point of the compromise was to establish a long-term stable relationship with Turkey. This aim was, however, qualified by adding that a new deal should be proportional to the needs of both sides. The EU wanted Turkey onside but not as a member. Turkey, it thought, was not ready to take on the requirements of full membership for some considerable time. Tributes to the importance of Turkey are a constant feature of the communiqués of the European Council. The term encapsulates the ambiguity of EU attitudes.

On the one hand Turkey is Europe's second European country in terms of population. Turkish construction and catering workers are to be found in every large city in Western Europe and the Russian Federation. To Western diplomats, Turkey's close relations with the USA and Israel reflect its geo-strategic position in the Balkans, the Caucasus, Central Asia, and the Middle East. By 1995, the so-called Quint states of Germany, France, the UK, Italy and Spain had taken upon themselves the task in European Political Co-operation of working for good relations with Turkey (Peterson & Bomberg, 1999: 237). Militarily, Turkey's army is second in size only to that of France, and has become battle-hardened by circulating all units through the mountains of south-east Turkey during a long civil war with the Marxist Kurdish guerrillas of the PKK. Moreover Turkey is the only NATO member with alternative alliance options, whether with Russia or with Iran and other Islamic states. To industrialists, Turkey's large economy has consistently shown that growth is compatible with inflation. To tourists, Turkey is second only to Italy in the number and quality of its classical and Christian artifacts, and has more beaches. Turkey has been serious about EU membership since 1984. Since that date it has moved from import substitution managed by state and family holding companies to opening itself to international competition. Turkey also contrasts itself favourably with the former communist states of Central and Eastern Europe in that it has had pluralist political parties since 1945. It has been an Associate Member of the EEC since the Treaty of Ankara came into force in December 1964.

On the other hand, the General Affairs Council had agreed with the Commission's 1987 Opinion, indefinitely postponing the opening of an accession process with Turkey despite recognising that Turkey was eligible for eventual membership. At a time when the Delors Commission was pushing for the addition of the single currency project to its single market programme, Turkey was generally considered too big, too poor, and too inflationary. The same factors decided the German-led EU after the end of the Cold War that to take on Turkey would be so costly as to put at risk the enlargement to Central and Eastern Europe. In terms of civilisation, Christian Democrat leaders are suspicious of Turkey as an Islamic country. After they met on 15 March 1997, Mr Wilfrid Martens claimed that 'The EU is in the process of building a civilisation in which Turkey has no place' (Nugent, 1997: 62). Socialist and liberal leaders are suspicious of Turkey's military establishment and police methods. The popular cultural prejudice against Turkish workers in all European countries led to the European Community's decision not to honour Article 12 of the 1963 Treaty of Ankara, by which freedom of movement for labour was supposed to be established by 1986. From a more nationalist perspective, Greek hostility to its larger neighbour has been strong since the Cyprus issue became salient in 1955, and Athens has pursued a policy of non-appeasement since the Turkish army took over Northern Cyprus in 1974 and allowed the Turkish Cypriots to rule it. Their thesis that the presence of a large number of Turkish troops in Northern Cyprus, said to be about 30,000 (Dodd, ed.1999: 208), is an affront to the sovereignty of small states has been generally supported by the smaller European states.

Completing the Customs Union in industrial and processed agricultural goods seemed to the larger states enough to keep on board this large and important European country. It would assuage American pressures to reinforce Turkey's pro-Western orientation at a time when the USA was winding down its Cold War military aid programme. It would remove Turkish tariffs against European goods and lower the tariff against American goods to European levels. It would end the dubious trading practice of imposing a quota on imports of Turkish textiles. It would fulfil the commitment under the

Additional Protocol of 1970 that the final stage of the Customs Union would be completed by December 1995, twenty two years after it came into effect in 1973. In June 1990 the package of measures drawn up at the request of the Council by Commissioner Matutes to further co-operation with Turkey included completion of the Customs Union by the end of 1995. All the member states had agreed to this timetable at a meeting of the EEC-Turkey Association Council of 9 November 1992 (see below).

Mrs Tansu Çiller's diplomatic calculation
In 1994 Mrs Çiller's government made a hard-headed diplomatic calculation. Greece and the Greek Parliament would not be alone among member states in rejecting a renewed Turkish application for membership. The European Parliament would also refuse the assent which is required under the terms of the Treaty of Maastricht. On the other hand, the completion of the Customs Union could be presented as a further step in Turkey's westernisation and acceptance as a major European state. In internal politics a success was needed against the advocates of a more Islamic policy that was winning support in the cities, and against those nationalists who wanted Turkey to adopt a more independent stance between Islam and the West. The removal of tariff protection would consolidate the late President Turgut Özal's more open economic policy and the adoption of Value Added Tax in 1993. It would remove the quota on Turkish textiles, important now that Turkey was replacing Hong Kong as the top exporter to the European Union. It might, as with Iberian and Greek EU membership, bring in foreign direct investment. The Government could expect the EU to make a contribution to compensate for the loss of tariff revenue to the state. It hoped for some of the $1.2bn it calculated had been blocked over twenty years (Middlemas,1995: 659). Moreover, to Mrs Çiller personally the economic aspect of the Customs Union was sufficient in that as a former professor of economics in an American university, she was more committed to westernisation than Europeanisation. She was to demonstrate her ignorance of the EU by suggesting that France make a bilateral trade deal with Turkey. Again in a speech to foreign ministers at the 1996 Dublin summit promoting Turkey's

case for EU membership, she trumpeted Turkey's NATO credentials without assuaging the distrust felt by some EU foreign ministers with respect to Turkey's military policies.

The Greek veto on the Customs Union
On 19 December 1994 Greece refused to agree to the final stage of the Customs Union to be put before an Association Council with Turkey. As all member states have to agree beforehand to what are called common positions to be put by the Presidency to Associate countries, the effect was to impose a veto. This was expected in that all Greek governments, backed by Greek public opinion and the Greek Members of the European Parliament, have been implacably hostile to appeasing Turkey so long as it remains in military occupation of Northern Cyprus and refuses to acknowledge Greek rights of jurisdiction in the Aegean. Since Greece became a member in 1980, it has prevented the distribution of funds legally due to Turkey under the Fourth Financial Protocol agreed as far back as 30 June 1980 with Turkey. Greece opposed payments under the Mediterranean Development Assistance (MEDA) programme on the ground that Turkey is an Asian country. However, the legal basis of its opposition to the Customs Union with Turkey had been weakened by what appears to have been a tacit deal reached in 1992 (Ugur, 1996: 21). In this instance Greece withdrew its opposition to the package of measures drawn up by Commissioner Matutes to fulfil the promise of 'increased interdependence and integration' made on 18 December 1989 in the Commission's Opinion postponing Turkey's membership. The Matutes package included the completion of the final stage of the Customs Union. This Greek concession was part of its campaign to prevent EU recognition of the Former Yugoslav Republic of Macedonia (FYROM). The unilateral Greek embargo on trade with the Former Yugoslav Republic of Macedonia had caused the Commission to cite Greece before the European Court of Justice for breach of the Common Commercial Policy. As a small country, Greece has to focus its attention on one issue for any realistic chance of success in the Council. This temporary re-focusing on Macedonia accounts for the Greek concession on the future Customs Union, which in any case was unlikely to surmount

the hurdle of assent from the European Parliament. In return, the other member states allowed Greece to maintain its veto on the 600m ecu due to Turkey under the Fourth Financial Protocol.

The diplomacy of the French Presidency
Nevertheless, the Member States accepted that the tacit deal of 1992 and the timetable set out in the Additional Protocol of 1970 did not bind Greece to accept the common position for completing the Customs Union with Turkey at the Association Council meeting planned for 19 December 1994. The incoming French President of the EU General Affairs Council of Foreign Ministers, M. Alain Juppé therefore laid contingency plans in expectation of the Greek veto. On the same day, he announced that after France took the Presidency in January, he would call simultaneous meetings on the following 5-6 March of a General Affairs Council and the thirty-sixth meeting of the Association Council with Turkey (Council of the EU, 1995a: 424). At the beginning of February 1995 a meeting took place in London of the foreign ministers of France, Germany, the United Kingdom, Italy and Turkey. Whether Cyprus was discussed is unclear, but the Greek Government protested to other member states that discussion of the Customs Union should not take place outside the Community framework (Pace, 1995: 9). Another meeting was held in Brussels between the Cypriot Foreign Minister and officials of the Commission to discuss the French plan to set a definite date for opening accession negotiations.

The Greek price for lifting its veto on the Customs Union with Turkey was that a date for beginning negotiations on membership should be offered to the Government of Cyprus. Although this would no more be a commitment to admit Cyprus than it would for any other applicant, it did imply negotiations in good faith to that end. It was frequently reaffirmed that the opening of negotiations might be a catalyst for a settlement of the Cyprus problem. The Greeks claimed that waiting for a settlement gave a veto on accession to Mr Denktaş.

The Commission in its 1993 Opinion on Cyprus had prepared the way for dropping this long-standing requirement of a prior settlement of the dispute by suggesting reconsideration in January

1995 in the light of progress, or lack of it, at that time. Its author, M. Serge Abou, recommended to the Council in January 1995:

> Now, more than ever before, the EU must actively support the UN Secretary-General's efforts. It must also spell out its intentions regarding Cyprus's accession, as required by the Council decision of October 1993 (Dodd, 1998: 180).

At this juncture, Mr Richard Holbrooke, fresh from his success in bringing the Bosnian protagonists to agree terms in Ohio, was widely expected to become President Clinton's representative on Cyprus.

On 6 February, the General Affairs Council discussed draft conclusions 'on the reconsideration of Cyprus' application for membership'. A copy found its way, via the UK mission to the United Nations in New York, to the Turkish mission in New York, who forwarded it to the Turkish Cypriots in Lefkoşa. At the meeting the ministers agreed, subject to the agreement of their governments, to accept the Greek demand for a definite date for the beginning of negotiations with Cyprus, even in the absence of a prior political settlement. It was to begin six months after the conclusion of the intergovernmental conference on adapting the EU institutions for enlargement, which itself was to begin at the end of March 1996. The foreign ministers rejected a Belgian and German proposal to defer negotiations until after the completion of the ratification process of what was to become the Treaty of Amsterdam. After the bad experience of delays and near-failure in ratifying the Maastricht treaty, this suggestion indicated German reluctance to accept the French package.

On 9 February 1995, Athens demanded further amendments (Necatigil, 1995: 28). The Greek Government wanted the definite phrase, 'will start' instead of the ambiguous 'can begin'. It wanted Cyprus to be put on a par with the candidate countries from Central and Eastern Europe by establishing a 'structured dialogue' with the EU. The others agreed to both changes. However, the Member States refused to give an explicit assurance that negotiations would not be linked to a solution of the 'Cyprus problem'. The Greeks had to be satisfied with the omission of what had hitherto always been explicitly stated as a precondition. The text hoped for the establishment of 'civil peace and reconciliation' under UN auspices. On the subject of the Customs Union with Turkey, a side payment of 400 mecu ($500m) was demanded in compensation to Greek textile interests; this demand was met although it does not appear in the formal conclusions. However, the Greeks did not obtain two further demands. One was that no specific figure be offered to the Turkish Government in compensation for its loss of tariff revenue. The second was that Turkey drop its legal objection to Cyprus joining the EU without first resolving its dispute with the Turkish Cypriots (*Agence Europe*, 1995: nos 6419-6420, 13-15 February). Germany and Greece obtained the agreement of the other member states that the troika of foreign ministers of past, present and future presidencies, accompanied by Commissioner Hans van den Broek, should take a stronger line in Ankara on the issue of human rights in south-east Turkey.

The package deal

This compromise enabled the Presidency to go ahead with the two meetings it had planned for 6 March. One was an internal EU General Affairs Council from which the passage cited above is taken. The language of 'reaffirmation' did not conceal from the parties the significance of setting the date for opening negotiations or of removing the requirement that there first be a government whose jurisdiction was recognised throughout the territory it claimed. The other was the Association Council of the EU15 with Turkey at which, subject to the assent of the European Parliament, the Customs Union with Turkey would be fully realised by 1 January 1996. At the working dinner held that night, the foreign ministers of France, Germany and Italy were unanimous on the relative significance of the two meetings. To Alain Juppé, Klaus Kinkel and Douglas Hurd, agreeing the final stage of the Customs Union with Turkey settled the general political framework of EU-Turkey relations. In their speeches this was the historically significant event. It was *'aussi un moment historique'* for Cyprus. The linkage was as clearly expressed in the rhetoric of the foreign ministers of the larger states as it had been in the negotiations. What mattered to them was that Greece would help establish a stable relationship with Turkey, and that Turkey would use its influence on the Turkish Cypriot leadership to secure the settlement on Cyprus that the EU ministers and other 'internationals' hoped would follow. However, immediately the governments of the two states principally involved at the regional level, Turkey and Greece, set out why in their view there was no *'compromis global''*. Turkey had negotiated for the finalisation of the Customs Union; Greece had negotiated a timetable for beginning talks with Cyprus. That was it.

Turkish denials

The Turkish Foreign Minister, Mr Murat Karayalçın, at that same dinner of 6 March, chose not to adopt the self-congratulatory tone appropriate to historic achievements. He attacked the inclusion of Cyprus without a prior settlement. He insisted that the Turkish objective remained full membership. His carefully phrased statement was designed to be made public to counter the powerful objections in Turkey and Northern Cyprus that a dishonourable deal had been struck.

Murat Karayalçın was well aware that the Turkish Cypriot leadership felt betrayed by the Turkish Government's decision to interpret the Turkish national interest as requiring the completion of the Customs Union in the full knowledge that on the same day the same EU ministers were agreeing to add Cyprus to the first wave of the EU enlargement process. From a legal perspective, the Turkish Government could insist that they had not been present at the General Affairs Council which that day had agreed to set a definite date for negotiations by the wholly Greek Cypriot government of Cyprus on behalf of the whole island. Politically, the Turkish Government could hope that Turkish Cypriot dependence would ensure a measure of silence. However, they also had reason to fear that Mr Denktaş might use his standing with mainland opinion to denounce this mistake on Turkish television. The Turkish Foreign Minister therefore reiterated his Government's full support for the Turkish Cypriot position that the Greek Cypriot Government was not entitled to make an application on behalf of the whole island before there was a settlement, and that no Cypriot government, even after a settlement, was entitled in international law to make an application to join any organisation of which both Turkey and Greece were not already members. So far from promising to work for a smooth settlement or accession process, he made it clear that Turkey would not confine itself to merely verbal protests. He repeated Turkey's threat that the integration of Greek Cyprus with the EU would be matched by integration of Turkish Cyprus with Turkey. He did not support the task delegated to the Commission of persuading the Turkish Cypriots of the economic benefits of reunification within the EU framework.

Murat Karayalçın was also well aware that many Turks on the mainland, pro-European as well as anti-European, criticised the acceptance of the Customs Union as a mistake. Turkish pride was at stake in several distinct aspects. Those who wanted full membership and those who did not were at one in finding it hard to swallow that Greek Cyprus was acceptable to the European Union when Turkey was not. Without exception, Turks regarded the Greek veto as another unjustifiable action that should not have been taken seriously by the European Union. Legally, as the final stage of the Customs Union was being completed in accordance with a timetable agreed in 1970, the Turks argued that it did not require either the assent of the hostile European Parliament or the pursuit of a unanimous 'prior position' in the Association Council. Morally, the Turks did not regard themselves as being in the wrong over Cyprus in implementing their right as a Guarantor to protecting their own interests and the rights of Turkish Cypriots. They did not accept any obligation to compromise with Greek demands over the Aegean or over Cyprus. Therefore the Foreign Minister reiterated that Turkey would continue to seek full membership. Turkey did not accept that the Customs Union was a sufficient framework for a satisfactory long-term relationship.

Greek denials
The Turkish statement prompted Mr Georgios Mangakis, the Deputy Foreign Minister of Greece, to write to M. Juppé on the evening of 6 March with a demand for an extraordinary meeting of the General Affairs Council. In his view, the Turkish threat to counter the

accession of Cyprus undermined the deal and should be countered by suspending the decision to proceed to the final stage of the Customs Union. M. Juppé refused the next day to unravel what had been achieved with such difficulty. He told Mr Mangakis that Turkey, as a third country, was not bound by internal EU decisions. Therefore Mr Karayalçın's statement did not alter the internal agreements reached by the EU15 on the timetable for Cypriot accession.

This was not the end of the matter. The Greeks and Greek Cypriots at the next EEC-Cyprus Association Council in June wanted the communiqué to state that there was 'no junction' between the agreements made on 6 March. Moreover the Greeks did not accept the French Presidency thesis that the basis of the compromise was that negotiations with Greek Cyprus had been agreed in return for getting relations with Turkey on a more stable and friendly basis. The Greek Cypriots interpreted Mrs Çiller's gesture of allowing a Turkish basketball team to compete in the Republic without travelling via the TRNC as a sign of weakness rather than goodwill. The Greek Government did not, and probably could not, persuade its Members of the European Parliament to vote for the Customs Union at the end of 1995. It did not lift its veto on payments due to Turkey from the Mediterranean funds or under the Fourth Financial Protocol. By 30 January 1996, tension between the Simitis government newly installed in Greece and the unpopular Çiller government in Turkey had reached the point that both fleets were ordered to sail against each other in the dispute over the uninhabited islet of Imia/Kardak.

Thus the French view that Greece was bound by this global compromise to end its hostile stance towards Turkey, and in particular to work with Turkey to create a Cypriot Federation, was not shared by Greece. In short, the package deal was not a package deal in the eyes of either Greece or Turkey, the regional actors most directly concerned.

European Union doubts

The reservations of other member states of the European Union can also be detected in the diplomacy leading up to the 6 March package and in the lack of publicity accorded to it. On several subsequent occasions, in public as well as in diplomatic exchanges, the argument would be made that what had been agreed was a package; therefore the continued Greek refusal to improve relations with Turkey absolved member states from any obligation to promote the accession of Cyprus.

One reservation is implicit in the use of the word 'Cyprus' in the communiqué of 6 March, cited above. This was no casual avoidance of the usual designation of the Republic of Cyprus, preferred by the Government side and therefore regularly enclosed within apostrophes by the Turkish side. The designation of 'Cyprus' left open the possibility of arguing that the EU was committed not to opening negotiations with the now wholly Greek Cypriot Government of the Republic of Cyprus, but with a future 'Federation of Cyprus'. This interpretation would have fitted well with the international community's public position that it wanted a 'bizonal, bicommunal Cyprus in accordance with the relevant UN Resolutions'. As far back as 1977 the High-level Agreements between Makarios and Denktaş had specified the aim of both communities in their talks as being the creation of a federal state in Cyprus. This designation would completely undermine what was being sought by Greece on behalf of the Republic of Cyprus, namely the promise of accession without prior agreement on a federation. In June, the French Presidency again used this weapon as a debating point. The Greek demand for a statement that there was 'no junction' between the two agreements disappeared off the table when the French countered with the suggestion that 'Cyprus' be clarified to be the 'Federation of Cyprus'. The architect of the 6 March compromise, French Foreign Minister, Alain Juppé, spelled out the French view that the Community decision was intended to lead to a federation. The accession of the Republic of Cyprus was intended to promote reconciliation. Its justification was an increase in the security and prosperity of both communities. On 6 March 1995 he wrote to Mr Mangakis:

> Ces résolutions prévoient la création d'une Fédération bizonale et bicommunautaire, permettant à tous les Chypriotes de vivre dans la paix, la concorde, et l'attachement à leur commune patrie. C'est

dans cette perspective que l'Union place clairement leur démarche, quand elle déclare que l'adhésion de la République de Chypre devrait concourir à la paix civile et à la réconciliation, consolider la prospérité et la sécurité de chacune des deux communautés de l'île.

The more important reservation is that if the Greeks did not accept that the accession of Cyprus was part of a package to secure good relations with Turkey, then the states which had agreed to Cypriot accession as part of a package were no longer bound to take on the problems of a divided island. We shall see in Chapter 3 that over the next five years French ministers Hervé de Charette and Pierre Muscovici in particular were willing to make this point in public. The near-war over Imia/Kardak in January 1996 led to acrimonious private exchanges between Greece and the larger member states. The public expression of this internal dispute lay in the absence of firm public support from the foreign ministers for the stance of a fellow member. The reticence of the foreign ministers in the framework of European Political Co-operation is the more pointed in that the Greek Government was able to substantiate the legality of its claim by producing a December 1932 supplementary appendix to the 1923 Treaty of Lausanne, which mentioned the islet by name. Unlike the European Parliament, which on 15 February robustly identified the frontiers of Greece as the frontiers of Europe, the Council of Foreign Ministers adopted a tepid, equidistant and non-interventionist stance (Catsiapis, 1996:157). The British and German Governments obstructed the Greek proposal to refer the case for decision by the International Court at The Hague. President Chirac reportedly told President Simitis that the accord of 6 March 1995 was '*un tout indissociable*' (*Le Monde,* 24/25 February 1996). If Greek actions paralysed European relations with Turkey, then this could be expected to compromise the accession of Cyprus. On 26 February 1996, the Council made a statement of concern to the Parliament. The British Government had successfully prevented the statement from being given the status of a declaration. At the Florence summit of 21-22 June the European Council of Heads of State invited the Turkish Prime Minister, Mr Mesut Yılmaz, to join them at their dinner. The European Council, 'recalling the decisions of 6 March

1995, stresses the priority it attaches to strengthening and deepening of relations with Turkey'. Romano Prodi and Jacques Chirac publicly criticised the Greek veto on payment of 365m ecu due to Turkey under the MEDA programme. The Greek veto was lifted after a further compromise by which the EU on 15 July took a stronger position on Imia/Kardak. The seriousness of this internal row may account for the absence of any stress on the historic significance of the 6 March accords in the Council's annual report on its work in 1995, published in 1996.

Meanwhile, the Member States had bound themselves to begin negotiations. It was still possible for the Commission, the European Parliament, the Parliament or the government of any member state to turn the Greek argument that opening negotiations would be a catalyst for a settlement into a reason for refusing Cypriot accession until there was a settlement. What had been in March 1995 a serious expectation that collaboration between Western Europe, the Clinton Administration and the UN Secretary-General would bring reconciliation between the two communities and their respective motherlands became increasingly unlikely as the course of enlargement negotiations drove Turkey and Turkish Cypriots into increasing alienation from the European Union. France, Italy, Belgium and Germany in particular over the next four years were not averse to pointing out the dangers for the EU itself of attempting to implement EU law in a territory where the Government's jurisdiction had been successfully contested for so long. In short, the EU was not bound to bring the negotiations to a successful conclusion.

In Chapter 3, the sequel to the European Union's commitment to include Cyprus will be described. But first it is important to sketch out the previous history of the relations between Cyprus and the European Communities. This is as essential to understanding the hostility of the Turkish Cypriot community to accession as it is to understanding the political enthusiasm of the Government side for a process which would prove costly to sectoral economic interests.

| 2 |

Association and Even-handedness before 1995

At the beginning of this period, the other organisations of the Cold War period: the Non-Aligned Movement and NATO, the United Nations General Assembly and Security Council were politically much more important than the EEC to the bi-communal Republic of Cyprus. By the end of this period, the wholly Greek Cypriot Government was stressing its European vocation, seeking full membership of the European Union. The origins of Greek Cypriot enthusiasm and Turkish Cypriot indifference lie in the attempt, and then the progressive failure, of the Member States to balance their recognition of the legitimacy of the Government with a policy of even-handedness towards the Turkish Cypriot community. As well as trying to understand the changing political relationship between the EU and the two sides on Cyprus, this chapter seeks as a secondary objective to examine the conflicting legal claims stemming from the Association Agreement of 1972 and the Government's application for membership in 1990.

The 1963 EEC offer of Membership or Association to the Republic of Cyprus

In the Treaty of Rome, it is easier for the Community to establish an Association with a third state, a union of states or an international organisation than to admit a new member. Article 237 restricts membership to European states. They must apply to the Council, which can only act after receiving an Opinion from the Commission. The terms of membership must be submitted for ratification by all the Contracting States in accordance with their respective constitutional requirements. Article 238 by contrast allows agreements establishing an Association to be 'concluded by the Council acting unanimously after consulting the Assembly'. The Council could negotiate any content it chose for an Association agreement with an international organisation, a union of states or an individual country. The status was probably designed to accommodate the UK, which had refused to join either the Coal and Steel Community or the European Economic Community.

As early as 1959, the Cypriot issue was important to the first two applications for Association. The EEC6 seems to have been more romantic in its attitude to applications from other European states than is conceivable today. In June, Greece, the 'fountain of democracy', became the first country to apply to become an individual Associate. Greece was followed six weeks later by Turkey, 'bastion of the West'. This sequence reflected Greek-Turkish rivalry, with Turkey determined not to be outdone by its Aegean neighbour. Greece had joined NATO in 1951 and Turkey in 1952; Greece became an Associate of the EEC in 1961, Turkey in 1963; Greece became a member of the EU in 1980 while Turkey became seriously interested in applying for membership after 1984 (Ozülker, 1999). For present purposes, however, it is also relevant that after a Turkish initiative in the margins of the UN General Assembly in September 1958, the two foreign ministers, Mr Rüştü Fatin Zorlu and Mr Evangelos Averoff met in February 1959 to draw up the outlines of the future Cypriot Constitution (James, 199: 13). If Zorlu and Averoff had not brought about a transformation in the previously hostile relations between their two countries by removing the 'poison thorn' of Cyprus, it is unlikely that the EEC would have entertained their applications in the summer of 1959.

The fact that both Greece and Turkey had applications pending for Associate status had some importance in July 1961 when Mr Harold Macmillan submitted Britain's application to become a member of the EEC. One minor consequence of this application was that Cypriot exports to the UK and Ireland became an item in the 1962 negotiations. Under GATT rules, the phasing out of British Commonwealth preference entitled the Republic of Cyprus to demand compensation for any foreseeable consequent loss of historic trading privileges. Moreover, despite initial British reluctance, Cyprus had by then become a member of the Commonwealth. The British Government had committed itself to negotiate the best possible deal on behalf of each of the Commonwealth countries. The Brussels' negotiators were able to offer Cyprus a choice between full membership or Associate status. (Droutsas in Axt, 1997: 102 cites Greek sources mentioning only association.) This was possible because Greece and Turkey were simultaneously negotiating their own Association. Three Articles of the 1960 Constitution of Cyprus might otherwise have been invoked to preclude this offer. As they have since become so contentious as part of the Turkish and Turkish Cypriot case against the 1990 accession application, it is worth setting out here why they were not a problem in 1961.

Article 50 of the Cypriot Constitution gives the Greek Cypriot President and the Turkish Cypriot Vice-President a right of separate veto over any act or decision by the Cypriot House of Representatives in foreign affairs. However neither the President nor the Vice-President could prevent 'the participation of the Republic in international organisations and pacts of alliance in which the Kingdom of Greece and the Republic of Turkey both participate'. At a meeting in London on 12 February 1959, the British Foreign Secretary had specifically asked whether it was intended to preclude Cypriot membership of organisations such as a European Free Trade Area. Both principal negotiators made it clear to the British Foreign Secretary 'that there would be no objection to Cypriot membership of international associations of which both Greece and Turkey were members' (Mendelson, 1997: 39). As the EEC in 1961 was on course to give both motherlands Associate status in what now seems a singularly unconcerned spirit, Article 50 was not a problem. It has also to be said that the Turkish Vice-President did not use his veto to prevent President Makarios joining the Non-Aligned Movement and attending the Belgrade Conference in September 1961 (Kyrris, 1996: 379). This must have been on the advice of the philhellene Turkish ambassador, Mr Emin Nirvana. Also Mr Fazıl Küçük, the Turkish Cypriot Vice-President, accepted Cypriot membership of the British Commonwealth, of which again neither Greece nor Turkey were members.

Article 170 of the Constitution requires the Republic of Cyprus to accord Greece, Turkey and the UK most-favoured-nation treatment in trade. The intention of this article was to prevent an economic union between Cyprus and Greece. As both Greece and Turkey were then negotiating the stages of their own customs unions with the EEC, this article was not contentious. Article 170 was one aspect of the general prohibition against union with Greece set out in Article 1(2) of the Treaty of Guarantee by which the Republic of Cyprus undertook 'not to participate, in whole or in part, in any political or economic union with any State whatsoever'. Nobody in 1961 seems to have thought that membership of the EEC implied that Eire was rejoining the UK, or Denmark joining West Germany. The EEC was not a state. In any case, the negotiations in 1961 did not progress far enough for anyone to contend that either Cypriot membership or Association implied union with Greece or Turkey.

Full membership was not seen as a problem for Cyprus. Its population of 600,000 was similar to that of Luxembourg. Cypriot sovereignty had been accepted by the United Nations even though its Constitution was so bound up by the international treaties of Guarantee, Alliance and Establishment that there were reasons for doubting whether it could be constitutionally self-determining. Cypriot non-alignment was of no more concern to the EEC than Irish neutrality. Cypriot trade was small. It was complementary to that of the EEC6 at a time when no member state produced early potatoes or sherry. From the Cypriot perspective, the EC6 ranked as their most important trading partner after the United Kingdom (Redmond, 1997: 91).

The Republic applied for full membership in 1962 (Bıçak, 1997:

245). The Turkish Government was well disposed to Cypriot EEC membership. Turkey and the bi-communal Republic of Cyprus signed a Trade Agreement on 9 November 1963 which made specific provision for Cypriot membership of a 'Customs Union, free trade area or an economic community' (Crawford et al, 1997: 14). It would appear that no objection was raised by the Turkish Cypriot Vice-President. This has some polemical importance in that the Turkish Republic of Northern Cyprus, supported by Turkey, now claims that Article 50 of the Constitution cited above, implementing Article 8 of the Basic Structure agreed at Zurich, precludes Cypriot accession until Turkey as well as Greece becomes a full EU member. The absence of objection by Mr Küçük does not settle this polemic. By Article 179 a veto has to be cast within fifteen days of a vote by the House of Representatives. The negotiations never reached this decisive stage. Cypriot interest in the EEC evaporated when de Gaulle pronounced that the United Kingdom had insufficient European orientation. The Cypriot negotiation itself was not motivated by any European vocation. Cypriot concerns went no further than the protection of historic commercial privileges in the British and Irish markets.

The Association of 1972/3
The second British application in 1967 was accompanied by an initiative from Malta, independent since 1964, which led in 1970 to the negotiating and signing of an EEC-Malta Association Agreement which envisaged embarking on a Customs Union in 1980 (Pace, 1995: 5). Cyprus did not follow suit. In August 1970, the UK application was successful at the third time of asking. It again included an assumption of responsibility to sponsor negotiations on behalf of countries losing their Commonwealth trade preferences. President Makarios chose to distance himself from Europe. He opted for an Associate status which did not include membership even as a possible objective. Within Cyprus, this choice enabled him to assuage opposition to the EEC from the Communist party, AKEL. Externally, he was better able to preserve his considerable standing in the Non-Aligned Movement. In March 1971 the now wholly Greek Cypriot Government appointed Mr Titos Phanos as its

Ambassador and Head of Mission to Brussels. The Commission President and Council Presidency accepted his credentials. The fact that the Commission did not reciprocate by establishing a Delegation in Nicosia has no diplomatic significance. Thirty years ago the Commission had little external representation outside the Community.

As the proposed EEC-Cypriot institutions were limited entirely to trade matters, the EEC side chose not to question the right of the UN-recognised Greek/Cypriot Government of Cyprus to sign the Agreement. Both communities were consulted during the negotiations (Necatigil, 1995: 25). In 1972 human rights were still the exclusive preserve of the Council of Europe's Commission and Court of Human Rights in Strasbourg. The EEC as a community of merchants did not object to accepting as an Associate a country where communal strife had for eight years necessitated the presence of 6,000 UN troops. After UK accession, the revised Treaty of Rome specified in Article 227 that the European territories of member states did not include the ninety-nine square miles under British sovereignty in Cyprus.

Negotiations for an Association Agreement between the Cypriot Mission in Brussels and the European Communities were begun, according to Cypriot sources, in March 1971, and took twenty-one months to complete (Cyprus, 1998: 1). According to the Commission, the process began in January 1972 and wound up on 6 December (*EC Bulletin,* 12/1972: 92). It was signed on 19 December 1972. It was adopted at the General Affairs Council of foreign ministers on 14 May. Regulations 1246-1253/73 were published in the Official Journal of 21 May 1973 (OJL: 133/73). They came into force on 1 June 1973. The Agreement, Protocol, eight regulations, and an exchange of correspondence amount to 117 closely written pages of the Official Journal. In contrast to the Association Agreements with Greece and Turkey, the Cypriot Agreement followed the model of the 1971 Agreement with Malta in not envisaging membership even if all went well.

The armed self-governing Administration of the Turkish Cypriot enclaves objected to the conclusion of the Agreement (Crawford, Haffner, Pellet, 1997: 7). Before 1974, the Turkish Cypriot enclaves excluded Government officials from 3.86 per cent of the island's territory. The EEC disregarded the objections on the ground that the matter was internal to Cyprus. Turkey did not suggest that Association for Cyprus would breach Article 1 Paragraph 2 of the Treaty of Guarantee. Turkey's concern about possible discrimination against the Turkish Cypriots was met by the inclusion of Article 5:

> The rules governing trade between the contracting parties may not give rise to any discrimination between the member states or between nationals or companies of these states *or nationals and companies of Cyprus.* (my italics)

This convoluted clause is unique to the Association Agreement with Cyprus. There is no such clause in the Association Agreement with Malta of 14 March 1971 (OJL: 61/71). It might be interpreted as a reassertion of the EEC principle of non-discrimination on grounds of nationality, directed against any privileges arising from the UK's historic role on the island. However, the reference to nationals and companies of Cyprus only makes sense as acknowledging the separation of the Greek Cypriot and Turkish Cypriot economies on the island, a gap which had been widening since 1964. There would have been no need for this unusual clause if the nationals of Cyprus had been perceived as individual citizens. The wording seems therefore to recognise the obligation not to favour Greek Cypriots.This clause is the origin of the EEC's assumption of a duty to be even-handed in dealings between the two communities. How to interpret this obligation became a contested practical matter after the events of August 1974. The treaty obligation not to discriminate between the nationals of Cyprus provided the Commission with a way of resisting the Government's categorisation of the entire Turkish Cypriot community as secessionist rebels. It was important in deciding to whom aid should be distributed. It complicated decisions on whether to accept imports of products from land in all areas of Cyprus whose ownership was legally questionable. It provided a justification for accepting products from Northern Cyprus until set aside in 1994 by a ruling of the EU Court of Justice.

Remarkably, no other reference is made to a dispute which in

1964 and 1967 had nearly caused war between Greece and Turkey. To meet the GATT rules exempting customs unions from the normal rules of trade between sovereign states, there was provision for an Association Council to show that this was indeed a Customs Union in the making. It comprised ministers from Cyprus and members of the European Commission and Council. It was to meet at least once a year, acting by consensus so that both sides had a veto. Both the EEC and Cyprus were entitled to restrict trade unilaterally, merely informing the Association Council. However the trigger for such unilateral action was specified in Article 10 as 'serious disturbances' in an economic sector or in the balance of payments. Political disturbances whether inside the island or as a result of outside intervention were not mentioned. Article 11 repeated the provision in the Treaty of Rome that allows member states unilaterally to break the treaty in an emergency. Breaches have to be justified on 'grounds of public morality, public policy, public security, the protection of health and life of humans, animals or plants, the protection of national treasures possessing artistic, historic or archaeological value, or the protection of industrial or commercial property.' Emergency rules are void if they discriminate on grounds of nationality or constitute a disguised restriction on trade.

This apolitical stance is underlined by the absence of detail on the membership of a joint parliamentary delegation. The only reference to the possibility of a joint parliamentary delegation is in a declaration annexed to the final act (OJL133/73: 85):

> The Contracting Parties agree to take all appropriate measures in order to facilitate co-operation and contacts between the European Parliament and the House of Representatives of the Republic of Cyprus.

The origin of the problem was that since December 1963 the Cypriot House of Representatives had ceased to meet the entrenched bi-communal requirements of the 1960 Constitution. The Constitution provides that 15 of the 50 members must be elected by a separate voting register of Turkish Cypriots. These members had not taken their seats since the outbreak of intercommunal violence which had followed President Makarios' thirteen proposed amendments to the Constitution. The Turkish Cypriots refused to return to the Parliament on the Greek Cypriot conditions that they accept the amendments passed in their absence and that they agree to a new electoral law abolishing separate Greek and Turkish Cypriot electoral rolls. Despite the urging of Turkey's President, İsmet İnönü, the three Turkish Cypriot ministers in the ten-man Executive, and all Turkish Cypriot officials in al: government departments (where the same ratio of 70:30 governed the allocation of posts) did not return to their offices. The Government argued that, out of necessity, Greek Cypriots had taken over all the paid jobs deserted by Turkish Cypriots.

This was treated as a matter internal to Cyprus by all European governments, the USA, the USSR, and the organs of the United Nations. However, the members of European Parliaments meeting in the Council of Europe Parliamentary Assembly, and the majority of ministers meeting in the Council of Europe Ministerial Council, after 1964 refused to accept the credentials of the Cypriot delegation because it included no Turkish Cypriots. The EEC Assembly resembled the Council of Europe in that its members were not then directly elected but chosen from the Parliaments of the Member States. European parliamentarians, while generally more hostile to Turkey than the European governments, were more sympathetic to the Turkish Cypriot case on this one issue of the rights of members of Parliament excluded by force. It was not until 4 July 1973, one month after the Cypriot Association came into force, that the European Parliament put forward its proposals for a Joint Delegation of the two Parliaments to meet twice a year, alternately in Brussels and Nicosia. It nominated fourteen members, to be drawn from its committee on external economic relations, a significant choice indicating its perception of the limited scope of the Agreement. The European Parliament followed the lead of the Assembly of the Council of Europe by asking for the inclusion of two elected Turkish Cypriots in the seven-member Cypriot delegation. The same proportions were suggested for the list of alternates. As no delegation could be brought together on this formula, the Joint Delegation of the Cypriot and European Parliaments remained a dead letter until 1992. Moreover, to judge from the few and short general debates on enlargement to the EEC9, the mostly 'Northern' members of the EEC Parliament in 1972 had little interest in Cyprus. They were preoccupied with future relations with the rival group of EFTA (European Free Trade Area) countries now bereft of the UK and Denmark. They were also interested in the joint arrangements involving the Parliament in the Lomé Agreement with the former colonies of the ACP (African, Caribbean and Pacific), where for idealistic reasons the Community liked to emphasise its egalitarian institutional philosophy.

Practical arrangements

Association with Cyprus was a practical, not to say bureaucratic, arrangement. Fifteen pages of the Official Journal were devoted to the design and use of two forms of movement certificate specific to Cyprus:

> Each certificate shall measure 210 x 297mm. The paper used must be white sized writing paper not containing mechanical pulp and weighing not less than $64g/m^2$ or between 25 and 30 g/m^2 if airmail paper is used.

The Agreement envisaged a Customs Union in two stages. The general idea was that EU tariffs would be gradually abolished on Cypriot exports. This would preclude any claim under GATT rules for any other compensation for the loss of Commonwealth preference (ROC, 1982: 6). The EEC committed itself only to the first four-year phase, to 30 June 1977. Negotiations on the second stage were scheduled to begin in January 1976. If the Association Council did not agree to the terms of this second 4-5 year phase before 1978, the first phase would continue on a rollover basis. For the first five years the UK and Ireland could continue to apply their preferential import regime to early potatoes fruit and vegetables. Community producers were carefully protected. Cypriot citrus exports were not to compete by price (Regulation 1252/73). The import regime for sherry could end in December 1975. Exporters from the EC6 to Britain and Ireland were entitled to a subsidy under

Regulation 1253/73 for 'wine products produced in the Community as originally constituted which are similar to the wine product exported under the label of "Cyprus sherry"'. The 183,600 hectolitres of Cypriot sherry allowed into the UK without charge, and the 1,400 hectolitres allowed into Ireland, could not be re-exported to other member states. Temperate agricultural products were excluded from the agreement so that Northern farm interests could not be harmed.

The specific concessions to Cyprus were not generous, and circumscribed by very detailed descriptions of the items to which rules of origin applied. The reduction of 40 per cent in the Common Commercial Tariff on Cypriot hesperids—lemons, limes, oranges and grapefruit—put Cyprus on a par with Israel and Spain. Greece at this time benefited from a reduction of 100 per cent while for the Maghreb countries of what used to be French North Africa it was 80 per cent. Carob bean was the only product on which the levy was removed altogether. As the Carob tree is commercially exploited in Crete and Spain, both still outside the Community, the full EEC levy on this product was only 10 per cent. On industrial products, the tariff reduction of 70 per cent was combined with a quota limiting imports into the Community of outer garments and man-made fibres, the only sectors in which a non-industrialised Cyprus was competitive. Petroleum products were not eligible lest Cyprus develop its own refineries. Finally, the Community refused a Cypriot request for inclusion in the negotiations defining the EEC's global approach to Mediterranean countries. The point was that although the global Mediterranean policy was intended to rationalise the Community's successive agreements with particular countries, impending negotiations with Israel, the Maghreb and other citrus exporters could be expected to affect the competitive position of Cypriot producers. Instead the EEC promised to consult with Cyprus, and take the interests of Cyprus into consideration (OJL133/73: 86).

For its part, Cyprus reduced its tariff by 15 per cent at once on 43 named agricultural products. After three years there was supposed to be a further reduction of 25 per cent, to be followed two years later by one of 35 per cent. Industrial tariffs were abolished, although

Cyprus retained the right to keep quotas and tariffs on fifteen categories of what it defined as products sensitive to its own manufacturers, and on petroleum imports. The Cypriot government reserved the right to delay reductions in order to protect its balance of payments. Mr Vassiliou, the future President of Cyprus and then chief negotiator in the accession talks, calculated at the time that the average marginal preference of EEC exporters over third parties at the end of the third stage was only 5 per cent, whereas the average preference for Cypriot exporters in EEC markets amounted to an even less stimulating 1.6 per cent (Shlaim & Yannopoulos, 1976: 213). On these figures, the balance of commercial advantage lay with EC exporters.

European Political Co-operation and the 1974 crisis

> Foreign policy has always been one of the most difficult areas in which to cooperate. It raises immediately, and most visibly, issues of national sovereignty (E.Regelsberger in Axt and Brey, eds, 1997: 20).

The Cyprus crisis of 1974 demonstrated the weakness of the EEC in dealing with a military crisis within the Western European geographical area. Since the 1969 Hague Summit, the European states had talked of co-operation in foreign policy. However, the procedures for consultation elaborated in 1970 by Commissioner Etienne Davignon avoided any suggestion of a common secretariat like the Commission to articulate a European interest. During the 1973 oil crisis the EEC states could not maintain a common reaction to the Arab embargo on the Netherlands, to the OPEC demands or to Secretary of State Henry Kissinger's counter-organisation of consumer states in the International Oil Agency. The EEC governments published a long document on 'the European Identity' on 14 December 1973, 'determined to defend the principles of representative democracy, of the rule of law, of social justice...and of respect for human rights'. In March 1974 they created an 'urgent consultation mechanism' for use in crises. It built on the secure communication network, COREU, through which the foreign ministries of the EEC express their solidarity by informing each other of all separate dealings with third countries. The question whether this Community of Information would lead to a Community of View and then of Action was tested in July 1974 when Greek officers led the Greek Cypriot National Guard in deposing President Makarios.

The Commission and member states began well enough. The Commission held up food aid to the value of 945,000 EUA (equivalent to the same number of U.S. dollars) to signal disapproval of the Greek Cypriot coup (Tsardanidis, 1988: 150). On 16 July, four days before the first Turkish landing, they instructed the French Presidency to make known their opposition to any intervention that might bring into question the independence and territorial integrity of Cyprus. This did not prevent the landing of Turkish troops on 20 July, but may well have been an important aspect of the diplomatic pressure which induced Turkey to agree to an early cease-fire on 22 July in accordance with UN Security Council Resolution 353. Having met fierce resistance in Kyrenia/Girne, the Turks had by then only established a very narrow corridor to Nicosia. Moreover, the cease-fire left their salient in Famagusta/Mağusa exposed. That same day the French Presidency persuaded all the EEC ambassadors in Paris to back the British effort to get the parties to negotiate.

The British position as the leading European state on Cyprus was not in doubt. The British were a Guarantor Power. It was through British bases in Cyprus and Malta that Archbishop Makarios had made his escape to London. It was the British Foreign Secretary, Mr James Callaghan, who called the meeting in Geneva of all three Guarantor Powers which agreed that the Greek Cypriots should evacuate the Turkish Cypriot enclaves, that the Turkish occupation zone should not be extended, and that the leaders of the two Cypriot administrations should be brought to Geneva for a conference in August to be chaired by Mr Callaghan. However, the British were determined not to take action on their own. To them international involvement meant an American initiative. On 9 August the British Foreign Secretary at dinner stressed to Mr Clerides, the leader of the Greek Cypriot delegation at Geneva, that 'Britain was no longer a superpower, that it could not afford another Suez and that, therefore, no "dynamic" action on the part of the United Kingdom could be contemplated otherwise than in the context of either the U.N. or a general American initiative' (Polyviou, 1976: 328).

At no point during the Geneva Conference did Mr Callaghan contemplate that there might be a 'dynamic' European initiative. Like Mr Harold Wilson, the other European leaders, Willy Brandt, Georges Pompidou, Mario Andreotti and Garret Fitzgerald did not regard themselves as bound by the Declaration of European Identity to mount a counter-intervention to protect human rights or the rule of law in Cyprus. The European understanding of national interest at this time precluded military action unless the lives of nationals were at stake. In 1967 the EEC had suspended the Association Agreement with Greece to show collective disapproval of the Junta; and Sweden and the Netherlands had referred cases on behalf of Greek nationals to the Commission of Human Rights. However, no European state, or group of European states, had contemplated military action against Greece to restore democracy and protect human rights. That this was well understood by all parties at the Geneva Conference is shown by the fact that the only reference to the EC9 recorded by the Greek Cypriot side came from the Turkish Foreign Minister, Mr Turan Güneş. In arguing against adjourning the Conference on 12 August he said the Turkish proposals 'had been communicated to many countries, the Community of Nine, the countries of NATO, etc.' (Polyviou, 1976: 363). Mr Clerides, who spoke next, ignored this solitary mention of the Community as irrelevant. He 'first expressed surprise that Mr Güneş had discussed his plan with so many countries; but how could this be relevant?'

On 14 August Turkey risked international isolation by landing more troops accompanied by 200 tanks. By 16 August the Turks controlled 37 per cent of the island. They halted to the north of a line they had proposed ten years earlier to the UN mediator, Galo Plaza. The army claimed military justification for moving inland from the exposed coastal enclaves established at the initial landings. It could have been worse. Mr Erbakan, then the Turkish Deputy Prime Minister, wanted Turkey to take over the whole island and then negotiate from a position of military strength.

This raises the question whether the UK and other European states, presumably in liaison with the USA, would have intervened militarily if Turkey had gone this far. Their initial political sympathy for Turkish intervention under the Treaty of Guarantee had quickly evaporated as Turkey had clearly decided not to limit itself to the restoration of the safeguards provided by the Constitution. If it is true that the British came close to war with Turkey for partitioning the island, then the total subjugation of the Greek Cypriot population might well have provoked a counter-intervention. From a military perspective, if they could have intervened to prevent the take-over of the whole island, they could have done it to prevent the take-over of one third of its territory. Instead, on 1 November the Europeans chose the option of diplomacy. In common with all 117 members of the United Nations, including Turkey, they voted for the United Nations General Assembly resolution 3212, which called even-handedly for 'the speedy withdrawal of all foreign armed forces' and commended 'the contacts and negotiations taking place on an equal footing, with the good offices of the Secretary-General, between the representatives of the two communities'. This was endorsed by the UN Security Council on 13 December 1974.

Ethnic cleansing?
In hindsight, what has to be explained is why the international community did not depict the Cyprus crisis in Holocaust terms as ethnic cleansing. In the summer of 1974, 140-160,000 Greek Cypriots left their homes and farms for the South, leaving some 20,000 in the Karpas peninsula. By the summer of 1975 only 10,500 Greek Cypriots remained in the Karpas (ROC, 1997: 11) and thereafter the number rapidly declined to the present remnant of a few hundred mainly elderly residents. Some 40,000 Turkish Cypriots and nearly all the 14,000 gypsies fled from the South. The shift of population is more complete than in Bosnia or Kosovo where 'ethnic cleansing' has been routinely condemned since 1994 in EU communiqués.

Ethnic cleansing may be an inappropriate term in that there were no bureaucratically managed extermination camps in Cyprus or in the Balkans. Despite atrocities, in Cyprus neither side set out systematically to murder either those fleeing or those who were too slow in fleeing. There is evidence that the Greek Cypriots who fled in August were expecting to return, as they had done after the initial flight in July. It is possible that the majority of the 3,000 Greek Cypriot dead and 'missing' met their fate in internecine fighting within the Greek Cypriot community and not by the hands of Turkish partisans (Kyle, 1997: 19). However, as in Bosnia and Kosovo, the nationalist leaders of both sides in Cyprus were determined to control territory from which potential 'traitors', defined as those of the other community, had been removed or rendered safe. Those who committed atrocities were not brought to justice by their own community because returning harm was widely accepted by both communities as retribution for the harm done by the other side.

The main reason why the emotive term 'ethnic cleansing' was avoided seems to be that Greece and Turkey, as well as the leading countries in NATO and the UN, were themselves willing to consider an exchange of population as a possible solution. The model for state creation in the Eastern Mediterranean was accepted to be the Treaty of Lausanne of 1923. The international recognition of Turkey and its borders included an agreement for the exchange of 1.1 million Orthodox Christians from Anatolia for 380,000 Muslims, mainly from Macedonia and Crete (Mango, 1999: 90). This exchange was regarded as better than the mutual slaughter of Armenians, Turks and Greeks which had taken place during the ten years of warfare which had ended with the substitution of the sovereign nation-state of Turkey for the Ottoman Empire. Mr Dean Acheson's plans for Cyprus in 1964, supported by the British Foreign Secretary, Mr Peter Carrington, were based on the movement of populations who were of the wrong religion or the wrong culture. The American solution envisaged that Greece could take over Cyprus with territorial enclaves for Turkish Cypriots in the North protected by a Turkish base on the Karpas peninsula. The plans were roundly condemned in 1965 by the UN mediator, Galo Plaza, as being against 'all the enlightened principles of the present time'. Despite this appeal to the Enlightenment, similar proposals were put to the Turkish Government by the Greek Junta. At NATO's Lisbon Conference in 1971 discussions were begun between Greece and Turkey on these lines (see Chapter 4). The United States in the Vietnam war period did not display the enthusiasm for human rights later shown by President Carter. It was not until 1975 that the EEC became interested in promoting human rights in Eastern Europe as the Helsinki process provided an opportunity for improving access to German nationals behind the Iron Curtain. It was not until 1980 that the European Community defied the Americans by recognising in the Venice Declaration the rights to statehood of Palestinians who had 'fled' in 1948.

In short, in 1974 even more than in the aftermath of Srbrenica in 1995, there was considerable support on pragmatic grounds of the need for establishing order by accepting ethnic cleansing as a concomitant of preserving sovereignty seized by force. Both sides housed refugees in the properties of those who had fled. The Turkish Cypriot authorities took over abandoned properties to lease and sell later to soldiers and new settlers from Anatolia. About one hundred houses in the empty village of Karmi were leased to foreigners who rebuilt them as suburban villas. The British unilaterally transferred to Turkey 9,390 Turkish Cypriots who had taken refuge in the Akrotiri base, knowing that they would then mostly relocate in Northern Cyprus. This was denounced by the Greek Cypriot Government. However, in August 1975 President Makarios himself agreed to the transfer of some 30- 40,000 Turkish Cypriots from the South directly to the North under UNFICYP auspices. The Turkish Cypriots claim that this was an agreement to relocate populations (Necatigil, 1989: 128); the Greek Cypriots deny this interpretation lest it imply international recognition of the legitimacy of the Turkish Cypriot authorities (ROC, 1997: 128-9, Appendix 8, Vienna press communiqué of 2 August, 1975).

Meanwhile, the initial success of the new intergovernmental European Political Co-operation in expressing united support on 16 July 1974 for the territorial integrity of Cyprus became quickly devalued. Faced with actual partition, western European states chose to marginalise themselves in a crisis where their primary objective was to avoid war. As with Hungary in 1956, the Greek coup in 1967, and Czechoslovakia in 1968, none of the governments thought it was a matter of national interest to risk their nationals individually or collectively in any military counter-intervention. The EC9 wanted to leave the matter as far as possible to the UN, where Britain and France were permanent members of the Security Council, and to the United States. They all supported intercommunal negotiations under the auspices of the UN Secretary-General on the powers of a pan-Cypriot federal government and on geographical aspects of a future settlement.

The EEC and Cyprus from September 1974 to the accession of Greece in 1980

> The Community was less successful subsequently in dealing with the situation. Part of the reason lay in its unwillingness, or its constitutional inability, to throw its relationship with Greece, Turkey and Cyprus into the balance by deploying the Association Agreements with these countries. More important was the abandonment of a neutral stance between Greece and Turkey, when Greece applied to join the Community following the collapse of the Colonels' regime (Simon Nuttall in Regelsberger *et al*, 1997: 20).

Simon Nuttall's assessment has the authority of a senior official in the External Relations Department (DG1) of the Commission. His categories of unwillingness, inability and, eventually, partiality are useful in explaining the Community's lack of success in dealing with the Cyprus problem. If the Community and its member states had seriously wanted to influence the political outcome in Cyprus, and in so doing, develop its profile as more than a regional economic organisation in the Mediterranean, then it had several levers to hand. Immediate European emergency aid was needed by all the communities on the island. Nearly a third of the population were refugees. The second lever was the recent Association Agreement. The EEC had a range of options from suspending the Association to moving to the second stage of a Customs Union. In practical terms, the EEC had to decide whether to accept exports of citrus which might or might not have been grown on the farms of the dispossessed of both communities. This carried with it political implications on the vexed issue of recognition in that the wholly Greek Cypriot Government had embargoed all trade with the Turkish

Cypriots while the Turkish Cypriots contested the legitimacy of the Government. The third lever was the restoration by the EEC of its Association with Greece after the junta's disastrous bid to take in Cyprus had brought about its own collapse in July 1974. The new Prime Minister of Greece, Mr Constantine Karamanlis, made full use of the Greek diaspora in a sophisticated campaign to secure full membership of the EEC. This provided many avenues for influencing Nicosia through Athens even though Greece now claimed that Cyprus was just another independent country. The fourth lever was perhaps less obvious. The isolation of Turkey at the United Nations might have been seen as an opportunity to extract a compromise over Cyprus instead of providing a further reason for the EEC to keep its distance.

Unwillingness

In 1974 the Member States of the EEC had no intention of countering the Turkish intervention with their own troops. Mr Clerides' demand at Geneva for the restoration of the 1960 Constitution was a poor rallying cry for war in that all Greek Cypriots had consistently claimed that the Constitution had been imposed on them against their will. Now the Turkish Cypriots for different reasons were also saying that the Constitution was unworkable. Secondly, the UK did not want the EEC to have any role in Cyprus. The British Government under Mr Harold Wilson lacked Mr Edward Heath's enthusiasm for the EEC as a regional framework of peace. The UK reverted to its preference for acting in consultation with the USA though the United Nations. The UK at its own expense contributed the single biggest contingent of troops to UNFICYP, the UN peacekeeping force. Thirdly, the USA did not want the EEC to get involved in the politics of the Eastern Mediterranean. A year later, European Political Co-operation was able to develop a high profile in the Helsinki process in Eastern Europe because there the USA chose to stay in the background on the issue of recognising the frontier changes made by Stalin. Fourthly, the Member States had different views. Public opinion in France, Ireland and Luxembourg identified with the Cypriot Government line that a small state had been occupied by a militarily powerful neighbour. The British, Germans and Dutch were more inclined to support American efforts to mediate between Turkey and Greece and UN Secretary General Kurt Waldheim's brokerage of negotiations in Vienna between the 'two separate administrations' on the island whose existence had been acknowledged in the Geneva Declaration of 30 July. Fifthly, unlike today, the Community made it a point of principle not to get involved in the internal affairs of member states or Associated countries. The idea of even aid to Associated states being conditional on their behaviour to minorities was not then on the agenda.

Constitutional inability

In 1974 it could be plausibly argued that even if the member states and institutions of the EEC had wanted to intervene or mediate in the Cyprus conflict, this was beyond its ability. Like Germany and Japan, its influence outside its borders was limited to that of a civilian power. Moreover, the Europeans could tell themselves that the UN was a more appropriate forum particularly because European states were still over-represented in the UN Security Council with at least one elected member in addition to Britain and France. Successive enlargements have increased the relative influence of European diplomats in New York; the EU-15 contributes to the UN 35.4 per cent of its regular funding and 37.9 per cent of the peacekeeping budget. Member states keen on the principle of sovereignty were reluctant to create a Community secretariat for foreign policy with powers of the kind wielded by the Commission in trade. The distinction between the meetings of foreign ministers in the intergovernmental framework of Political Co-operation and their meetings as the General Affairs Council could be carried to ludicrous lengths. During the October 1973 oil crisis the foreign ministers meeting as the General Affairs Council in Brussels had then flown to Denmark, the country holding the Presidency, to make the point that they were meeting an Arab delegation in the new intergovernmental framework of Political Co-operation. The Commissioner for External Relations attended the General Affairs Council as of right; in the EPC framework he might be invited to lunch but was usually not invited to dinner. This compartmentalisation in external relations also affected the development of an Association Agreement. Before an Association meeting, the Presidency had to bring the Member States to reach a unanimous common position. Only the Commission could negotiate on aid and trade matters, on the basis of a mandate unanimously agreed by the Council of Ministers. This rigidity made it very difficult for the EEC to cast itself in the role of a flexible negotiator in a complicated dispute.

On the other hand, this division of labour did enable the Member States and their Council to maintain the same useful fiction that the same states also allowed themselves in the UN context. In the UN only the Government of Cyprus enjoyed recognition; but the UN Secretary-General was mandated by the Security Council to arrange meetings between the two Cypriot communities on the basis of their equality. In the EEC the Government of Cyprus was recognised as the sole legitimate Government; but the Commission, and special representatives appointed by the Presidency, were mandated to meet the leaders of both Communities in order to inform themselves, to convey information, or to consult. This interpretation by the Community institutions of the rule of law enabled the Commission, the UK and the permanent ambassadors of the Member States in Brussels to collude in continued trade with the 'unrecognised' Turkish Cypriot Administration. This flexibility became difficult after Greece became a member, and impossible after the Court judgement in the Anastasiou case in 1994 insisted that only the certification issued by a recognised government had validity.

Partiality

The Community stance of impartiality and even-handedness between Greek Cypriots and Turkish Cypriots was never wholly convincing, and wore thinner and thinner as the decade came to an end with the accession of Greece. Eurocrats felt a greater cultural affinity to Greece than to Turkey.

Politically, few Eurocrats drew the conclusion that therefore they should take extra care in Cyprus to be even-handed between the two communities (Heinze, 1986). Internationally isolated by its military occupation of Northern Cyprus, economically weakened by the effects of the oil crisis, and politically weakened by a polarisation of left and right which spilled over into street violence, Turkey did not set great store by its Association with the EEC. In 1976 Turkey asked for the suspension of its commitment to an annual programme of dismantling its tariff protection. In 1978 Mr Bülent Ecevit unilaterally suspended Turkey's undertakings for five years. The suggestion by the German Foreign Minister, Hans-Dietrich Genscher, that Turkey be admitted as an observer when the Council discussed matters of mutual interest, including terrorism, was rejected by other member states (Brewin, 1996: 37). The Community offered to relaunch the Association with Turkey in June 1980 as reassurance before Greek accession. This relaunch was pre-empted by the military coup of General Kenan Evren.

For its part, the Greek Government overcame an unfavourable Opinion from the Commission to become a full member of the European Community. Mr Karamanlis' withdrawal of Greek troops from NATO did not harm him in Brussels, which shared French suspicions of American dominance. Mr Karamanlis adopted what was from the EEC viewpoint an impeccable low-key policy on the intercommunal negotiations in Cyprus, encapsulated in the slogan 'Cyprus decides, Greece supports' (Zervakis in Axt & Brey, 1997: 141). Although it had been under his Conservative premiership that the terms of Cypriot independence had been agreed with Mr Adnan Menderes in 1959, talks with the Turks at Montreux in 1978 did not touch on Cyprus. French sponsorship of Greece secured Greek accession. President Giscard d'Estaing was supported by the Hellenophile Herr Genscher. Greece was helped by the attitude of some states to the Cyprus problem. Ireland could identify with the claim that a community in the North was trying to secede with help from an over-mighty neighbour; German opinion could identify with the Greek view of Cyprus as partitioned by an over-mighty Eastern neighbour which had forced many of the inhabitants to flee to freedom.

The asymmetry is evident from the Council's desultory attempts at securing guarantees from Greece that its membership would not involve the Community in its campaign against Turkey. The EC promise to Turkey that relations would not be affected by Greek accession (5 February 1980, *EC Bulletin* 1980, 2: points 1.3.1 -

1.3.5.) proved empty. The Greek Parliament did not ratify the Association Agreement with Turkey until April 1988. The Greek Government was able to veto implementation of the Fourth Financial Protocol of 1980/1, even after it was reinitialled in 1988, insisting on a link with the Cyprus problem. Greece did not lift its blocking of benefits due to Turkey under the revised Mediterranean policy (MEDA payments) until the EC reaffirmed its position on the Cyprus problem in June 1992 (*Agence Europe*, 5767 & 5759).

European Political Co-operation
The states throughout this period maintained a working group on Cyprus in the inter-governmental framework of European Political Co-operation. The members of this group were officials from their respective foreign services who reported directly to the Political Committee. These are the Political Directors, the most senior civil servants in the nine Foreign Offices, who meet monthly. The chair of this Committee is the same as that of the Presidency, and therefore changes every six months. They prepare the agenda of ministerial meetings. This is made known by the Presidency country to the American Government. The US State Department is therefore in a position to use its influence on matters such as Cyprus usually by talking to the German, Dutch or British governments. The Presidency country also makes known its assessment of the conclusions reached under EPC to other western governments. Most of the documents and reports produced in this framework are not made public, with the exception of formal declarations issued on behalf of the Member States. These are often issued by the Heads of Government who in December 1974 agreed to hold summits at least three times a year, accompanied by their foreign ministers. Each September the Presidency country also makes a statement on behalf of the EEC at the opening of the UN General Assembly in New York.

Between 1970 and 1987, 12 of the 299 intergovernmental declarations in the framework of European Political Co-operation concerned Cyprus (Pijpers,1990: 184). They follow a standard pattern. The Community's commitment to the independence, sovereignty, territorial integrity and unity of Cyprus is reaffirmed.

Appeals to the communities to end the island's partition on the basis of UN resolutions are not accompanied by any suggestion of EEC action such as mediation. Moral support is offered for the efforts of the UN Secretary General in promoting dialogue between the two communities and for the indispensable role of UN peacekeeping forces. In the early years the EEC welcomes the Vienna Agreement of 1975 and the High-level Agreement of 1977 on a federation. In the later years 'interested parties' are asked to refuse all recognition to the Turkish Republic of Northern Cyprus. This followed an unusually blunt EPC communiqué from Athens on 16 November 1983. However, in December 1983 another declaration prepared by the Greek Presidency was not issued after the break-up of a rancorous meeting of the heads of state (Ifestos, 1987: 272).

What is not in the public domain are the reports on Cyprus produced by the Political Committee or the working group. Some of these reports were produced at the request of the EEC Commission. The Commission's purpose was to secure a political mandate, or guidance, on whether to resist pressure from the Government of Cyprus to proceed with the Customs Union which the Association Agreement had envisaged as constituting the second stage of the economic linkage between the EEC and Cyprus. Mr Panayiotis Ifestos was told: 'It is the impression of some of the officials involved that the EPC reports on this issue influence considerably both the attitudes of the Member States and the attitudes of the EEC Commission (Ifestos, 1987: 236). He was not told of any *démarches*, the unpublicised enquiries whereby the weight of the Community is effectively exercised on behalf of individuals at risk.

While happy with any formula putting responsibility on the two communities under the aegis of the UN, the EEC nevertheless had to decide whether to distribute aid to the Turkish Cypriot side as well as to the recognised Greek Cypriot Government. It had to decide whether, and how, to implement the first commercial stage of the Association Agreement amid conflicting claims that citrus was being exported from land stolen from its owners. It had to hold meetings under the Association Agreement with a recognised government which regarded the constitutional rights of its Turkish Cypriots to participate in government as no longer operable.

Commission emergency aid to both sides

At the second Geneva Conference, Mr Callaghan spoke of the whole island of Cyprus becoming one vast refugee camp (Polyviou, 1977: 341). He had plans to evacuate British nationals. He may have had some inkling of what became a large-scale diaspora from both communities to London. In no way was he thinking European. Other member states would not be asked to offer shelter in their own countries to Cypriots. Instead, 'feeling keenly for refugees', their foreign ministers, meeting under political co-operation procedures, announced that the Commission would send on their behalf financial assistance and food aid. The European Development Fund, a fund for contract work in former colonies controlled directly by the Member States, could also be used.

The Commissioner for Development, M. Claude Cheysson, interpreted his mandate with a robust even-handedness. He arranged that food aid should be distributed roughly in proportion to the population size of the two communities. At independence in 1960 the Turkish Cypriots had constituted 18 per cent of the inhabitants. In answer to a question in the European Parliament (518/78) the Commission could report that between 1974 and 1978 the northern sector had received 16 per cent of the cereals, 20 per cent of the milk powder and 19 per cent of the butter oil sent to Cyprus. As early as 12 September 1974 supplemental aid was assigned to Cyprus in addition to the regular aid being sent before the crisis erupted (*EC Bulletin*, 1974, 9: 56). In March 1975, 5,000 tons of wheat and 300 tons of butter oil from the Community's intervention stocks were sent as emergency aid; in April 1976 twice these quantities were allocated.

Commissioner Cheysson's even-handedness implied a strong self-distancing of the Community from taking sides. The Commission made no judgements of either need or desert. Food aid was distributed from Community intervention stocks through the Red Cross and UNHCR, the United Nations High Commission for Refugees. M. Cheysson was happy to tell the European Parliament on 29 April 1975 that his purpose was to avoid complications from the '*de facto* or legal authorities now controlling the island'. Although the Community recognised only the Greek Cypriot

Government, the Commissioner did not let the Government decide who in the North should receive aid. Moreover the Commissioner faced down the initial refusal of the Government to allow existing regular aid to be distributed as emergency aid. M. Cheysson's attitude was supported by Turkey. The Parliamentary Committee of the EEC-Turkey Association asked the Commission 'to ensure that the Community's food aid to the population of the island is effectively delivered and distributed, regardless of the ethnic community to which they belong or the area in which they live'. (*EC Bulletin* 1975, 4: point 4 of 24 April).

Financial protocols
The same principle was applied in distributing non-emergency financial aid. In November 1978 the First Protocol on Financial Aid allocated just under 20 per cent to the Turkish Cypriots (Şakir Alemdar in Dodd, ed., 1993: 94). These financial subsidies for the benefit of the whole population were some compensation for the EEC reluctance to move towards the Customs Union envisaged by the Association Agreement. Thirty million European ECU were disbursed between 1979 and 1983. The grant element of six million ECU was small. Four million ECU of special loans drawn from the Community's own budget could be lent to commercial ventures as risk capital. The remaining twenty million ECU consisted of loans at reduced interest administered by the European Investment Bank (EIB) in Luxembourg.

Under the Second Protocol only 4.5 per cent of the 44m ECU administered by the European Investment Bank went to the North between 1984 -1988. By then Greece had become a full member of the Community and the Turkish Cypriots had declared an independent republic. Between 1989 and 1993, the only money transferred to the Turkish Cypriots under the Third Protocol of 62m ECU was for a sewage project in Nicosia. It is unfortunate that the principal joint project financed by the EU takes sewage from the South of Nicosia for disposal in the North. Cited by the European Court of Justice in 1994 and trumpeted in all Community brochures on Cyprus as evidence of EC even-handedness, it provokes a certain wry ribaldry among Turkish Cypriots. They make nothing of the unusual flexibility shown in this instance by the Greek Cypriot side. The Municipality in Nicosia arranged that the transfer of EIB funds via a London bank to the North would not be challenged by its own Government as EC aid to an unrecognised entity.

This discontinuation of the policy of proportionality and even-handedness did not require any change of policy on Cyprus by the European Investment Bank. Its own explanation is that its capacity to raise money at the lowest rates on the open market is a function of getting its lending guaranteed by the Central Bank of whatever country is receiving the loan. Now that its lending has shifted from the financing of government projects to the underwriting of private companies this need for an effective guarantee has become absolute. The Turkish Cypriots refuse to recognise the authority of the Central Bank of Cyprus. They will submit no projects to the Central Bank for its approval nor accept EIB loans by that route. The responsibility accorded for supervision to the Commission delegation in Cyprus since 1990 has not been interpreted as enabling the EU ambassador to approve projects in the North, even with respect to loans guaranteed by the EEC budget. It would take a very secure ambassador to defy local opinion in Nicosia and the views of the Greek EIB governor. Instead, Ambassador Gilles Anouil went along with his hosts. Neither the Commission nor member state representatives on the island showed any sensitivity to the effect on Turkish Cypriot opinion when credit was repeatedly taken by the Greek representative on the EIB Board of Governors for financial aid to the Republic of Cyprus. Personnel from the European institutions regarded the 'intransigent' Turkish Cypriot leadership as having only itself to blame for not submitting projects.

The grant element in financial aid to Cyprus was not generous for an island suffering economic disruption and political division. Over the fourteen years between 1979 and 1993 grants totalled 29m ECU. At an annual average of 2.07m ECU, or $4 per Cypriot, this was not going to induce dependency. Most EC financial aid was in the form of repayable loans, amounting to 92m ECU, to which should be added 10m ECU in special loans and 5m ECU in risk capital. There was no aid between 1993 and 1995, the years between the Commission Opinion and the Council's decision to set a date for the opening of negotiations. However, the marked change in distribution of EC financial aid between the First and Third Protocols helps to explain the hostile indifference of the Turkish Cypriots to the Fourth Protocol 1995-98, in which the Community for the first time offered aid 'to promote a settlement of the Cyprus question' (Council Decision EC 95/485 of 30 October 1995), a subject for the next chapter.

Trade and recognition

The Community was even less forthcoming in offering trade concessions to restore economic confidence and prosperity on the island. For three years after 1974 it took the line that the Association Agreement was to be implemented on an interim basis 'due to the lack of normality on the island' (Gaston Thorn, Third Association Council, 4/76). Mr Ernst Glinne MEP asked the Commission on 27 September 1976: 'Is a deliberate effort being made to ignore Cyprus, a tactic used elsewhere in other Mediterranean areas where the situation is volatile?' (OJC: 226/76).

The Community refused to negotiate on the second stage of the Association, namely the Customs Union due to start in 1977. If this stance was intended to pressure the Government to discuss a federal constitution with Mr Denktaş, the participants in the high-level talks sponsored by UN Secretary-General Waldheim have left no record of it. The alternative speculation is that the Community judged that if it were to complete a Customs Union with the Government side, this would make the Turkish Cypriots less willing to settle the Cyprus problem. 'The EC sought to adopt a strictly neutral position and any enhancement of the Association Agreement might have been perceived by the Turkish Cypriots (and by Turkey itself) as unduly favouring the Greek Cypriots' (Redmond, 1993: 93fn).

It took another ten years before agreement was reached on implementing the Customs Union. The negotiations could be seen as hard-headed and acrimonious, but they also involved two issues of fairness. On the one hand the Greek Cypriot Government recognised by the Community thought more was due to it for the failure of the European side to implement the UN Security Council resolutions. On the other hand, the European negotiators wanted to protect the unrepresented Turkish Cypriots. The Greek Cypriot demand that the Turkish occupation, and Turkish Cypriot take-over of Greek Cypriot property, should not be recognised by the Community conflicted with the duty under Article 5 not to discriminate in trade between different nationals. The Commission tried to square this circle by claiming that exports to the UK took place under the aegis of what was left of the Commonwealth preference system. It offered to examine exports to other member states, an empty gesture as Northern Cyprus had no export outlets other than the UK and Ireland via Rotterdam (Tsardanidis, 1988: 159).

The partition of the island in 1974 had caused severe economic losses for both communities. The Greek Cypriots lost most in the short term. They had to abandon their citrus groves in the best agricultural land around Morphou; they could no longer operate their new hotels, hitherto concentrated at Varosha close to Famagusta, and at Kyrenia. The Turkish Cypriots had a bigger long-term problem. Already, during the decade since 1964, they had been forced to develop a separate and poorer economy in the enclaves covering the 3.86 per cent of Cyprus to which they had mainly retreated. Since 1964, in addition to jobs lost in 'unsafe' areas, they had been deprived of all government jobs, pensions, and access via government agencies to international relief. Turkish pensions were an inadequate substitute which served politically to underline their dependency on the Turkish motherland. After 1974, they additionally had to face the economic disadvantages consequent on the lack of international recognition. International airlines cannot land except at airports listed by recognised governments. The Greek embargo on 'Turkish-occupied Cyprus' made shipowners in a sector dominated by Greek shipping interests reluctant to accept the hassle of being blacklisted for landing cargoes at Famagusta/Mağusa. The lack of recognition precluded the development of offshore financial services, a shipping flag of convenience, sporting links and, for a time, universities with internationally recognised qualifications. The international embargo on exports of agricultural products which might come from Greek-owned property affected Turkish Cypriots at a time when their market was already being undermined by competition from better financed, and sometimes subsidised, producers in Spain, California and Israel, who enjoyed easier access to the European market.

Trade involved institutions, notably the Association Council. The second meeting of the EEC-Cyprus Association Council was scheduled for July 1975. Mr Denktaş announced that he was coming to Brussels that week as President of the Turkish Federated State of Northern Cyprus. The assumption of this title on 13 February 1975 had been 'regretted' in March by the UN Security Council in UNSC Resolution 367. Mr Denktaş was persuaded to defer his visit until 23 July, one week after the Association meeting with the Greek Cypriot Government. No representative of the Council would meet with him. Commission officials would see him as the representative of the Turkish community without insisting that he return to calling himself Vice-President of the Republic of Cyprus. The Commission established a precedent that in receiving Mr Denktaş they were ready to inform him and to listen, but not to negotiate anything. Mr Denktaş' position was complicated by the ambivalence of Turkey's view of the legitimacy of the Cypriot Mission to the EEC of the Government of Cyprus. This is illustrated by a complaint from the Turkish delegation on 29 January 1975 that if accusations were entertained against Turkey before informing Turkey and hearing its point of view, 'matters could come to a point where Turkey would have to inform the Community officially that the Turkish Government does not recognise the Cypriot mission to the EEC as representing the whole of the island, and to ask the EEC not to recognise it in their manner either' (Tsardanidis, 1988: 160). This threat only made sense if officially Turkey still recognised the Cypriot mission to the EEC as representing the Republic. It is one of the oddities of the Cyprus story that no statement was made by Turkey in 1964 or 1974 officially withdrawing recognition of the Government, or of the Republic, of Cyprus; in 1983 the reasons for recognition of the TRNC circulated by the Turkish Foreign Minister (UN doc. A/38/602 of 23 November, 1983) do not indicate what kind of entity exists south of the border. As the Turkish Embassy in Cyprus happened to be in the Turkish quarter of Nicosia/Lefkoşa, the Turks did not need a decisive break with what they now habitually describe in inverted commas as the 'Republic of Cyprus'.

In 1975 Commissioner Christopher Soames (Redmond, 1993: 66) re-affirmed that the European Communities had a duty of even-handedness with respect to the Greek and Turkish Cypriots. This obligation did not mean that the unique bi-communal nature of the 1960 Constitution might entitle Turkish Cypriots to negotiate any matters within the framework of the Association. Still less did it accord the leader of the Turkish community a veto on procedure or on any results that might be achieved. Even-handedness was understood by the Commission to mean that the benefits to the two communities should be in proportion to their populations. There was no implication of either equal or proportionate status for those who saw themselves as representing the Turkish Cypriots. As for the Member States, their Committee of Permanent Representatives in Brussels, COREPER, on 22 July 1977 made a 'gentleman's agreement' among themselves to interpret the new 1977 Regulation on co-operation between customs authorities in a way that would allow trade with Northern Cyprus to continue. An agreement among gentlemen implies a disregard of the principles of legality and publicity. The Greek and Greek Cypriot governments were not informed of its existence (Tsardanides, 1988: 163). Based on a draft from the Commission's Legal Service it allowed for the continuation of exports to England and a further 1,000 tonnes to Ireland via Rotterdam from the North of Cyprus. The Legal Service took the following view:

> It should not be entirely excluded that the Communities and/or the customs authorities of the member states could legitimately approach the Turkish occupation power in matters of movement certificates and customs co-operation. Such contacts would not be likely to involve or prejudice any recognition of the status of the Turkish Cypriot community in general of the Northern part of the island.

For their part, the Cypriot mission wanted the EEC and its governments to be more generous in trade concessions to compensate for the economic losses suffered by the Government side. Their secondary objective was to reorient Cypriot trade back to

Europe and away from the Arab countries to which nearly half its trade had been diverted in the wake of the oil price hike. Urgency was lent to its requests in that on 1 January 1976 the UK was to complete its alignment with the Common Commercial Tariff. Already since December 1974, sherry had been exported on an interim basis. In a memorandum to the Commission, the Government of Cyprus on 29 September 1975 made it clear that they wanted EEC co-operation in the embargo on trade and contacts with the illegal occupation authorities in the North. The Government wanted the EEC to use the opportunity presented by the end of Commonwealth Preference to amend the rules of origin to exclude Turkish Cypriot exports that might include products from property stolen from Greek Cypriots. The Government also wanted concessions to Cyprus to be increased in the light of advantages accorded to the Maghreb countries and Israel under the Global Mediterranean Policy.

Negotiating slowly the second stage of the Customs Union
However, the Commission took until the following year before asking, in February 1976, for a mandate from the Council to open negotiations on the second stage of the Customs Union. Mr Denktaş continued to lobby the Commission as a hostile outsider. A letter of protest to the Commission about the working of the Association Agreement, dated 30 March 1976, is couched in terms which do not anticipate a friendly outcome:

> Despite specific provisions of the Agreement to the effect that the two communities in Cyprus should benefit from the Association Agreement without discrimination (Article 5), the implementation of the first stage of the EEC-Cyprus Association Agreement has proved unsuccessful as far as the Turkish community in Cyprus is concerned. The reason for this outcome lies in the denial of Turkish Cypriot participation in this Agreement at the stages of negotiation, signing and implementation. This constitutes a denial of entrenched legal and constitutional rights of the Turkish community to participate on an equal footing with the Greek Cypriot community at all levels and in every stage of the Cyprus-EEC relations.

It was not until May 1976 that the Council was able to agree on a mandate for the Commission. The problem of amending the rules of origin was complicated by internal quarrels among the Member States. British and Irish generosity to Cyprus would establish precedents which would in turn affect the ongoing negotiations with the Maghreb countries. The EEC in this period was trying to rationalise its historically separate arrangements with Mediterranean countries from Morocco to Israel, an effort subsumed under the title of a Global Mediterranean Policy. The French and Italian governments had to balance their political aims for improved relations with their neighbours against the threat to their own producers implicit in opening up the market for citrus to their regional competitors. Thus the May mandate to Cyprus was linked to agreement on a 10 per cent increase in the reference price for selling wine in the Community market. These delays in turn required an extension for the third time in July 1976 of the interim agreement whereby Cyprus could export 198,000 hectolitres of sherry to the UK and 2000hl to Ireland.

The reticence of the Council can also be partially defended as a holding operation until the warring parties reached agreement on how Cyprus would be governed as a federation. The third meeting of the EEC-Cyprus Association Council had been held the previous month, in April 1976. M. Gaston Thorn, of Luxembourg, explained that delays were due to the lack of normality on the island. The implication was that the delays would disappear if a solution were found. This expectation was kept alive by the High-level Agreement between Archbishop Makarios and Mr Denktaş in February 1977 that they would negotiate for an 'independent, non-aligned, bi-communal federal republic'.

On 16 May 1977, a few months after this apparent breakthrough, negotiations began on the content of the second stage of the Customs Union. Again, the talks in Brussels were inconclusive and abrasive. The Cypriot Government twice rejected as inadequate EEC proposals for moving to the second stage of the Customs Union (*EEC Bulletin* 1977,12: 2.2.51 & *EEC Bulletin* 1978, 1: 2.2.370). Understandably, the government took the view that the victim of aggression was being penalised. In response, the EEC showed who

The European Union and Cyprus

had the power to make decisions in the framework of the Association. It unilaterally extended the 1977 deadline for moving from the first stage of tariff cuts, extending its validity by an Additional Protocol of 15 September 1977 to the end of 1979. Belatedly, on 7 February 1980, a Transitional Protocol extended the first stage a second time until 31 December 1980. Cyprus was compensated to the extent that the First Financial Protocol was signed and the EEC abolished all remaining duties on industrial products (Redmond, 1997: 93), a measure of little value to a non-industrialised island.

Exploratory talks on the second stage recommenced on 29 January 1980 (*EEC Bulletin*, 1980, 1: 2.2.42) and a second round of talks on this and the consequences of Greek accession on 19 March 1980 (*EEC Bulletin*, 1980, 3: 2.2.53). Again, political disagreements among member states precluded success. After October 1981, negotiations were not helped by the election of the populist Greek Prime Minister, Mr Andreas Papandreou. Although he was the first Greek prime minister to visit the island, his scorn for both the EEC and NATO did not make for success in negotiations. However, Turkey's military government was not in a position to capitalise on the disfavour courted by Mr Papandreou.

On 24 November 1980, the EEC-Cyprus Association Council (*EEC Bulletin*, 1980/11: 2.2.54) decided that the process of entering into the second stage of the Agreement should begin on 1 January 1981 (OJL 174: 29). The protocol is unusual in spelling out that the negotiating process itself would be so unhurried that discussions on the conditions and procedures of the second stage would not begin until 1982. The Turkish Cypriots were to be included in the benefits, but not the process, of the negotiation. The British sovereign bases were excluded by a formula which based the unity of the island on human rather than physical geography: 'It is understood that the advantages envisaged must benefit the island's population as a whole'. Meanwhile the conditions applying to the first stage were extended to December 1981 by a unilateral EEC protocol. Bilateral talks, beginning in 1981, were to make arrangements for continuing the first stage on into 1982 and 1983 by mutual agreement. However it was not until October 1982 that the Council agreed on the mandate to be given the Commission negotiators. Meanwhile, by a protocol of 24 June 1981, various concessions were unilaterally added. The pettiness of the advantages envisaged can be illustrated by the arrangements for new potatoes. After the 15 May each year the tariff reduction of 60 per cent on 60,000 tonnes was reduced to 55 per cent for the subsequent six weeks.

The Turkish Cypriots chose not to take advantage of the low standing in Brussels of the other parties to the Cyprus dispute. It was during the transition period from military to civilian rule, before Prime Minister Özal had established himself, that the Turkish Cypriot National Assembly proclaimed the Turkish Republic of Northern Cyprus. The capitals of Europe were not prepared for this sudden step towards independence under the protection of the Turkish army. The Commission, the Council and the European Parliament reacted as quickly and as negatively as the UN Security Council and General Assembly:

> The Commission deeply regrets and rejects the unilateral declaration of independence of the Turkish Cypriot community. The Government of Cyprus is the sole legitimate representative recognised by the European Community.

On 16 November 1983, the ten Member States rejected the 'declaration purporting to establish a "Turkish Republic of Northern Cyprus" as an independent State... The Ten reiterate their unconditional support for the independence, sovereignty, territorial integrity and unity of the Republic of Cyprus. They continue to regard the government of President Kyprianou as the sole legitimate government of the Republic of Cyprus. They call upon all interested parties not to recognise this act'.

In 1983 the Republic of Cyprus protested in vain to the Commission that exports from Northern Cyprus were in breach of its embargo. Its *note verbale* claimed that the Commission's practice of allowing imports into the Community from Northern Cyprus was in clear contrast to the legal requirement that 'only products accompanied by movement certificates issued by the official Government and exported from sea or airports under its control satisfied the conditions of the Association Agreement' (Anastasiou, 1994: 51). In 1984   the issue of a Customs Union was again postponed, the Germans going so far as to claim that Cyprus was not capable of entering a Customs Union. The EC seemed content to continue unilateral extensions of the provisions of the first stage of the Association Agreement—to 1983, 1985 and 1987, each time incorporating adjustments in line with concessions to other Mediterranean countries. Meanwhile full membership for Spain and Portugal came into effect on 1 January 1986, albeit with a long transitory period before their agricultural products could enter the EC without any restriction.

Exploratory talks on the Customs Union with Cyprus began again in November 1985, and at last serious negotiation got under way in a second round in February 1986. That summer Herr Hans Schweb, the Commission's experienced desk officer with responsibility for Cyprus, Malta and Turkey, visited Northern Cyprus. He did not accept the argument put by his hosts that the consent of both community leaders was required by international and constitutional law for the conclusion of international agreements. Although the Turkish Cypriots themselves no longer regarded the 1960 Constitution as valid, they argued that because the Community accepted the Greek Cypriot side as legitimate by virtue of that Constitution, no agreement was possible because there was no Turkish Vice-President in a position to exercise the veto to which he was entitled by Article 50 of the Constitution.

The Protocol for the second stage of the Association Agreement was eventually signed on 19 October 1987, ten years after it was supposed to commence. It was approved by the European Parliament in December 1987, concluded by a Council decision of 21 December 1987 (OJL: 393) and came into force on 1 January 1988. In Cyprus the House of Representatives ratified it by 31 votes to 17, the opposition coming from the communists of AKEL and the socialists of EDEK. Two phases were envisaged before the Customs Union could be realised at the end of another fifteen years. In the first phase, 1988-1997, the EC agreed to abolish the remaining quotas on Cypriot textiles. Cyprus agreed to adopt progressively the Common Customs Tariff before the end of 1997. Cyprus was allowed to exclude temperate agricultural imports from the European Community. Cyprus would reduce duties and quotas on forty-three agricultural products and on most industrial products. Cyprus could continue to protect petroleum products and fifteen categories of industrial products, defined by its Government as sensitive because they were made in Cypriot factories. By an exchange of letters, recorded in the Official Journal, Cyprus undertook 'to ensure that, in future, its exports of [new potatoes] will be principally channelled towards its main traditional suppliers' (sic)! A Trade and Economic Co-operation Committee was instituted. Disputes would be referred not to the Court of Justice of the EU15 but to three arbitrators. In the second phase, the Customs Union would be fully realised between 1997 and 2002/3. All tariffs, the remaining quotas on industrial and agricultural products and rules of origin on manufactured products, would be eliminated.

Towards the application for membership
The second Greek Presidency of the European Community in 1988 provided the opportunity to build on the commitment to the Customs Union to promote Cypriot membership. This was the period between the Turkish application of 1987 and the Commission Opinion on Turkey in 1989. The political decision to apply for full membership with Greek support had been signalled by the Cypriot Prime Minister, Mr Vassiliou, in 1987/8, well before the end of the Cold War. The driving force behind the application however came from the Greek Prime Minister. Mr Papandreou was finding increasing difficulty in getting majorities in the UN General Assembly and Security Council for resolutions hostile to Turkey. However, the timing of the application was delayed by Mr Vassiliou. His government's dependence on the anti-European communist party, AKEL, made him inclined instead to non-alignment and to securing intercommunal agreement with the Turkish Cypriots within the UN framework (Zervakis in Axt & Brey, 1997: 144). The delay, and the option of an alternative policy, had the positive consequence that the ground for the application in 1990 was carefully prepared.

The application was encouraged by a Resolution of the European Parliament on 10 March 1988. Its uniquely considerate language stands out from the run of resolutions fully committed to Greek-Cypriot condemnation of the Turkish occupation. It is the only Resolution which Parliament asked to be forwarded to the Turkish Cypriots:

> The European Parliament...calls on the Council, in order to facilitate the resumption and successful outcome of negotiations between the two communities, to devote special study to the possibility of an *economic opening* by the Community towards the Republic of Cyprus *as a whole*, the practical arrangements for such a move and its consequences, and also, in the long term, the question of Cyprus's *possible accession* to the Community. [my italics]

On 18 July 1988 the Council made a political gesture by favouring the Republic of Cyprus with a formal invitation to begin political dialogue with the Member States of the European Community (Regelsberger et al, 1997: 80). The status of being engaged in political dialogue is a recognition by the EC of the special importance of some third countries. It establishes an institutionalised regularity of meetings alongside normal ad hoc diplomatic relations and commercial contacts. The focus is on the foreign policy agenda of European Political Co-operation. Usually the foreign secretaries of the present, past and future Presidency countries commit themselves to holding a meeting on at least an annual basis. The small size of Cyprus, in the Council's perspective, is underlined by the fact that until 1995 the Community was represented by the Presidency foreign secretary alone, and not the usual troika of past, present and future presidencies. Another mark of European favour was that in 1989 Nicosia was chosen as the venue for the launch of the Charter of Euro-Mediterranean Basin Co-operation on the Environment.

With the end of the Cold War, the Dublin summit of 28 April, 1990 celebrated a Europe 'which, having overcome the unnatural divisions imposed on it by ideology and confrontation, stands united in its commitment to democracy, pluralism, the rule of law, full respect for human rights, and the principles of the market economy'.

The European Community tried to balance the new opening to the East with some ill-prepared gestures focused on the Mediterranean. One was a proposal for a forum in which the five Mediterranean EC countries would meet with the five countries of North Africa, an innovation killed off by UN sanctions on Libya. Another was the Spanish proposal to emulate the success of the Helsinki process in promoting human rights and respect for frontiers in Eastern Europe by establishing a Conference on Security and Co-operation in the Mediterranean, to include Cyprus and Malta. A third was a premature attempt to revive the Euro-Arab dialogue. Finally, the Irish Presidency linked the development of relations with Turkey inter alia to a change in Turkey's attitude on the Cyprus problem.

The following month, on 24 May 1990, the Commission established a permanent delegation in Nicosia. The head of delegation is accredited as the Commission's official representative to the Government of Cyprus with the courtesy title of Ambassador. His role includes the monitoring of financial protocols and the dissemination of information on EC programmes. As those interested parties include Turkish Cypriots, it might have considerably improved the two-way communication process if the opportunity had been taken to insist that the Cypriot authorities condone the employment by the Ambassador of Turkish Cypriots in proportion to their population. As all Turkish Cypriots resident before 1974 are entitled to apply for a passport from the Republic of Cyprus, it would have been difficult for the authorities to refuse this request. The fact that it was not done may have helped Ambassador Gilles Anouil in establishing good relations with the Government, but was a missed opportunity to re-establish its commitment to even-handedness in dealing with both main communities. In the same month the Republic of Cyprus affirmed its pan-European credentials by signing the Agreement establishing the European Bank for Reconstruction and Development, intended as a conduit for money to the transitional regimes in Central and Eastern Europe.

The application for Cypriot membership of the three European Communities was formally submitted to Sr Gianni de Michelis, the President of the Council of Ministers on the 4 July 1990. The newly elected Greek government of Mr Constantine Mitsotakis 'concurred with Vassiliou's government that an EC membership for Cyprus would also entail tangible benefits for the Turkish Cypriots. This would also facilitate the ultimate acceptance of Turkey by the Community' (Zervakis in Axt & Brey, 1997: 144).

Turkish Cypriot objections
The Turkish Cypriot leadership immediately closed the crossing points on the frontier. This was condemned by the European Parliament on the 12 July 1990 as a violation of human rights. On the same day, a memorandum setting out the legal, political and practical objections of 'the Turkish Cypriot side' was submitted to Sr de Michelis, as follows:

> The present opposition to the Greek Cypriot application is of a fundamental nature. It arises *in limine*. The internationally unlawful character of the authority that purports to make the application deprives it of the capacity so to act, while the scope of the application and the manner of its making both taint the application with invalidity (para. 18).

The memorandum was written by Mr Necati Münir Ertekün, QC. On behalf of his community, he denies from the outset that a wholly Greek Cypriot authority has the capacity to act legally on behalf of the whole island. As the scope of the application would unite Cyprus with Greece, he argues that this is forbidden by the treaties of 1960, the validity of which is recognised by all parties. To back up this argument he sent Sr de Michaelis a supplementary note on 3 September 1990 containing the British records of a meeting in London of 12 February 1959. Additional arguments sought to persuade the Council that it would not be in its own interests to proceed with the application. Membership of the European Communities would be unworkable in a divided island. The application on behalf of 'Cyprus' was misconceived in suggesting a 'unity of the island which is not supportable either in law or in fact'. To admit Greek Cyprus would mean a second vote for Greece. The memorandum therefore asked the Council not to refer the application to the Commission for an Opinion, or at most to limit the reference to the question of the legality of the application. He extended an olive branch of a sort by linking a possible Turkish Cypriot endorsement of membership to a prior settlement:

> Notwithstanding this the TRNC does not wish to create the impression that it is opposed to the eventual membership of the European Communities by a State of Cyprus restored to legality and stability by a settlement freely negotiated between parties of equal standing (para.19).

The Turkish Cypriot leadership received oblique support from the UN Secretary-General Mr Perez de Cuellar. On 11 September 1990 he issued a press statement urging the EC to think of Cypriot membership within the framework of a comprehensive settlement.

On 17 September the Council chose to ask the Commission for its Opinion on the application in accordance with the procedure laid down in the Treaty of Rome. No member state was willing to question the legal standing of the Government of Cyprus, although it might have been different if Turkish membership had been in prospect. The fact that the Cypriot Government was the recognised locutor in the Association context was sufficient. The corollary was that the Turkish Cypriot leadership had no standing, and no reply was sent to their memoranda of July and September. However, the Council's doubts about getting involved in a divided Cyprus (Michaelides, 1996: 7) explain why it never criticised the delay of nearly three years before the Commission in July 1993 delivered its Opinions on Cyprus and Malta. This gestation period was longer than had been needed in 1987 for Turkey. During these three years the Commission produced Opinions on Austria (August 1991), Sweden (July 1992), Finland (November 1992), and Norway (March 1993). The enlargement to the EFTA countries of Northern Europe had brought down the average time taken by the whole membership process to a total of six years from the time of first application. The Brussels institutions could not doubt the commitment of the Cypriot Government to its European project. In 1992 it adopted VAT, albeit with many zero-rated items, and tied the Cypriot pound to the ECU. The Commission took its time in the hope of a breakthrough in the intercommunal negotiations over Cyprus between Mr Vassiliou and Mr Denktaş brokered after 1991 by the new UN Secretary-General, Mr Boutros Boutros Ghali.

The 'Set of Ideas

As permanent members of the UN Security Council, Britain and France endorsed in UNSC 750 a package of 100 proposals drawn up after consulting the parties separately in proximity talks. The proposed Federal Republic of Cyprus was to be 'bi-communal as regards the constitutional aspects and bi-zonal as regards the territorial aspects'. The aim was the 'effective participation of both communities in all organs and decisions'. Legislation would require the separate approval of representatives of both communities in a Lower House elected on a 70:30 ratio between the communities and an Upper House chosen on a 50:50 ratio. Officials of the Federal Government would be appointed on a 70:30 ratio. Two federated states would have 'equality and identical powers and functions' in their separately administered territorial zones. Turkish Cypriots were asked to reduce the territory they controlled to 26 per cent of the island, giving up Famagusta and Morphou. Membership of the EC would be put to the two communities in separate referenda (para.92). It was left open whether these referenda would take place at the same time as those on the framework agreement, as Mr Vassiliou wanted, or delayed until after Turkey had first become itself a member state, as Mr Denktaş wanted. There was nothing on what might happen if the Turkish Cypriot community voted negatively.

Both Parliaments strongly reaffirmed their views of the principles being compromised (Necatigil, 1996: 375-87). Mr Denktaş objected strongly to nine of the draft points; the UN Security Council in Resolution 789 of 24 November 1992 blamed the Turkish Cypriots for not adopting positions 'consistent with the Set of Ideas'. Mr Vassiliou accepted the proposals as a basis for discussion but not for negotiation. In February 1993 Mr Clerides' victory over Mr Vassiliou in the presidential elections reduced the possibility of intercommunal agreement. According to Mr Clerides, the UN Set of Ideas would 'block Cyprus' course towards Europe' (Dodd, 1998: 51). In power political terms, this meant that the Greek Cypriot position would be relatively stronger if the Republic of Cyprus were admitted. In terms of principle, Mr Clerides wanted the UN Ideas to take more account of EC principles of free movement, the individual human rights and majoritarian democracy protected by the European Convention, and international law that recognised the legitimacy of the existing Republic and the illegitimacy of self-rule in the North. His new foreign minister, Mr Alecos Michaelides, articulated this European orientation, arguing that accession without a settlement was the best way of promoting a settlement:

> We shall give priority to actions which aim at promoting the accession of Cyprus to the European Union. We shall undertake every effort to persuade the European Union that progress in Cyprus' accession assist in the efforts to solve the Cyprus problem. If Europe wishes to solve the Cyprus problem, it should help by expressing its readiness to accept us as a member (Michaelides 1996: 6).

Support for Cypriot accession in the European Parliament
In this the Cypriot Government could count on sustained support from the European Parliament. On 17 March 1992 the European Parliament set up a new EC-Cyprus Parliamentary Committee. Sir James Scott-Hopkins, European co-chairman, at a press conference said that the Community should examine the Cypriot application irrespective of the internal problems of the country (Necatigil, 1995: 27). Meeting twice a year with four or five agenda items prepared a month in advance, this joint delegation has proved useful both formally and informally in disseminating the Cypriot Government's enthusiasm for accession. It built on consistent sympathy in the Parliament since 1974 for resolutions attacking Turkey as the occupier of Northern Cyprus, and as having a bad record on human rights. After the accession of Greece in 1981, Greek Cypriot MEPs were able to count on greater support in the Parliament than they could look for in the Assembly of the Council of Europe. After 1984, with the exception of the more balanced 1988 Resolution discussed above, the Parliament gave unconditional support for resolutions acceptable to the Greek lobby. For example, on 14 March 1991 the

Parliament asked the international community to show the same
determination in implementing United Nations resolutions on Cyprus
as on Kuwait. On 17 May Parliament 'called on Turkey...to
withdraw all troops from Cyprus'. On 12 September the Parliament,
lamenting the Turkish military occupation and systematic attempt at
colonisation, 'considers that the lack of involvement of the European
Community is incomprehensible'. A resolution of 21 January 1993
welcoming the establishment of the joint Parliamentary Committee
established with the wholly Greek Cypriot House of Representatives
is worth citing at greater length because it links condemnation of the
Turkish Cypriots for the failure of the UN talks with a plea for
Cypriot membership before a settlement without waiting for the
outcome of the election:

> The European Parliament
> 1. Adopts the position of the Security Council that the talks in
> New York did not achieve their intended objective in particular
> because certain positions adopted by the Turkish Cypriot side
> were fundamentally at variance with the Set of Ideas;
> 2. Reaffirms its conviction that the continuation of the status
> quo in Cyprus is unacceptable and poses wider dangers for the
> region;
> 3. Calls upon the Turkish side to return to the new round of
> talks in March 1993;
> 4. Calls upon the Government of Turkey to withdraw its
> occupation troops from the Republic of Cyprus in accordance
> with the relevant UN resolutions and calls for the Turkish
> troops to be replaced by United Nations peacekeeping forces;
> 5. Calls on the Turkish side to accept without further delay the
> confidence-building measures adopted by Security Council
> Resolution 789;
> 6. Supports the recommendations of the EC-Cyprus Joint
> Parliamentary Committee adopted in Nicosia on 16 July 1992
> and, in particular, expresses the wish that the Opinion of the
> Commission on the application of Cyprus for full membership
> to the EC, and the decision of the Council that will follow,
> should contribute to the furtherance of the admission of Cyprus

to the Community, which will have positive effects on the efforts to resolve the Cyprus problem;
[7.] Instructs its President to forward this resolution to the Council and Commission, EPC, the Governments of the Member States, the UN Secretary-General and the Governments of Turkey and Cyprus.

The Turkish Cypriots with whom a complex settlement is supposed to be made in the talks beginning in March 1993 are not even mentioned. They are no longer named among those to whom the Resolution is to be forwarded even though this had been possible in 1988.

The Commission Opinion of 1993

In 1992 the Commission prepared a paper for the Lisbon summit entitled, 'Europe and the challenge of enlargement'. Its forthcoming Opinions on the applications of Cyprus and Malta would address the question of how micro-states might participate in the Community institutions. The Commission linked Cypriot accession with the Cyprus problem, stating that there was '*inevitably* a link between the question of accession and the problem which results from the *de facto* separation of the island into two entities' (point 30, my italics).

In Lisbon, the European Council decided that relations with Cyprus and Malta would be developed and strengthened by building on the Association Agreements and their application for membership and by developing the political dialogue begun in 1988. 'Each of these applications must be considered on its merits' (*EC Bulletin*, 1992, 6: 10). Turkey, on the other hand, would not be considered on the basis of its application but rather on the non-commital Article 28 of its Association Agreement. This was repeated in Copenhagen conclusions a year later (*EC Bulletin*, 1993, 6: 12). The importance of the Copenhagen summit, however, is that some new hurdles were erected to be applied impartially to all candidates. Where the treaty of Rome had required only that candidates be European, after Copenhagen the criteria were:

1. The applicant country must have achieved stability of

institutions guaranteeing democracy, the rule of law, human rights and respect for and protection of minorities.

2. It must have a functioning market economy, as well as the capacity to cope with competitive pressure and market forces within the European Union.

3. It must have the ability to take on the obligations of membership, including adherence to the aims of political, economic and monetary union.

At Copenhagen, France had wanted even tougher quantifiable criteria. The French led the demand for defined standards of social protection, a defined level of GDP per capita, a defined minimum of privately held assets, the application of the Maastricht criteria on public debt and inflation, a modern fiscal system, and proven administrative capacity to implement the 80,000 pages of EU law. Proven administrative capacity was added to the Copenhagen list at the Madrid summit in December 1995. The intention behind these moves had nothing to do with Cyprus. The idea was to prevent the development of a strong European Union being diluted by the addition of rickety Eastern states.

The relevance for present purposes is that the Copenhagen criteria would only cause major difficulties for Cyprus if the North were included. Greek Cypriot respect for the Turkish Cypriot and Turkish minorities would be difficult to demonstrate. The ability of Turkish Cypriot entrepreneurs to meet competitive pressures could be doubted. There was no way the Turkish lira could be expected to meet the limits on inflation set out in the Treaty of Maastricht. The additional criterion of administrative capacity added by the Madrid Council in December 1995 would cause a particular further difficulty for the TRNC in terms of both the will and the capacity to implement the mass of European regulations. What is surprising, however, is that the Commission's Opinion on Cyprus does not analyse the Cyprus situation in terms of the Copenhagen criteria published in the same month and much discussed beforehand. The following analysis of the Opinion, submitted on 30 June 1993, is organised around those criteria.

The Commission's Opinion was written by M. Serge Abou, the

French official responsible in the Commission for the dossiers of Turkey, Cyprus and Malta. Part One is very positive about the geographic, cultural, economic and political, but not racial, factors making Cyprus worthy of moving from the status of an Associate for over twenty years to that of a full member:

> Cyprus' geographical position, the deep-lying bonds which, for two thousand years, have located the island at the very fount of European culture and civilisation, the intensity of the European influence apparent in the values shared by the people of Cyprus and in the conduct of the cultural, political, economic and social life of its citizens, the wealth of contacts of every kind with the Community, all these confer on Cyprus, beyond all doubt, its European identity and character and confirm its vocation to belong to the Community (para. 44).

Stability of institutions guaranteeing human rights and respect for minorities

In terms of the first Copenhagen criterion, Serge Abou confronts the issue of stability of institutions. However, he side-steps the vexed question whether the Republic could respect or protect its Turkish Cypriot citizens, giving an ambiguously unfavourable verdict about the past while skilfully opening the way for reconsideration in January 1995.

Stability is treated as an institutional question. The international aspect is discussed in terms of the UN agenda without mentioning the five near-wars between Greece and Turkey involving Cyprus before 1993. The Government of Cyprus is entirely absolved from responsibility for the 'turbulent history' of the young Republic. The outbreaks of communal violence before 1974 are attributed to 'the existence of the Greek and Turkish communities side by side' without raising the question of why this longstanding coexistence had been peaceful and was now confrontational. The crisis of 1974 was due to influences from outside. There was 'a coup inspired by the supporters of integration with Greece. This resulted in a military intervention by Turkey'. The Turkish military occupation resulted in the *de facto* partition of the island. 'Until recent years...a mutually acceptable institutional solution had been blocked by the intransigence of both sides...The possibility of continuing disagreements can still not be ruled out.' At this point the Introduction confronts the challenge to the legality of the Government's application to the EU from the '*de facto* authorities of the northern part of the island':

> The Community, however, following the logic of its established position, which is consistent with that of the United Nations where the legitimacy of the government of the Republic of Cyprus and non-recognition of the 'Turkish Republic of Northern Cyprus' are concerned, felt that the application was admissible.

The Cyprus problem is not treated as one of instability. Rather, the problem has caused inconvenience 'in the technical preparation of this opinion. Data on the northern part of the island were therefore obtained from the Government of the Republic of Cyprus or from available international sources'.

Respect for human rights and minorities is treated as a constitutional question. The Republic of Cyprus retains the constitution of 1960:

> Of course, all provisions relating to the participation of the Turkish community in the exercise of executive, legislative and judicial powers are no longer applied. Indeed, some have not been applied since the inter-communal crisis of 1963 (para. 15).

The phrase, 'of course' bears the burden of dispensing with the constitutional guarantees to the Turkish Cypriot community of a third of government jobs, separate voting lists, seats in separate communal legislatures and a third of the seats in the House of Representatives, a third of the judiciary, and a higher proportion of jobs in the Army and Police. Because the Copenhagen criteria are formulated in terms of minorities, it is correct to say (Paragraph 17) that the rights of the 'three minorities'—Maronites, Latins and Armenians—are respected. However Abou is disingenuous not to discuss whether the intention of the first Copenhagen criterion includes the rights of the Turkish Cypriot community even though Turkish Cypriots refuse to accept minority status. European Union officials and statesmen have raised the Kurdish question with Turkey despite Turkey's claim that Kurds are not listed with Greeks and Armenians as minorities in the 1923 Treaty of Lausanne. Voting registers and parliamentary seats are a human rights matter. The constitutional claims of the Turkish Cypriots are described with apparent even-handedness:

> The government in the north, which is not recognised by the international community, adopted a constitution by referendum in 1975. The constitution was later modified in 1985. Mr Denktaş was elected President under this constitution and re-elected in 1985 and 1990. He holds a large majority in parliament owing mainly to the Turkish settler vote (para. 16).

The last sentence contains two mistakes that would not have been made if President Denktaş had invited Serge Abou to see for himself the political situation in Northern Cyprus. The President has no place in the Parliament. Jonathan Warner's 1990 study of voting behaviour claims that the settler vote is evenly distributed across parties, and is not the main source of the Prime Minister, Dr Derviş Eroğlu's majority. The sentence is indicative of the degree of ignorance in Brussels about the Turkish Cypriots, whose isolation precludes them from the 'wealth of contacts of every kind with the Community' cited above.

Nevertheless, on the criterion of political stability, immediate accession is ruled out. 'Cyprus' integration with the Community implies a peaceful, balanced, and lasting settlement of the Cyprus question' (Paragraph 47). Paragraph 48 concludes that 'as soon as the prospect of a settlement is surer, the Community is ready to start the process with Cyprus that should eventually lead to its accession'.

Market freedoms: With regard to the question of the candidate country's capacity to cope with market freedoms, the Opinion is positive with respect to the South. Paragraph 10 points out to the Council that the fundamental freedoms of movement for capital, labour and services which 'could not today be exercised over the entirety of the island's territory...would have to be guaranteed as part of a comprehensive settlement'. Putting it this way accords with the view of both the Commission and the Government that the four freedoms of the Treaty of Rome should be enjoyed over the whole island. However, it conceals the fact that a comprehensive settlement could only be agreed if the Turkish Cypriots were convinced that the beaches and hotels of the North would not be bought up by the wealthier Greek Cypriots. This point is separate from the question of the return of property to those who were dispossessed during and after the 1974 partition.

Ability to take on the obligations of membership: Paragraph 21 expresses coded concern that the enmity between the two communities with or without a settlement will impede the making of new regulations in Brussels and their implementation in Cyprus:

> In this context [of a UN-brokered settlement] care should therefore be taken with a view of the possibility of Community membership to ensure that the decision-making process of the executive and legislature is compatible with the Community's discussion and decision-making apparatus and will enable the Cypriot authorities to adopt the *acquis communautaire* and to implement it effectively *throughout the island.* [my italics]

In Paragraph 39 the Opinion mildly admonishes the unwilling pupils in the North that 'considerably more effort will be required to adjust to the *acquis communautaire* than in the South'. Abou does point out that if Cyprus remains divided, this will further complicate the Union's formulation of foreign policy especially with respect to Turkey. He does not mention the Balkans. He says:

> In relation to the Common Foreign and Security Policy, the need to promote a political settlement is all the more paramount as the current situation would make it difficult for Cyprus to accept and implement commitments made under the European Union Treaty. The political problems linked to the status quo would inevitably have an impact on the Community's policies, especially those concerning Turkey. Cyprus must also give up its membership of

the Non-Aligned Movement of which it was a founder-member and in which it continues to participate actively (para.22).

The Opinion does not mention that non-alignment is a defining attribute of the North laid down in the TRNC's Constitution.

The Opinion shows a particularly light touch with respect to the implications for the Community's own institutions. It merely raises the question whether, as Turkish is one of the two official languages of the Republic of Cyprus, the Community would have to adopt Turkish as an official language (Paragraph 40). The Report does not carry out the promise made by the Commission to the Lisbon summit that it would set out the options for participation by micro-states in the Community institutions. It offers instead 'appropriate treatment in the decision-making process'. Nothing is said of how Community institutions would enforce Community law in the territory 'occupied' by the Turkish army, and whether sanctions on Turkey would be required by the principle of solidarity among member states.

The final paragraph deals in a totally different way with the question of what might happen should there be no settlement. The first suggestion is clear enough despite its opaque phrasing: 'the situation should be reassessed in view of the positions adopted by each party'. While no criteria are offered for assessing what positions adopted by the only two parties involved, the Greek Cypriots and the Turkish Cypriots, should lead to what consequences, it is reasonable to deduce that a negative stance by the Turkish Cypriots would open the way to admitting Greek Cyprus without a settlement. Abou's second point is that 'the question of Cyprus's accession should be reconsidered in January 1995.' The last line of the Opinion, which took three years to prepare, suggests a further delay of at least eighteen months before a reconsideration of the merits of the application.

Sequel to the Commission's Opinion
The General Affairs Council on 19-20 July 1993 welcomed the Opinion. On 4 October, a compromise 'broad consensus' was achieved which opened the way for 'substantial talks' on the *acquis* between the Commission and the Greek Cypriots. While no date was

set for accession negotiations, January 1995 was accepted for examining the question:

> The Council supports the Commission stance which proposes to make use of all the instruments contained in the Accession Agreement in order to contribute, in close co-operation with the Cypriot government, to the economic, social and political transition of Cyprus towards integration with the *European Union, without waiting for a peaceful, balanced, and durable solution to the Cypriot problem*. To this end, the Council invites the Commission to initiate, from now on, *substantial discussions* with the government of Cyprus to help it prepare, in the best possible conditions, for accession negotiations *which will later follow*, and to regularly inform the Council on the progress achieved (para.1). [my italics]

The next point implies that the Council agreed with the Commission and the Greek Cypriot Government that its application could not be a hostage to the perceived intransigence of the Turkish Cypriot side:

> In the eventuality whereby, *despite these efforts, a prospect of settlement is not forthcoming in a foreseeable future*, the Council has agreed to examine the situation in view of the positions adopted by each party in the intercommunal talks and to examine, in January 1995, the question of Cyprus accession to the European Union in the light of the situation (para.1 [my italics] See also forty-first review of the activities of the Council, 1994).

Between November 1993 and February 1995, the Commission held substantive productive discussions with twenty-three sectoral committees set up in Nicosia for this purpose.

In the first six months of 1994, Greece became the Presidency country for a third time. The Greek Foreign Minister, Mr Theodoros Pangalos told the European Parliament on 19 January 1994:

> Regardless of the progress on the Cyprus problem itself, Cyprus should accede to the European Union as soon as possible,

something which will significantly help the efforts to find a solution to that problem (Annexe to OJ, 3-441: 149).

On 9 February, he proposed that Cyprus and Malta took precedence over enlargement to Eastern Europe:

> We must make a decision on 1 January 1995. Later on we shall have to study the possibility of seriously tackling the request to participate in the Union by Central European countries like Hungary and Poland (Annexe to OJ 3-442: 141).

This deliberate coat-trailing expresses the view common to the leaders of Mediterranean countries that their concerns have again been displaced since 1989 by the priority accorded to the Central and Eastern Europe Countries, the CEEC. According to Pace (1995: 10):

> Long-standing relations have not given the Mediterranean countries any advantages, and the EU's behaviour, based naturally on the interests of the present member states, has led to some bewilderment on the part of the Mediterranean applicants.

At the Summit meeting it organised in Corfu, 24-25 June 1994, the Greeks proposed to redress the balance with a Euro-Mediterranean Partnership which would include the applicant states of Cyprus and Malta. The idea was that this partnership, to be launched a year later, would not threaten Southern member states with competing agricultural imports or threaten partner states with any systematic attack on their abysmal records on human rights. The Heads of State and Government 'noted' that Cyprus and Malta were to be involved in the next stage of enlargement. However the statement gave at least as much weight to the need for a settlement of the Cyprus problem that would respect 'the territorial integrity and unity of the country, in accordance with the relevant UN resolutions and high-level agreements'. This formula was repeated at Essen in December 1994. The underlying disagreement among member states on the question of a Cypriot settlement before its accession came into public view. While Foreign Minister Pangalos claimed that 'the question of the admission of Cyprus was dissociated from the political problem of Cyprus' (*Agence Europe*, 26 June 1994: 4), John Major in the House of Commons on 27 June implied that Cyprus could not join until after a settlement. Huntington's informants told him that 'the Greek behaviour as President of the EU Council in December 1994 exasperated other members, and Western European officials privately label its membership a mistake' (Huntington, 1997: 163). The Maltese and Cypriot leaders were not invited by the German Presidency along with Central and East European leaders to a meeting in Essen coinciding with the December summit on enlargement.

On 7 February 1994 the Council took the highly unusual step of mandating the author of the Opinion on Cyprus, a Commission official, as the Council's own Observer on Cyprus. He was to report 'on the implications for the requirements of the *acquis* of the Union of political developments in Cyprus.' This display of the Council's confidence also implied complete disregard for the fact that Abou was *persona non grata* to the Turkish Cypriots and therefore could not be expected to attend intercommunal discussions. Within the Commission, Abou, a desk officer, reported directly to the External Affairs Commissioner, Mr Hans van den Broek. Heinz Kramer says that the Council appointed an observer to the intercommunal talks in the summer of 1993 on the 'Set of Ideas' (Kramer, 1997b: 25), but if so it was not taken up. The earliest public reference to the appointment of a Council Observer is a proposal by the European Parliament on 27 October 1993; it was opposed by the United Kingdom. Although the Greek preoccupation with the status of the Former Yugoslav Republic of Macedonia is credited with reducing its focus on Cyprus, Abou's new role may have been a gesture to an Athens annoyed by the recognition accorded to FYROM by six member states. The Turkish Cypriots again refused to see him, preferring consistency in demanding legal recognition first to showing confidence in the strength of their political position. Serge Abou delivered two unpublished reports to the Council during the Greek Presidency, in April and June. However the political division over Europe in the two Cypriot communities was then transformed by Greek Cypriot joy, and Turkish Cypriot anger, at a ruling by all thirteen judges of the EU12 Court of Justice in Luxembourg.

The Court of Justice, 1994: the Anastasiou case
Since 1974 sanctions have proved a powerful weapon in the Government armoury directed against the Turkish Cypriots. In the absence of international recognition, the new airport built by the TRNC at Ercan is not listed as safe for landing by any country except Turkey. Commissioner van den Broek always landed at Larnaca, the internationally recognised airport built by the Government after Nicosia airport on the frontier line became unusable for both sides in 1974. If the Commissioner had flown to Ercan via Turkey, the Greek Cypriot Government would have found ways to sanction this action, as they did with commercial companies who traded with the North.

The significance of the case for EU relations with Cyprus is twofold. It closed the loophole in the embargo by ruling in favour of the Government argument that its certification was necessary for the importation of plants, fruit and potatoes into the territory of member states. This European ruling so immediately infuriated the TRNC Assembly that on 28 August it repealed all its previous resolutions envisaging a Federal Republic of Cyprus as an acceptable solution, though did not thereby exclude it as a possibility altogether. It demanded complete economic integration with Turkey. Secondly, the Turkish Cypriots drew the conclusion that they should be suspicious of any rights based on a treaty with the European Union. The Court discounted a treaty obligation as important as Article 5 of the 1972 Treaty of Association by prioritising the Community need for uniform rules of certification. It followed that any derogations in a future Treaty of Accession intended to protect Turkish Cypriot property could be trumped by the Court giving priority to the fundamental freedoms of free movement of capital, persons, goods and services. These four freedoms are more important as principles to the European Union than the requirements of mere administrative uniformity.

The Commission and the United Kingdom argued that, exceptionally, the United Kingdom had to accept movement certificates and phytosanitary certificates issued in the North for otherwise the UK authorities would be in breach of Article 5, by which they were forbidden to discriminate between nationals of Cyprus. The certification made no reference to the TRNC, and had not caused any problem of plant health or concealed imports from elsewhere. The United Kingdom, wrapping itself in a mantle of state sovereignty, separately provoked the European judges by contending that the Anastasiou company making the complaint could not rely on the wording of administrative protocols that were only applicable to states.

The Court followed the advice of its own Advocate-General in ruling that the company concerned was directly affected by the UK interpretation of the procedures (para.23). On the central issue it ruled that the UK could only accept certification from a recognised government (67). Article 5 was not essential to the aims of the Association. The Court's further argument (47) that 'Article 5 cannot in any event confer on the Community the right to interfere in the internal affairs of Cyprus' reiterates a contemporary principle. However, the Court judgement contains no sign that it attempted to reach any political understanding of why this unusual version of the Community's non-discrimination principle was included in the treaty. It does cite the transfer of sewage as evidence that the benefits of the Association 'have on several occasions been accessible to the whole population of Cyprus' (45). From a political perspective, to understand the requirement on member states not to discriminate between the nationals of Cyprus as amounting to interference is itself to interfere on the side of the wholly Greek Cypriot Government. In the same spirit the Court argued that the Community must obtain the agreement of the Government for any procedures of certification (46). The Court also argued that different national practices create 'uncertainty of a kind likely to undermine the existence of a common commercial policy' (53). This statement of principle does seem disproportionate in that the trade concerned was confined to Britain and Ireland via Rotterdam. The fact that some unspecified member states refused to recognise certificates from Northern Cyprus stamped in the name of 'Cyprus Customs Authorities' was therefore a potential rather than a substantial threat to administrative uniformity (52). Finally the Court rejected the Commission's argument that it was 'difficult' for exporters from the North to obtain certificates other than those issued locally. The Court found that the Turkish exporters had failed to apply for certification, implying that domestic remedies had not been exhausted (41, 48). As neither the Greek Republic nor the Turkish authorities permitted Greek Cypriot inspectors to cross the Green Line, the Court's observation is demonstrably absurd. It may be worth remarking that the European Court of Justice does not issue 'minority opinions', a relic of its insecure beginnings when it feared that established national courts might not respect its judgements.

The lack of impartiality shown by the Court of Justice in rejecting what remained of the basis for even-handedness between the two major Cypriot communities fits a general pattern shown by all the European institutions. Between the coup of 1974 and this case in 1994, the Parliament, the Commission and, to a lesser extent, the Council, show the same propensity to identify increasingly with the Greek Cypriot view of the situation on the ground in Cyprus. The Greek Cypriots interpret this as support for the justice of their case in law and morality. The Turkish Cypriots see this as a consequence of the absence of Turks, or Muslims, in the Commission, Parliament and Court. Clearly the isolation, imposed and self-imposed, of the Turkish Cypriots, did not help the smaller community disseminate its own views of where justice and morality might lie. No Turkish Cypriots or Turks appeared before the Court of Justice.

Greece vetoes the Customs Union with Turkey
The tightening of sanctions after the Anastasiou ruling did not endear the European Union to the Turkish Cypriot leadership or make them minded to compromise. In October 1994 Mr Denktaş rejected Mr Clerides' offer to accept a cantonal federation if the Turkish Cypriots would agree to participate in accession talks to the EU which might be delayed while the details were worked through (Dodd, 1998: 69). The Turkish Cypriot fear of being taken over was accentuated by Mr Clerides' suggestion that Cyprus be demilitarised—understood by Mr Denktaş as replacing the Turkish army with an international force paid for by the Government alongside the wholly Greek Cypriot National Guard.

The failure of Mr Clerides' 'notably courageous overtures' was reported by Serge Abou to the European Council in his third report of 23 January 1995 (Appendix 6 in Dodd, 1997: 172-180). The lack of progress had led to accentuating the international community's weariness with the problem, the military build-up, and the worsening economic problems of the Turkish Cypriot community. Nevertheless two essential points should not be overlooked. According to the EU Observer, all the cards were now on the table, 'If the political will is found, all the ingredients of a mutually advantageous settlement in accordance with the Security Council resolutions are at hand'. This line accorded with that of the UN Secretary General's representative in Cyprus, Gustave Feissel, to be discussed in Chapter 6. Abou's second point was that the time had come for the EU to take an active role in seeking a solution:

> The talks have shown that the issue of Cyprus' membership of the EU is now fixed in the minds of all those concerned, something which obviously *gives the EU a particular responsibility*, namely to flesh out the position adopted by the Corfu European Council *on the accession process and to play an active part in efforts to find a solution to the Cyprus problem* (para. II, 2 ii). [my italics]

This responsibility is implicitly linked in the next sentence to a change in EU relations with Turkey:

> In relations with Turkey the EU should try to find the means to establish a climate of confidence and a constructive dialogue on ways to achieve an overall settlement. A decisive step in this direction would be a successful outcome to the negotiations on the completion of the customs union and the *normalisation of EU-Turkey relations*, including the resumption of financial co-operation [blocked by Greece] and establishment of a level of economic co-operation and political dialogue in keeping *with Turkey's importance as a partner.* [my italics]

The significance of this linkage is that the Council's Observer on Cyprus, and simultaneously the senior Commission official responsible for Turkey, was taking a strong line against a Greek diplomacy which was now out of step with the views of the major states. A month before Abou's report, ferocious resistance on the part of Greece to the completion of the Customs Union with Turkey had led to a veto, in Community parlance, on 19 December 1994, at the thirty-fifth EC-Turkey Association Council (*EC Bulletin*, 1994,12: 424).

> However, in the absence of a joint position, the Community was unable to enter into a discussion with the Turkish delegation on the subject of completion of the Customs Union...the [incoming] French Presidency accordingly announced that it intended to hold the next Association Council meeting simultaneously with the meeting of the Council of Ministers of the European Union on 6 & 7 March 1995 with the aim of taking the decisions needed to move to the final stage of the EC-Turkey customs union.

The elements of the package deal were in place.

| 3 |

Negotiating Accession

Cyprus' accession should benefit all communities and help to bring about
civil peace and reconciliation (Council Conclusions, 6 March 1995).

1. Introduction

The idea that the accession process would stimulate reconciliation
between Greek and Turkish Cypriots proved as empty as the
Council's hope that relations between Greece and Turkey would be
normalised. For the five years after 1995, the Commission and the
Government of Cyprus collaborated successfully in harmonising
Cypriot law and institutions in readiness for integration into the
Community. However, this very success further alienated the
Turkish Cypriots. So far from accession becoming a catalyst for a
settlement, the EU had to reckon with the ever-growing integration
of Turkish Cyprus with Turkey anticipated by Murat Karayalçın at
the dinner on 6 March 1995. Graeco-Turkish relations became worse
rather than better. By the end of the year, the crisis over the islet of
Imia/Kardak beginning on 25 December was to escalate rapidly so
that in January both countries' fleets sailed against each other
prepared for battle. Again, the Council's aim of establishing in the
Customs Union a stable framework for relations with Turkey was
only partially realised. Although the Customs Union itself received
the assent of the European Parliament in December 1995, and proved
less problematic from Brussels' perspective than expected, it was
unacceptable to Turkey as a satisfactory basis for relations. Later, in
retaliation for the European Union's 'historic mistake' in December

1997 of formally excluding Turkey from the second wave of candidates for membership, Turkey took a strongly nationalist line stressing its independence between West and East. One consequence was that Turkey refused to talk with the EU about Cyprus. It remains to be seen whether the acceptance of Turkey's candidature by the EU15 at their Helsinki summit of December 1999 has provided a better framework for relations between the EU and Turkey, and between Greece and Turkey, changing thereby the conditions for a settlement in Cyprus.

In 1995, the European Union's relations with its neighbours in Eastern Europe and the Southern Mediterranean showed the same combination of magnetic powers of attraction combined with frustrating weakness in establishing a peaceful and protective milieu. Thus a ceremony in Paris, coincidentally also in March 1995, demonstrated how successfully the EU had dispelled initial hostility in Eastern Europe at EU interference in the domestic affairs of states which had recently recovered their full sovereignty (Peterson & Bomberg, 1999: 238). The occasion was the signing of the last in a series of 47 stability pacts between the EU or its Member States and individual countries of Central and Eastern Europe. Another 76 agreements had been signed bilaterally between neighbouring states after two years of conferences financed and promoted by the EU General Affairs Council. They were known as Balladur pacts in honour of the French Prime Minister who had initiated them. They were supported by a German-designed programme under OSCE auspices to monitor the treatment of minorities and implement cross-border co-operation paid for by the EU assistance programme, PHARE. On the other hand, the credibility of EU decision-making had been called into serious question by the Yugoslav crisis. The setting up of the Contact Group in April 1993 involving only Germany, France, the UK, the Russian Federation and the USA signified that the EU could no longer be expected to function as a single entity in promoting a settlement or keeping the peace in former Yugoslavia. The European failure to protect the human rights of Muslims in Bosnia had outraged influential opinion within the EU, in the USA and especially in Muslim countries. In 1995 the protected city of Srbrenica, 80 per cent of whose inhabitants were

Muslim, was given up by Dutch troops to Serb irregulars. Mutual respect between Washington and Brussels was at such an ebb that officials on both sides constructed a New Transatlantic Agenda to restore confidence (Krenzler, 1996: 9).

With respect to their neighbours in the Southern Mediterranean, EU member states were even more loath to sacrifice their own interests for the sake of milieu goals. On 8 March 1995, two days after the Council compromise on the Turkish Customs Union, the Commission outlined in a Communication to the Council and the Parliament what became in November the Barcelona process. It offered limited financial aid and eventual industrial free trade with 12 Mediterranean states, including Turkey and Cyprus (*EU Bulletin*, 1995, 3: 1.4.57). The Member States of the EU would not open their labour or agricultural markets to promote the regional stability of the Mediterranean. Given the lack of industrialisation in most of these countries, the offer of industrial free trade by 2010 was unlikely to transform the undemocratic regimes and abolish mass unemployment in these neighbouring countries. The exclusion of the United States from the Barcelona process was yet another indication of a European desire for greater regional autonomy after the end of the Cold War. But, as in Eastern Europe, the governments of the EU15 did not want the costs of transition to result in either higher taxes or greater competition that would hurt their own populations.

In their preparations for the forthcoming intergovernmental conference, at the end of which the EU had promised to open negotiations with Cyprus within six months, the EU governments and institutions showed their awareness of the need for greater EU decision-making capacity in foreign policy. It was a central concern of most of the position papers (e.g Schäuble/Lamers, 1994: 79). In June 1995, the first preparatory meeting of the IGC was deliberately held on the fortieth anniversary of the Messina Conference of June 1955. Its chairman, Sr Carlos Westendorp, made the point that this was the first intergovernmental conference intended to reform the institutions. The starting date of March 1996 had been written into the Maastricht Treaty by the defeated federalists who expected that the three-pillar structure acceptable to John Major would by then have proved unworkable. In terms of foreign policy, three elements were missing. The EU lacked an elected president who could, like the American president, tip the balance against state and sectoral interests where this was needed for reasons of external policy. Secondly, the EU lacked an institution which could emulate the Commission's role in domestic policy of formulating a common European policy to put to the Council for decision. Thirdly, the EU lacked soldiers, or even designated national contingents, which could collectively enforce peaceful outcomes and protect ethnic minorities in the Balkans or in the Southern Mediterranean.

It is against this background that EU decision making with respect to Cyprus has to be understood. Remarkably few personnel became involved in this issue—in the Council of Ministers, the European Council of heads of state and government, the Commission, the Parliament and the European Investment Bank. We begin with the Councils which since Maastricht have embodied the dominance of the nation-states in the post-Delors decade.

EU institutions: the Councils

The 6 March compromise on finalising the Customs Union with Turkey and setting a date for beginning accession negotiations with Cyprus was the work of the *General Affairs Council* of the European Union. Composed of the foreign ministers of all fifteen member states, or their deputies, it is attended by at least one, and often more, of the members of the Commission. The General Affairs Council meets more frequently than any other council, and its members also see a good deal of each other in other fora such as the Council of Europe, NATO and the United Nations. Foreign ministers, the EU Commissioner for External Relations and the President of the Commission also attend what is called the *European Council* of heads of EU governments. This frequency of social contact helps in reaching consensus among separate national interests. When ministers are dealing with Community matters like trade and aid, majority voting weighted according to the populations of the Member States is applicable. More informal conventions apply to matters on the intergovernmental agenda on foreign affairs. For example, where a member state has a particular interest in an issue, as do Greece and Britain with respect to Cyprus, other ministers are expected to show solidarity. For Community matters, including the *acquis*, the overcrowded agenda is prepared by the senior ambassadors of the Member States in Brussels (*COREPER II*) on the basis of Commission proposals. For intergovernmental business, the agenda is discussed by the *Committee of Political Directors* of the national foreign ministries, sometimes on the basis of unpublished papers produced by *Working Groups* of the Council Secretariat (Peterson and Bomberg, 1999: 35). Since 1974 Cyprus has merited a Working Group.

The distinction between Community matters, like accession, and foreign policy matters, such as supporting the UN in promoting a settlement between the communities, was all too useful as an excuse for not using accession as a lever for promoting a settlement. Moreover, a Council composed largely of fifteen sovereign states had other reasons for not wishing to take responsibility for settling the Cyprus dispute. The inhibition against Community involvement in internal political problems was still dominant despite the gradual reception of the doctrine that first the democratic, and then the human rights', credentials of applicant states were matters of Community concern. An explicit treaty basis for this doctrine was not available until the 1997 Treaty of Amsterdam. In the case of Cyprus, for the Council to seek a settlement was all the more difficult because the Turkish Cypriot claim to rule in the North had been denounced as illegal secession in the clearest possible terms. The institutions of Council, Commission and Parliament had all separately followed the lead of the UN Security Council in denouncing the 1983 declaration of independence of the Turkish Republic of Northern Cyprus. Greek nationals in all the institutions, with considerable support especially from Scandinavians, Irish and Luxembourgers, were keen to uphold this non-recognition stance as the only available effective means of protesting against the partition of the island by overwhelming external force. On the other hand, the Gaullist dictum applies to Cyprus that diplomacy, while paying great attention to form, only recognises realities. A military offensive against Turkey was impossible to contemplate for other members of NATO. Unlike the USSR in the case of divided Germany, Turkey was an ally. The enlargement of NATO to Poland, Hungary and the

Czech Republic needed the assent of Turkey. The creation of a European Security Defence Identity could be counter-productive if it excluded Turkey, an Associate Member of the Western European Union. After Kosovo, the determined moves to create a European force of 60,000 men for peacekeeping purposes would be immeasurably stronger in reassuring all sides of its potential impartiality and effectiveness if it included Turkish troops, the most battle-hardened troops in Europe. Despite its partiality for the Greek Cypriot cause, the Council members knew full well that no settlement on the island could be reached without the agreement of the elected leaders of the Turkish Cypriot community and of Turkey. None supported the Italian Foreign Minister, Sr Lamberto Dini, when he said in public on 27 August 1997, 'There are two republics in Cyprus, two entities, two governments'. Signor Dini retracted his remark, but the fact that it had been made by such a significant Mediterranean politician showed that EU solidarity on the legitimacy of the wholly Greek Cypriot Government of Cyprus could not be taken for granted.

The Council attempted to finesse the issue of recognition by institutional devices similar to those which the same European states and the USA used in the UN context. One device was the nomination of *Special Representatives*. While a regular diplomat accredited to the Republic of Cyprus could visit the North for talks, special representatives were different in that they could be mandated to talk to both communities on the basis of equality. There were so many special representatives on Cyprus that they could also be mandated to talk to each other. At Scottish hotels, in American university seminars, at the UN headquarters in New York, in seminars for businessmen in Brussels, the principal special representatives concerted their understanding of events. The American President had a 'special representative' and the US State Department a 'special co-ordinator'. The Russian Federation and Australia had special representatives. The UN Secretary-General and his special representative were mandated to talk to all parties interested in a solution. The Commonwealth of former British colonies appointed a special representative. Several member states demonstrated a particular national concern with the search for a settlement by appointing special representatives. The UK appointed Sir David Hannay, GCMG, on 23 May 1996. As a diplomatic heavyweight who had been UK Representative in Brussels and in New York, his appointment was indicative of British concern to keep the issue of the sovereign bases out of any negotiations, and to keep the EU to its role as supporting the efforts of the UN and the United States. Finland and Sweden, states which had contributed troops to UNFICYP, appointed special missions. The special representative of Germany until 1999 was Detlev Graf zu Rantzau. The Council Presidency, as distinct from the Council, appointed a succession of national diplomats to be its special representative for Cyprus, mandated to inform the Council of political developments on the island. The Italian Presidency on 29 January 1996 appointed Mr Federico di Roberto. Mr Kester Heaslip represented the Irish and then the Dutch Presidencies for the second half of 1996 and the first six months of 1997. Sir David Hannay represented the EU during the Luxembourg Presidency and then the UK Presidency in 1998.

A second UN device copied by the General Affairs Council was to mandate the Commission to carry out specified tasks that necessarily implied dealings with the unrecognised authorities of the North. In the UN case, the Security Council mandated its Secretary General to arrange talks between the two sides as though they were equals; also, every six months it mandated the UNFICYP to continue its peacekeeping mission on both sides of the Green Line even though the Status of Forces Agreement was signed only with the Government of Cyprus. In the same way, the General Affairs Council in March 1995 mandated the European Commission to make the necessary contacts with the authorities in the North to 'inform' them of the benefits of EU membership. The Commission was to 'consult' with the recognised Government of the Republic on how this might be done. Consultation is an ambiguous requirement. The Commission in Nicosia had a choice. The requirement was interpreted as implying a power of veto to the Greek Cypriot Government, with whom good relations were needed to prepare the way for accession. Alternatively, the Commission might have chosen merely to inform the Government of what it was doing to bring the Turkish Cypriots to look more positively on EU involvement. For example, if the Commission had deputed an EU information officer to work permanently in the North, his welcome in the North would have been warmer precisely because of the disapproval his appointment would have aroused in he South.

EU institutions: the Commission

In the Santer Commission, the Commissioner for External Relations responsible since 1993 for the enlargement dossier was himself an experienced former foreign secretary. In 1994 Commissioner Hans van den Broek from the Netherlands had defeated Leon Brittan's bid to take over the dossier on Central and Eastern Europe (Middlemas, 1995: 224).

The Southern Mediterranean was the responsibility of Sr Manuel Marin, the Commissioner for Development. When the Prodi Commission took over in 1999, the new Commissioner for enlargement, Herr Günther Verheugen, displayed a much deeper cultural sensitivity to the Turkish understanding of their European vocation, though what he had to say in Northern Cyprus did not endear him to his Turkish Cypriot audiences.

Within the Directorate-General for External Relations there has long been a unit with responsibility for the two tiny Associated countries of Cyprus and Malta and the huge Associated country of Turkey. The Unit has four A-grade (policy) officers, a desk officer for each country and the Head of Unit, Serge Abou remained in charge until his promotion in 1998, when he was replaced as head of Unit by Mr Erik van der Linden. M. Philippe Combescot, his deputy and the desk officer for Turkey, also covered for Cyprus in Brussels during his colleague's maternity leave. In Nicosia there was a long interregnum between Ambassador Anouil's departure in 1998 and the appointment of Sr Donato Chiarini. The tiny Delegation consisted of one executive B-grade and one clerical C-grade officer, with five locally recruited staff (Nugent, 1997: 63).

This very small band of officials was supplemented by others from M. François Lamoureux' group preparing enlargement and then from the Task Force for negotiations directed by Herr Klaus van der Pas. Also the Directorate-General for the political side of External Relations, DGIA, has special advisers who cover all aspects of the enlargement process. Finally, it was the Legal Service of the Commission which commissioned the only attempt at justifying to Turkey and the Turkish Cypriots the EU's rejection of their legal arguments that Cyprus' founding treaties invalidate the accession process. Turkey as a non-member could not bring an action before the European Court of Justice, and no member or institution would bring an action. Three academic lawyers, Professors James Crawford, Gerhard Hafner and Alain Pellet, were instructed to refute the arguments of Professor M.H.Mendelson QC, which queried on Turkey's behalf the legality of the EU acceptance of the Cypriot application. Professor Mendelson responded with a further Note on the significance to be attributed to the analogy they drew with the 1955 Austrian treaty. So in a Community founded on the rule of law, there is no authoritative resolution by any court of these conflicting legal Opinions (Summaries in Dodd, 1998: Appendix 10).

Other EU institutions

The Parliament and the European Investment Bank were even more partial than the Council and the Commission to the Greek Cypriot side. The dominance of the Greek lobby in the EU-Turkey and the EU-Cyprus Joint Parliamentary Delegations reflected a European public opinion which was at once uninterested in, and mildly hostile to, Turkey and the Turkish Republic of Northern Cyprus. Between 1995 and 2000, public opinion outside Greece and Turkey never seriously engaged with Cyprus in the way it did with Sarajevo or Kosovo. Even the Imia/Kardak incident was largely seen as a minor dispute about goats on an uninhabited islet. In Holbrooke's accurate phrase, President Clinton stopped the war fleets sailing towards each other 'while Europe slept'. The exception was the coverage of the killing in 1996 by Turkish Cypriot soldiers of two Greek Cypriot cousins, one of whom was attempting to take down a Turkish flag on the border. However, the exception proves the rule. This incident was the culmination of a bikers' ride from Berlin to Nicosia which was deliberately intended to bring the scandalous division of Cyprus back into the limelight.

The willingness of the European Parliament in plenary session to pass resolutions supporting the Government can be illustrated from the following resolution of 13 July 1995 in the wake of a natural disaster in the mountains encircling Kyrenia:

> Following the fires which devastated the part of Cyprus occupied by the Turkish armed forces, Parliament called on the Commission to provide the Cypriot Government with immediate material and financial assistance. It called on the Council and Commission to bring pressure to bear on the Turkish occupying authorities to allow the Cypriot Government to assist in extinguishing the fires and repairing the damage caused (OJC: 249, 25 September, 1995).

This hostility to the 'Turkish occupying authorities' was of a piece with the Parliament's earlier rejection of the completion of the Customs Union with Turkey on 16 February, citing Turkey's bad record in Cyprus and on human rights. It took intense pressure from the Commission and the Member States to persuade the two main parties in the European Parliament to dragoon their members to give a reluctant assent to the Customs Union with Turkey on 13 December 1995. So far the Joint Committee of the European and Cypriot Parliaments has regularly supported the Greek view that accession should not be conditional on a settlement. In April 2000 it additionally resolved that the negotiations for Turkish membership foreseen by the Helsinki Conclusions should not be opened until Turkish troops have been withdrawn from Cyprus.

Since the ratification of the Treaty of Maastricht, the European Parliament has won powers which could become very important to the ratification process of any enlargement. An absolute majority of all its members, not just of those voting, has to assent to the separate treaties negotiated with each candidate country. This is in addition to the needed ratification by the national parliaments of the Member States and of the applicant country.

The European Investment Bank has a desk officer for Cyprus. Since 1980 the EIB has lost any sense that even-handedness is required in Cyprus by the Treaty of Association. Like their counterparts in the Commission, EIB officials are uncomprehending of Turkish Cypriot indifference. They have come to the conclusion that the North has ruled itself out from the loans and grants on offer, and that the Turkish political calculations are more the concern of the Council and the United Nations. Under the Fourth Financial Protocol, loans of 50m EURO are earmarked for Cyprus, with an additional 2m EURO for use by the Cyprus Development Bank. It is worth pointing out that the 3bn EURO available for loans to foster enlargement are not specifically allocated to any particular country or purpose. It is remotely possible that the Council might look to this EIB allocation as a source for funding a settlement of the property issue in Cyprus.

Paucity and partiality

In the following discussion of the accession negotiations, and EU attempts to promote them as a catalyst for a settlement, we have to remember how few are the officials directly involved in the Council and Commission, and their inevitable partiality. The identification of the institutions with Greece and the Greek Cypriots has made it exceptionally difficult for either Commission officials or the special representatives of the Council Presidency to be accepted by Turkish Cypriots and Turks as equidistant honest brokers between the two communities and their respective motherlands. The degree of impartiality attempted by the Commission before 1980 has become a distant, as well as painful, memory. The division of labour established by the Council between the special representative responsible for facilitating a settlement and the Commission responsible for allaying Turkish Cypriot hostility was unlikely to be a decisive contribution towards peace. The Council has indeed made it plain that the political will for a settlement was a matter not for itself but for the two communities and their respective motherlands. The Council seems to have had no doubts in seeing its responsibility as to support, and not displace, the longstanding involvement of the UN and the USA in fostering a settlement between the other parties directly involved. In 1995 Cyprus was a hurdle on the path to enlargement to the East which the Council hoped that others would remove by negotiating a settlement before its accession.

2. Towards Accession

The conditions of admission and the adjustments to the Treaties on which the Union is founded which such admission entails shall be the subject of an agreement between the Member States and the applicant State (Article O, Treaty on European Union, 1992).

The compromise of 6 March committed the EU Council to work in good faith for the accession of the Republic of Cyprus. However, the existing framework of the EU's pre-accession strategy was based on three elements defined at the Essen Summit in 1994—*Europe Agreements*, *PHARE Agreements*, and *Structured Dialogue*. None of these elements strictly applied to either Cyprus or Malta, the two Associated Mediterranean countries of whose membership applications the Essen Summit had 'taken note'. The Europe Agreements with countries of Central and then Eastern Europe were called Partnership Agreements rather than Association Agreements. Partnership had become the preferred designation used for Northern European states of EFTA in the European Economic Area Agreements of the previous decade. The term 'partnership' was intended to conceal the actual dominance of the EU side; the term 'Association' had become devalued by the failure of the EC relationships with the non-European former colonies and with Turkey. PHARE Agreements financed the provision of advice on transition to political pluralism and capitalism by Western experts to Poland and Hungary, a measure extended to other Eastern European countries and supplemented by contracts for improving infrastructure. Unlike Marshall Aid, the money was not given to recipient countries to spend as they saw fit. Much of the budget went to consultants from EU countries, a result which accorded with Member State notions of national interest. The jargon term, 'structured dialogue', recognises that applicants have a special status with the Council and Commission expressed in regular and institutionalised arrangements for attending meetings in Brussels. The Treaty of Rome had made no provision for Observer status permitting favoured third parties to attend meetings but not to vote. After 1995 the EU maintained the legal bases of the differences between the CEEC countries and Cyprus. As a relatively developed capitalist democracy, Cyprus was not included in the PHARE programme. Its Association Agreement was not renamed as a Europe Agreement. However, its new status was recognised by developing structural dialogue, a change which did not require a new Agreement.

Structured dialogue

> The Council... intends adopting concrete proposals for a specific strategy in preparation for accession, including a structured dialogue in time for the next meeting of the Association Council with Cyprus (Draft Conclusions, 2 February 1995).

The content of the structured dialogue with Cyprus had itself to be negotiated. An annexe to the Conclusions reached on 6 March envisages that Cypriot ministers and officials could in future be invited on a regular basis to attend meetings under the three Maastricht pillars of Community, foreign and police business. Ministers and officials might be invited 'if necessary and as the need arises' (*sic*) to some first pillar, EEC Councils. Tourism, the environment, and maritime affairs were cited as examples. Ministers and officials might also attend intergovernmental meetings on the Common Foreign and Security Policy and on Justice and Home Affairs. The President and Foreign Minister would meet with the other heads of government in the margins of meetings of the European Council. At the nineteenth meeting of the Association Council in June the structured dialogue with Cyprus was instituted. However, the June minutes include a reminder of the link some saw between accession and a settlement by defining the purpose of the dialogue as 'to help to achieve the objective of Cyprus' accession, which both parties consider will benefit both of the island's communities and contribute to civil peace and reconciliation'. The modalities defined unilaterally a month later on 17 July 1995 at the General Affairs Council (*EU Bulletin*, 1995, 718: point 1.4.72) reflect a further compromise consequent on the dispute over whether Turkish Cypriots had to be included in this dialogue. On the one hand, the Cypriot Government is recognised as the sole legitimate locutor. On the other hand President Clerides is to attend only one summit each year:

> The Government of Cyprus will be the sole interlocutor in this dialogue, which will take the form of an annual meeting of heads of State or Government, on the fringe of a European Council, and six monthly meetings of foreign ministers.

In the event, President Clerides and his Delegation attended two summits in 1995, at Cannes and Madrid, and two in 1996, at Florence and Dublin.

Structured dialogue meetings were held at the ministerial level with Cyprus in November 1995, May 1996, and October 1996. There is a significant gap in this sequence before the next meeting in October 1997 because the February 1997 meeting had to be 'postponed'. The postponement was due to an impasse between the larger member states and Greece on whether to require the Government of Cyprus to include Turkish Cypriots in its Delegation when it came to formal negotiations on the terms of accession. The bitterness of the dispute is all the more evident because, under the rules of structural dialogue, member states may express differing points of view. However, the Dutch Presidency had timetabled the annual Association meeting with Cyprus for the same day, for which the Member States did have to agree unanimously a common position beforehand.

In September 1995 a Cypriot minister of Justice attended his first meeting of the Justice and Home Affairs Council, the third pillar of the Maastricht Treaty. However the Interior Ministers of the EU consistently maintained the difference between Cyprus and the East and Central European countries. On 5 December 1997, for example, the Justice and Home Affairs ministers met with their CEEC counterparts, 'and subsequently with the Ministers (*sic*) for Justice of Cyprus. On that occasion the ministers held an exchange of views on judicial co-operation in civil and criminal matters' (Press release 12888/97). Other ministers and their officials during the Italian and Spanish presidencies in 1996 attended meetings on police and immigration (Schengen) questions, transport, agriculture and environment policies. The Cypriot Government participated in meetings of EUROSTAT, of trans-European telecommunications and shipping networks, and nine Community programmes covering such matters as scientific research and educational exchanges.

Political dialogue

Just as significant of the Council's willingness to enhance the status of Cyprus is the commitment on 6 March 1995 to upgrade the political dialogue on EU external policy, which had been in place since the 1989 summit in Rhodes. The head of the Cypriot foreign service could henceforth be invited to meetings of the national political directors of the EU15 foreign offices. This insider status was underlined by the appointment of a Cypriot correspondent, receiving copies of telegrams issued by member states. Cypriot experts could also be invited to meetings with other national experts in working parties or *ad hoc* discussions on the OSCE, the UN, terrorism, human rights, disarmament and security. This increased the visibility of the Cypriot Government's candidature by associating Cyprus with EU declarations on issues from East Timor to Mostar. Cyprus could associate itself with the unpublicised *démarches* by which the foreign ministers intervened on behalf of political prisoners in third countries. In third countries, Cypriot ambassadors could be invited to the meetings of EU ambassadors where policy was concerted. In May 1995 the EU defence and foreign ministers agreed at a meeting of the Western European Union, the defence arm of the EU, that a dialogue with Cyprus would be initiated and expanded in line with progress towards accession (Emiliou in Axt and Brey, 1997:135). Cyprus also had a certain place in the European Union's largely cosmetic 1995 Barcelona process of balancing Eastern enlargement with a Euro-Mediterranean Partnership. The Cypriot Foreign Minister has attended the annual meetings although Cyprus has never been included among the problem areas discussed. Cyprus is a beneficiary under the EU budget heading, MEDA, which finances this process.

Preparation of the dossiers: March 1995 - March 1998

> [The Council] calls upon the Commission to continue its work of familiarising the Cyprus Administration with the *acquis communautaire* (Conclusions, 6 March 1995).

The *acquis communautaire* is about substantive law rather than status. Accession to the EU means accepting all the regulations, directives and decisions accumulated since 1958. Since the accession of Greece, the European institutions have been particularly keen to ensure that applicant countries have prepared effective mechanisms to implement transposed legislation such as VAT collection and the distribution of subsidies to farmers. The application by Cyprus of common rules on goods and persons coming from outside the Community is of particular importance to the EU because of Cyprus' geographical position.

From the Commission's perspective, Cyprus posed the fewest problems of economic and legal adjustment to the EU of all the candidate countries. It is small. It is more prosperous than the other applicants. On the basis of data from what EUROSTAT calls 'the territory under the government's control' Cyprus in 1997 had a per capita GDP expressed in purchasing power parities (PPS) of 78 per cent of the average for all member states. The comparable figures for other applicants range from 23 to 68 per cent of the EU average (figures for 1998 in *Frontier-free Europe: Eurostat supplement*, 3-2000). Cyprus has a disproportionately large, underemployed and well-educated civil service. Cyprus has a strong Progressive Party of the Working People (AKEL) but no problems of transition from communist rule. The problems associated with too much protection for manufactures, and too little for the environment, are familiar throughout Southern Europe.

Within the Commission, the job of preparing for enlargement was given to François Lamoureux of the DGIA, the Directorate-General for external political relations. He could call on officials seconded to GISELA, *la groupe interservice élargissement*. They came from all the directorate-generals, the Legal Service, the Statistical Office, the *Cellule Prospective* (a think-tank with a long-term horizon), the task force assigned to the 1996 inter-governmental conference, the task force dealing with immigration and crime, and EURATOM. On the Commission side, preparing accession was seen as different from the 'us-and-them' negotiations with third countries in that the Commission was socialising the 'future us'(Avery & Cameron, 1998: 67) Socialising Greek Cypriot officials was eased by the Government's sense of urgency. It had adopted Value Added Tax in 1992 and established more than twenty working groups to examine the sectoral differences between Cypriot and EU law.

The absence of Turkish Cypriot officials made progress easier and quicker for both the Greek Cypriot and the Commission officials involved. They did not have to consider derogations on the freedom of movement for capital and labour, or the question of Turkish Cypriot competence in implementing the *acquis*. They did not have to deal with immediately disputatious problems like assigning the money from the Fourth Protocol of 1995 to joint projects, or the practicalities of ending the embargo on trade with the illegal Turkish Republic of Northern Cyprus. There is little sense of regret in the Commission Report of 1998 on Cyprus which told the Council that 'The Turkish Cypriot civil administration does not seem to be prepared to adopt the *acquis*'. The Commission author identifies completely with the Government line on the Constitution, 'The fundamentals still apply but without the power sharing element'. This one sentence demonstrates the Commission's incomprehension of the Turkish Cypriot position that power sharing cannot be an optional element which the majority may remove at will. By March 1995, the Commission services had finished helping their Greek Cypriot counterparts prepare their reports on the extent of the changes that would be needed in adapting Cypriot law and procedures. The second stage was to establish with the Cypriot authorities the deadlines for transposing the *acquis* into Cypriot law. In May 1995, the Commission's White Paper on the Preparation of the Associated Countries of Central and Eastern Europe for Integration into the Internal Market is notable for maintaining the distinction between preparing the CEEC countries and preparing Cyprus. The Commission opened to Eastern Europeans, but not to Cypriots, the training workshops run by its technical assistance information exchange, TAIEX, originally set up to help member states cope with the Single Market. Neither the Commission's *Newsletter for Central and Eastern Europe,* nor its in-house successor, *European Dialogue,* were targeted at Cyprus. However its readers were given an accurate impression of the Brussels perspective on Cyprus:

> Although Cyprus' political tensions continue to make its accession to the EU an emotive and controversial subject, on a purely technical level it has for the most part been accepted already (*European Dialogue*, 1997, 4 July).

Towards a mandate for negotiations

They pretend to want us, and we pretend to be ready (Anon).

In June 1997 at Amsterdam the European Council of Heads of State and Government was able to conclude the inter-governmental conference on schedule by postponing decisions on reforming the institutions. They agreed that, once the number of member states had reached twenty, the linked issues of weighted voting in the Council and the number of Commissioners would be decided at another intergovernmental conference. The significance for Cyprus is that if it were to join as the same time as the other five applicants in the first wave, the EU membership would reach twenty one. The Cypriot Government could also be pleased that the Member States, mindful of their promise to open negotiations within six months of the conclusion of the Conference, avoided the ratification problems requiring referenda and judicial review that had so delayed the implementation of the Maastricht Treaty.

On 15 July the Commission published its ideas on managing the enlargement process, memorably and misleadingly entitled Agenda 2000. Even though a note in the Introduction recognises that the Council has decided that Cyprus 'will be involved in this phase of enlargement', the Commission's proposals reinforce the elements of an approach wholly inappropriate to Cyprus. The PHARE programmes remained the basic element of aid, committing 70 per cent of increased expenditure to be spent on infrastructure mainly to improve transport in Eastern Europe. Agricultural aid and incentives for regional co-operation were focussed on the Central and East European countries. Aid would be conditional on timetables to be set out in new Accession Partnerships with each candidate. The Commission recommended that negotiations begin with five CEEC countries within six months of the ratification in October of the Treaty of Amsterdam. The Commission's low-profile approach on Cyprus was limited to a country profile in Volume II of its Communication to the Council. This avoided the need to explain why a Cypriot settlement now seemed more distant than envisaged in either the Opinion of 1993 or the Council Conclusions of March 1995. The Commission suggested that its Opinion of 1993 was sufficient, when taken together with the Council decision of March 1995, for Cyprus to be added to the first wave of five Central and East European countries:

> If progress towards a settlement is not made before the negotiations are due to begin, they should be opened with the government of the Republic of Cyprus, as the only authority recognised by international law (Commission, 1997a: 66).

That same month the Commission referred again to the importance the EU attaches to the achievement of a just and lasting settlement. The occasion was a Communication to the Council on 'going beyond the customs union...with Turkey' (Commission, 1997b).

At Luxembourg, 12-13 December 1997, the Heads of Government slightly modified the Commission's suggestions. It decided it would be tactful to open the accession process with all ten candidates, plus Cyprus, 10 + 1. Eleven countries would become Accession Partners (APs). These were formally approved together on 25 March 1998. Although Associate Partnerships were billed as replacing the multilateral structural dialogue, environment and justice ministers continued to meet in what were now called 'pre-accession ministerial meetings'. A Pre-Accession pact on Organised Crime showed the continued vitality of these meetings (*Uniting Europe*, June 1998,10: 5). Nevertheless, the essence of the Commission proposal to limit the opening of real negotiations to five countries plus Cyprus was simultaneously adopted in that the

Council decided to convene bilateral intergovernmental conferences with the five leading countries of the Czech Republic, Hungary, Poland, Estonia and Slovenia, plus Cyprus (5 + 1). The formality of separate negotiations with each candidate allowed for accession negotiations proceeding at different speeds, the regatta model. In practice, similar agendas were timetabled with each candidate's negotiation team over one or two days.

Negotiations were officially begun on 26 March 1998 by the foreign ministers of the EU15 + 5 + Cyprus.

Screening

Hans van den Broek, the Commissioner responsible for enlargement, is credited with dubbing these six states the 'ins' (Soveroski, 1999: 20) to distinguish them from the second wave of five countries, the 'pre-ins'. Preparing negotiations with the Luxembourg 'ins' became the responsibility of a dedicated Enlargement Task Force of forty officials under Mr Klaus van der Pas. Van den Broek explained:

> It is right to separate preparation from the negotiation. Negotiators do not want to be bothered by trade disputes, accession partnerships and PHARE agreements. These will remain with M. Lamoureux. The task force will be responsible for the direct negotiations.

Van der Pas had been the Commission's Spokesman for the previous three years, and intimately involved with the negotiations over the European Economic Area and Swedish enlargement. On being appointed, he spoke of the magnitude of the task:

> This is the first time we have negotiated at the same time with six countries wanting to join the Union, and never before have we had six countries which have such a long way to go. You cannot expect in a multilateral setting to get clarity from countries and a readiness to put individual cards on the table (*European Dialogue*, 1998, 4, July-August).

Given the small number of officials, its senior members had to take on responsibility at once for particular dossiers and for liaison with the negotiating team from one country. For Cyprus, the task force official was an Austrian, Mr Leopold Maurer. He was also in charge of negotiations with all six applicants on the commercial matters of some relevance to Cyprus—small and medium enterprises, company law, taxation matters, and statistics. More important was his responsibility for three of the 'free movement dossiers'— for goods, services, and capital—all of which would be more complicated if derogations protecting the Turkish Cypriots were to be offered to promote a settlement. Maurer was unequivocal in telling a committee of the Cypriot Parliament on 15 January 1999 that 'there should be no transitional periods, no deviations for the date the *acquis* will be taken over'*(Cyprus Mail*, 16 January 1999).

The task force began by screening the 'ins' individually. Through questionnaires and meetings the Commission tried to reach a common definition of the progress being made by each applicant in adopting the *acquis*. For negotiation purposes, the *acquis* was divided into thirty negotiating chapters, plus one for miscellaneous matters. To establish a common rhythm, the Commission officials began by spending one day on each chapter with all six applicants, followed by one day with each separately. The Commission wrote its own position papers summarising the information supplied by each candidate team, paying attention not just to whether each state could transpose the legislation, but also the more difficult question of whether there were implementing institutions in place. The task force divided the chapters into three categories of difficulty. The two easiest were the chapters where both sides found no problems, and the chapters where the candidate could adopt Community legislation by the working target date of 1 January 2003. The third category concerned requests for transition periods or other derogations, requiring negotiations at ministerial level. Between April and July 1998, the task force held detailed discussions on the twelve least problematic chapters — science and research, education and training, telecommunications and information technologies, culture and audio-visual policy, industry policy, small and medium-sized undertakings, common foreign and security policy (with officials from the member-states), company law, statistics, consumers, free movement of goods (*European Dialogue*, 1998/4 July-August). This left agriculture, regional and social spending and free movement of labour, and environmental questions to be examined before the target date for finishing the screening process of July 1999 (Soveroski, 1999: 17). Progress in the preparatory screening process by the Enlargement Task Force and applicant administrations was formally recorded at monthly sessions which symbolised the dominance of the Union in the proceedings. The Presidency representative sat at one end of the table, flanked by the Council secretariat and the Commission, plus the ambassadors or ministers of the fifteen Member States. The negotiator for the applicant state sat at the other end. The screening of the difficult chapters continued even after the beginning of substantive negotiations between the applicants and the Member States.

Ministerial negotiations
The shift to the stage of ministerial negotiations was agreed by the General Affairs Council on 5 October 1998. Again there was a question whether Cyprus should be treated separately from the others. The Council regretted that the 'situation' in Cyprus made comprehensive screening and universal implementation of the *acquis* there impossible. However, after debate, it also decided that Cyprus should participate in the ministerial-level negotiating process on the same basis as for the other five. On 7 December, still affirming that accession would be for the benefit of both communities and contribute to a settlement, the Council finally adopted a specific pre-accession strategy for Cyprus. It provided a legal basis for Cypriot participation in TAIEX and PHARE programmes targeted on training judges and officials, thus excluding Cyprus from aid for infrastructure projects. It enabled Cyprus to participate in the EU programmes and agencies open to other applicants. For example, on 20 May 1999, Cyprus became a member of the EU research programme, COST. Cyprus was to bear the costs of adjustment in terms of loss of manufacturing, agriculture, service industries or government revenue.

In the ministerial sessions themselves the EU treated Cyprus as a model candidate. The only permanent derogation it sought was to exempt Co-operative Banks. The most difficult chapter concerning Cyprus, namely institutions, would be the last to be discussed. The timing was to enable the Member States themselves in the IGC 2000 to reach a consensus on whether every sovereign state should be entitled to appoint one Commissioner and to hold the Council Presidency in rotation. The EU also had its own difficulties in the areas where Cyprus might want to delay its implementation of the *acquis*, such as telecommunications and the free movement of persons.

The first ministerial session on 10 November 1998 set the pattern for negotiating chapters which continued into the Portuguese Presidency of 2000, by which time all thirty-one chapters except those on institutions and miscellaneous matters had been opened. The Permanent Representatives of the Member States in Brussels (COREPER) reported to the Council on 28 October, summarising the Commission's position papers on each Conference. On 29 October 1998 the COREPER met the chief negotiators of the 5 + 1 applicants for the first substantive inter-state talks on the first seven chapters. On 5 November these talks were continued at the level of deputy foreign ministers, so that the ministers on 10 November were able to agree four of the chapters, and leave only a few questions remaining on the next three chapters. By the end of January 1999, the Luxembourg Six had presented their negotiating positions on the next eight chapters. In preparing a report on Cyprus for February 1999, Maurer and seven accompanying officials regarded five chapters as sewn up—external relations, telecommunications, company law, free movement of goods, justice and home affairs—four nearing completion, and eight more including competition and state aid, ready for negotiation. The ministerial meeting of 22 June 1999 was prepared by substantive negotiating sessions between the chief negotiators of the Six and the COREPER, on 19 April and 19 May. Throughout the negotiations, the Member States co-ordinated their positions at a Council working group which met twice weekly (Soveroski, 1999: 17).

Despite the success of these negotiations on a technical level, there was still considerable political uncertainty with respect to the enlargement process in general, and with respect to Cyprus in particular. At the March 1999 Summit in Berlin the heads of state ringfenced 57bn EURO for pre-accession spending on the assumption that enlargement would begin in 2002. On the other hand, the defence of national interests in agriculture and redistributive structural funds, and xenophobia on potential immigration, suggested grounds for doubt whether the ratification by all states could be completed by 2004. In December 1999, the decision to allow the Helsinki Six of second wave states the opportunity to catch up with the Luxembourg Six was a further cause of uncertainty. Whereas German reunification had stirred the imagination, the historic significance of the reunification of West and East Europe and the possible reunification of North and South Cyprus excited little interest outside the elites directly involved. It did not help that the process of accession negotiations had exacerbated the political division between the two communities in Cyprus, between the EU and Turkey, and between Western Europe and Islam.

3. Away from a Settlement?

The ambiguity in the European Union thesis that setting a date for accession negotiations would be a catalyst for a solution was apparent from the evening of 6 March 1995. The Greek Deputy Foreign Minister, Mr Mangakis, wrote to the Council President, French Foreign Secretary Alain Juppé, demanding that the Council be recalled for an extraordinary session. He complained that Murat Karayalçın had provocatively questioned Cyprus' right to membership. Karayalçın's statement that 'Turkey would be left with no option but to take steps towards a similar integration with the Turkish Republic of Northern Cyprus' was a threat to annex part of Cyprus if negotiations were to begin without a prior settlement. Therefore the final stage of the Customs Union should be delayed because Turkey has shown itself 'directly opposed to the Conclusions of several European Councils and the common position' (Dodd, 1998: 65).

M. Juppé refused to unravel the deal. He pointed out that Turkey was not a member of the Council that had set the date for accession and so was not bound by its decisions. He reminded Mr Mangakis of the Council's expectation that setting a date was meant to lead to a compromise settlement between the parties on the island, promoted by Greece and Turkey in co-operation, following the route set out in UN Security Council resolutions:

> Ces résolutions prévoient la création d'une Fédération bizonale et bicommunautaire, permettant à tous les Chypriotes de vivre dans la paix, la concorde, et l'attachement à leur commune patrie. C'est dans cette perspective que l'Union place clairement leur démarche, quand elle déclare que l'adhésion de la République de Chypre devrait concourir à la paix civile et à la réconciliation, consolider la prospérité et la Ces résolutions prévoient la création d'une Fédération, bizonale sécurité de chacune des deux communautés de l'île.

Greece, however, did not want better relations with Turkey at the price of accepting the presence of Turkish troops in Cyprus or in compromising its claims to sovereignty over the sea and airspace surrounding its Aegean islands. Where the Presidency hoped prospect of accession would bring the Turkish Cypriots to settle as Muslim harbingers of eventual Turkish membership, Greece supported Nicosia in its desire to exclude the Turkish Cypriots until after the accession had been completed. Accession first by the Government side would strengthen both its immediate security and its eventual negotiating *vis-à-vis* the Turkish Cypriots and Turkey. The fact was that the Council's determination to push through the March compromise was not matched by any comparable determination to use the lever of accession to force the Greek Cypriots to negotiate a bi-zonal settlement. Still less could the Council insist that Greece negotiate a settlement of its bilateral disputes with Turkey when the Greeks were so confident that the international law of the sea supported their claim that their chains of islands should be the basis for determining the locus of sovereignty. For Greece to accept a diplomatic 50/50 division of the Aegean along the line of the Continental Shelf rather than this legal approach would be to recognise that Turkey as a big naval power could not accept that all routes to the Dardanelles and the Aegean should be subject to Greek control. For all its irritation with the Greek Government and Greek public opinion in precluding better relations with Turkey, the Council backed the legal theses of its fellow member. On the Aegean, it regularly called for referral of the dispute to the International Court of Justice at the Hague. On Cyprus, it called for implementation of the UN resolutions which accorded sovereignty exclusively to the Republic of Cyprus. The 6 March Conclusions reiterated that 'the EU intends to continue to support with all means at its disposal the United Nations' efforts to achieve a comprehensive settlement of the Cyprus question'.

The EU concept of elements

The Council hoped that the accession process would be a catalyst of the same elements which the UN Secretary General had identified in his 1992 'Set of Ideas' (see Stavrinides, 1999b) as a possible diplomatic compromise. In its statement of 6 March, the Council repeated Serge Abou's claim that the stalled intercommunal talks had identified 'elements which could be useful for defining an agreement'. The chemistry metaphor of elements that could be combined in varying strengths to secure an overall package agreement between the parties on the island expresses at once the sense and the limitations of the European understanding of the Cyprus question.

The four principal elements on which Abou had focused were constitutional, territorial, security and property concerns, marginalising other issues like the past fate of the 'missing' and the future provision of water and electricity. The Constitution of 1960 would be amended in the direction of a federation of the two territorial zones as indicated by Makarios and Denktaş as long ago as 1977. It did not matter to the EU whether the two communities compromised on the side of the stronger central institutions favoured by the majority community, or the stronger cantonal arrangements favoured by the Turkish Cypriots. The nature of the constitutional compromise would be linked to a compromise on territory. The more the compromise favoured the Turkish Cypriot cantonal demands, the less territory they could be expected to retain. What mattered here was the future of the agricultural land around Morphou. On the security issue, the reduction of the Turkish military presence would be balanced by the continuation of the Treaty of Guarantee in some form that would recognise the legitimacy of a Turkish presence and right of intervention. In December 1997, Commissioner van den Broek told his Turkish Cypriot audience at the Ledra Palace: 'If the parties themselves agree to a settlement which includes such security provisions as the [1960] Treaty of Guarantee, I see no reason for the Union to find any problem with that in relation to membership'.

On 12 April 2000 his successor, Commissioner Verheugen, went a step further. He rejected any linkage between the negotiations with Turkey anticipated after the Helsinki summit of 1999 and the withdrawal of Turkish forces from Cyprus. He pointed out that his own country, Germany, had had to accept the presence of foreign troops.

Security is also linked to three property issues requiring costly decisions from the European Union. The first issue is that of the carefully documented rights of Cypriots from both communities to homes and fields abandoned in 1974. The nationalist leaders on both sides claim for opposed reasons that an external compensation fund is not needed. The Greek Cypriot Government maintains that the courts will sort the matter after a settlement, enabling Greek Cypriots to return to the North, which before 1974 was the most prosperous agricultural and touristic part of the island. The Turkish Cypriots argue that at today's prices the property abandoned by them in the South is roughly equal in value to the property they have taken over in the North. All that needs to be done is to recognise that each community has compensated its own with the land deserted by the others. The UN 'Set of Ideas', however, suggested that a compensation fund will be needed, with large contributions from the EU and the United States. The need is related to the insecurity which individuals fear if they return to their former homes. In a poll in Southern Cyprus in April 2000, 80 per cent of Greek Cypriots responded that they would not live in a Turkish Cypriot canton. Turkish Cypriots are nearly unanimous that they would not live under Greek Cypriot local rule. It follows that many individuals would prefer to sell their property rights if they were compensated financially by some fund to which the EU could be expected to make the biggest contribution.

The second costly decision required from the EU is again one that the communities negotiating between themselves prefer to ignore. Soldiers from EU countries will be needed to monitor and perhaps intervene where members of one community are at risk when travelling, working or eventually living in the sector ruled by the other. If Cyprus becomes a member state, this obligation would better be fulfilled by police and troops seconded from other member states than by the United Nations. The post-Kosovo creation of a force of 60,000 troops to be trained together in peacekeeping might usefully be based in Cyprus.

The third decision is more costly to EU principles than to its budget. A bi-zonal Cyprus divided between two hostile communities implies some limitation on the EU's fundamental principles of free movement of capital, labour and perhaps some services. Turkish Cypriot rulers of a zone in the North would be unlikely to tolerate the richer Greek Cypriots buying up all the beaches and development land. A public order situation might arise in which Turkish Cypriots might intimidate any of their number who chose to sell their land to Greek Cypriots, rather as Palestinian Arabs tried to prevent sales of land to Jews. The Treaty of Rome does allow for the suspension of its obligations on grounds of public order. An apposite illustration is that Turkish nationals with work permits in an EU country are not allowed to move freely in Greece, a derogation which the Greek Government insists is necessary for reasons of Greek national security. Commissioner van den Broek alluded to the difficulty in December 1997 at the Ledra Palace. He said, 'If they decide that certain basic freedoms should be introduced in a particular way, as mutual trust and confidence develop, this is something which the European Union would make efforts to accommodate'.

His meaning was unmistakable to a Turkish Cypriot audience. Freedom of movement for capital and labour might not be applied until mutual trust had improved. However, the Commissioner was not facing up to the fact that his audience were looking for a permanent derogation. Three precedents in EU law are relevant. Although Finnish citizens, the 25,000 Swedish-speaking Åland islanders constitute an autonomous community within a bi-zonal state. Residents not having the right of domicile cannot participate in elections, or stand for office, or own real property, or exercise a trade or profession except by license from the Älanders' autonomous authorities. Earlier the EU had permitted Denmark to refuse Germans permission to purchase second homes in Denmark, an analogous example of differentiation within the Community's legal order. Thirdly, the Amsterdam treaty established a legal basis in Article 130 for adopting special measures for 'the outermost regions', provided they did not undermine the integrity and coherence of the Community legal order. This ambiguous legal base envisaged permanent derogations favouring the Inouit in the Arctic regions of Sweden, rather than merely peripheral regions like Cyprus, but the precedent of possible permanent exceptional measures on a treaty basis is there.

However, van den Broek's allusion was expressed so opaquely, and conformed so well to the doctrine that derogations must be limited in time, that the suggestion of dispensing with fundamental principle aroused no comment in the European Parliament and press. The point is that such debate is needed if the implications of Cypriot accession are to be understood. To take up again the reference to freedom of movement for Turks in Greece, this could be sorted out if Turkey and Greece, like contemporary West Europeans and Scandinavians, ceased in the future to fear military invasion from each other.

The principle of freedom of movement, however, raises another more immediate problem which has to be addressed because it is an issue of European human rights as well as a matter for national authorities. If it is right for Greece to deny freedom of movement to citizens of Turkey by invoking its national security, the Federation of Cyprus would *a fortiori* be justified in denying freedom of movement to Turkish citizens in Cyprus. In Greek Cypriot eyes, the tens of thousands who have come to live in Cyprus from Turkey since 1974 are Turkish citizens, categorised as illegal colonists, who should not be counted as Turkish Cypriots.

The EU concept of political will

The Council's consistent position is that it is for others to show the political will needed to catalyse the elements into an acceptable solution. On 6 March 1995 the Council repeated its call for 'all parties to step up their efforts to achieve a comprehensive settlement of the Cyprus question in accordance with UN Security Council Resolutions, based on the concept of a bi-communal and bi-zonal Federation'. The EU would support the international effort to get an agreement between the parties. In defence of the EU stance, this accorded with the entrenched claims of both communities that a solution 'imposed' from outside would not be acceptable. The implication that the EU was not going to mediate between the parties or impose a settlement was welcome to both Cypriot communities, both motherlands, the UN and the United States.

Secondly, the institutions of the European Union have avoided involvement in 'internal' disputes even when they have an international aspect, as in Gibraltar, Ulster or the Tyrol. The EU institutions lack the resources in terms of personnel, budget, federal courts and federal troops. The Spanish, Italian, Irish, Dutch and Luxembourg presidencies were unwilling to take as tough a line with the Greek Cypriot Government as the French Presidency had done over the Turkish Customs Union. Especially after the failures of unilateral EU involvement in Bosnia from 1992-5, support for the established involvement of the UN and the USA in Cyprus can be defended as a sensible common front, thereby maintaining the unity of the internationals and the Member States. The EU has to show solidarity with Greece and the UK, which both have particular interests in Cyprus. A variation of this argument that the EU does not need to take on the risks of itself brokering a settlement, is that much will change before the accession of Cyprus occurs. Elections in EU states, upsets in Eastern Europe, a change in Turkey one way or the other, better or worse relations between Greece and Turkey, the end of the Anglo-Saxon UN-authorised mission in Iraq, all these future possibilities are invoked to justify caution on the part of EU officials.

Thirdly, the partiality of the Member States and its own institutions over decades makes it difficult for the EU to act as broker in drawing up a settlement to be put to separate referenda in both parts of the island. One difficulty was well expressed by the German special representative, Detlev Graf zu Rantzau on 11 March 1999. With unusual clarity he explained to the Greek Cypriot journalists at Larnaca airport why the internationals' call for talks without preconditions was unacceptable to Mr Denktaş:

> All UN resolutions speak about the political integrity and sovereignty and territorial integrity of the Republic of Cyprus. If you negotiate on the basis of these resolutions, then this means you insist on the sovereignty of Cyprus. Therefore I say it is the reference to these resolutions in the eyes of Mr Denktaş [which is] a precondition he cannot accept.

On the other hand, the EU willingness to negotiate accession while leaving a settlement to the parties under the auspices of the UN was itself making a settlement less likely. The accession negotiations strengthened the hand of the Greek Cypriot nationalists, who were prepared to risk deepening the division of the island rather than compromise on their view that Cyprus is a Hellenic island which should be ruled democratically by the majority, with protection for the rights as individuals of the Turkish Cypriot minority. The accession negotiations strengthened the hand of the Turkish Cypriot nationalists who are prepared to integrate *de facto* or *de jure* with Turkey to preserve Turkish rule over all the land they occupied in the North and to prevent Cyprus becoming another island base in the Greek encirclement of Turkey.

By refusing to take responsibility, the EU was not playing the cards which make its hand stronger than that of the UN or the United States. The dependency of the Turkish Cypriot nationalists on Turkish subsidies and troops means they can sometimes be induced to change tack when this is deemed in the Turkish national interest, as it was in 1959, in 1995, and perhaps again after 2000. The secular authorities in Turkey, including the army, want Turkey to be accepted as not merely eligible for EU membership but on track to becoming a member of the European Union. The commitment of the Greek Cypriot Government to EU accession makes it vulnerable should the EU take the Government's claim to rule all Cyprus at face value and insist that it show itself capable of implementing democracy and human rights over the whole island before accession. The EU has not yet offered the cash and troops which would be needed to establish a bi-zonal federation.

However understandable, the EU's unwillingness to take a strong line on the need for a bi-zonal settlement poses risks to itself. As the EU recognises the Government as having jurisdiction over the whole island, then accession must mean that the whole island is deemed to be within EU boundaries. It could be argued that this situation was similar to that of divided Germany, where the Federal Republic claimed jurisdiction over the 1938 boundaries but everybody accepted that EU policies could not be applied in the Deutsche Demokratische Republik. Alternatively, it could be argued that the present *de facto* and possible *de jure* integration of the TRNC with Turkey is very different from the DDR case both because East Germany never integrated its economy or currency with that of the Soviet Union, and because each successive EU treaty has strengthened the EU stance against changes of borders in Europe without consent. The EU would face an immediate challenge to its authority in foreign policy as well as in legal terms. The EU would have to respond by economic sanctions against Turkey. This would not be popular in Washington. Accession without a settlement would increase tensions between the two parts of the island, between Greece and Turkey, and between Islam and the West.

In 1995, however, the Council did not accept that it needed to show a will of its own to promote a settlement. It hoped that the Customs Union with Turkey would be enough to avoid complicating enlargement to Eastern Europe by simultaneously taking on the issue of Turkish membership. It hoped that taking on the tiny island of Cyprus would remove the threat of a Greek veto on its Eastern enlargement, and persuade the Turkish Cypriots that their security and prosperity would be enhanced by participation in an accession process that would be a catalyst for a settlement under UN auspices. The Council envisaged two separable tracks, one preparing for accession and the other promoting a settlement. The accession process was largely an administrative matter for the Commission and the Republic of Cyprus, but the Council retained final responsibility and put some effort into requiring the Government to sponsor a Turkish Cypriot participation which neither Cypriot community wanted. The promotion of a solution was largely a political matter for the Council and its leading member states in concert with the Clinton Administration and successive UN secretaries-general. As ever, the key to a settlement lay in good relations between Greece and Turkey, which until 1999 were notable for their absence. We shall begin with the EU failure to promote a settlement.

Informing the Turkish Cypriots

> The Council considers that this [Turkish Cypriot] community must perceive the advantages of E.U. accession more clearly and its concern at the prospect must be allayed. The Council calls upon the Commission to organise the requisite contacts to this end with the Turkish-Cypriot community, in consultation with the Government of Cyprus (Council Conclusions, 6 March 1995).

In its communiqué the Council listed the advantages of accession to both communities as first, increased security and then, increased prosperity. The Greek Cypriots were convinced that they would be more secure from an attack by the Turkish army if Cyprus were a member state. However, the EU did have a problem in convincing the Turkish Cypriots that their security would be enhanced. To the EU, the arms build-up on both sides after 1993 seemed reason enough for the European Council at successive summits to endorse Mr Clerides' proposals for demilitarisation. At the Edinburgh summit of February 1998, Mr Robin Cook's praise for demilitarisation was a way of mending fences with Mr Clerides after the heavy pressure exerted by the Council to get him to invite the participation of the Turkish Cypriots in accession talks. However, to Turkish Cypriots, demilitarisation meant that the dominance of the Greek National Guard would be restored. The Council's attitude and the Commission's lack of interest in what to the isolated Turkish Cypriots was a more important issue than prosperity meant that the problem was not even addressed by the Commission's information campaign.

It might be thought that the Commission's new duty of informing the Turkish Cypriots of the economic benefits of accession would be easier to discharge. The end of the international embargo would facilitate Turkish Cypriot exports and enable tourists to be flown directly to the North. The end of an artificial frontier across an island would itself open up trading possibilities. Foreign investment, European Investment Bank loans at the lowest possible rates, grants from the Community budget in regional and special aid programmes would all become available to stimulate economic growth. The Turkish Cypriots, moreover, did not have large economic sectors like the unregulated shipping fleet and the subsidised production sector of the South which stood to lose from accession. Ambassador Gilles Anouil set about his task of producing information brochures, sending them to an 'information office' in the Eastern Mediterranean University in Famagusta. He crossed over the border to attend seminars for the young businessmen, the trade unionists, the leaders of Opposition parties, and the women's groups whom the Commission thought would be the most receptive audiences in a hostile community. In 1997 Commissioner van den Broek spoke to Turkish Cypriots on each of the two trips to Cyprus he made that year. He and Richard Holbrooke held a much publicised joint seminar in Brussels attended by representatives of both communities.

The total failure of this campaign may be explicable in terms of the hostility of the Turkish Cypriot leadership, and of the hostility of the 'consulted' Greek Cypriot Government to any form of contact with the North. However, in addition to these basic obstacles, the Commission's unimaginatively bureaucratic interpretation of its mandate did not help. Turkish Cypriots were not hired to write or publish the brochures. Turks were not hired to estimate the costs of 'Non-Cyprus' on the lines of the UN Consultancy report discussed by Abou in his 1995 report to the Council. No EU brochure addresses the Turkish Cypriots' fear that the richer Greek Cypriots would return to develop the North, and that the Europeans' remedy for the economic disparity was a 'combination of Greek-Cypriot know-how and financial aid' (Redmond, 1993: 92). The Commission Delegation's '*Newsletter*' is not interested in repeating to its largely Greek Cypriot audience the arguments on recognition of the Turkish Cypriots or of the Muslim identity within the EU made by the EU's

Ambassador to Turkey, Mr Michael Lake in the *Herald Tribune* of
19 December 1996:

> For the Turkish Cypriots, who are effectively stateless because of
> the international embargo on them, it would mean a secure
> prospect of recognition as part of the world community. They
> would also become the first identifiably Muslim community inside
> the EU.

No lawyers were brought in from the sovereignty-minded EFTA
Secretariat to help those in the North understand the advantages of
providing good information to Brussels and using the law to oil the
machinery instead of concentrating on rights, historic wrongs and
duties. None of the roving Commission officials from DGIA were
sent to the North on long missions to show respect to their TRNC
hosts. (It is worth recalling that Kurt Waldheim when he became
Austrian Foreign Minister spent six months in Italy to demonstrate
commitment and respect before attempting his successful resolution
of the Tyrol dispute.) It is perfectly understandable that
Commissioner van den Broek was doing all he could within the
conventions by going to Cyprus in December 1997 for a second time
to limit the damage to be expected from the Luxembourg Council's
Conclusions excluding Turkey. However, what was required was a
well-prepared but uncharacteristically dramatic political gesture,
such as landing at Ercan airport. The predictable outrage from
Nicosia, Athens, and some EU governments would have done much
to overcome Turkish Cypriot alienation without seriously putting at
risk the irreversible Greek Cypriot commitment. The fact that the
Commissioner and Council could not grasp the nettle of Turkish
Cypriot rule in the North shows the unreality of their hopes for a
settlement, and their practical and perhaps intellectual commitment
to the Greek Cypriot Government. The EU's activities produced few
protests from its Greek Cypriot hosts. In December 1997, Mr
Denktaş therefore lost nothing when he decreed an end to all EU
information activities in the North. The Turkish Cypriot regime was
all too happy to share the Turkish Government's disaffection with
the EU after the Luxembourg Summit.

The Opinion of Crawford, Hafner and Pellet

During this low point in EU relations with Turkey and the Turkish Cypriots, the Commission's Legal service produced a clear and uncompromising Opinion, as mentioned earlier, by three independent lawyers defending the legality of the Cypriot Government's application for membership. It does not mention the Opinion commissioned from Professor Mendelson by the Turkish Government setting out Turkish Cypriot arguments, but seems nevertheless to be a formal reply to that Opinion. Its principal value lies in its understanding of the nature of the EU as a constitutional entity. It sets out why the EU is not a state in the sense envisaged by the Treaty of Guarantee in its Article 1, Paragraph 2, forbidding any attempt to unite Cyprus with Greece, or any partition of Cyprus between Turkey and Greece. It recounts why membership of the EU does not have the implications with respect to most-favoured-nation treatment of Turkey which Mendelson derived from Article 170 of the Constitution. It provided a relevant, although not decisive, analogy with Austria. The Austrian commitment under Article 4 (1) of the Austrian State Treaty of 1955 not to 'enter into political or economic union with Germany in any form whatever' did not rule out Austrian accession to the European Union.

On Cyprus, however, the Opinion is less convincing. The claim that Cyprus is an independent state like any other is upheld by discounting any need to discuss questions of the 'interpretation, continuing validity or legal effect' of the Treaty of Guarantee. This avoids any consideration of Turkey's legal right to uphold the bi-communal 'state of affairs' established by the Constitution. The absence of a Vice-President to exercise the veto under Article 50 of the Constitution is treated as a purely internal constitutional matter for Cyprus as though there was no interlinking of international treaties with the Constitution. The constitutional difficulties since 1963 and the *de facto* division of the island since 1974 are dismissed as a matter for the Greek Cypriot Government. The European Court of Justice is quoted with approval for saying that 'The problems resulting from the *de facto* partition of the island must be resolved exclusively by the Republic of Cyprus, which alone is internationally recognized'. This splendid assertion of sovereignty removes the treaty rights of all three Guarantor Powers. It completely discounts relevant developments in human rights law which have made the rights of individuals and groups a legitimate international concern.

Like the   Mendelson Opinion, the Opinion of Crawford, Pellet and Hafner seems intended to provide a rallying point for the converted before some imaginary court where the number of supporters is crucial. The approach is that of the propagandist, careful to document the facts selected to give an account so misleading that all virtue is to be found only on one side.

Financial Aid

In the Commission's perspective, the grants which it could disburse in the Fourth Financial Protocol 1995-1998 were evidence of its goodwill and commitment to a settlement. While only 5m EURO were allocated to pay for the costs of pre-accession, including training and research on the harmonisation of the *acquis*, 12m EURO were available for projects whose purpose was to prepare the reunification of Cyprus (*EC Bulletin*, 1995, 1.4.70 & Council Decision 95/485/EC of 30 October 1995). Article 5, Paragraph 2, of the Protocol makes provision for the possibility of Cypriot accession 'during the period covered by this Protocol'. In addition 5m EURO were allocated to bi-communal projects such as joint seminars attended by individuals from both communities in Brussels or the Ledra Palace. (Other EU and American and Norwegian funding for this purpose of stimulating favourable publicity was available. For example, between 7-18 April 1997 fifty women from both communities were brought to Brussels on the initiative of the European Parliament at the expense of the MEDA programme.)

The Commission's officials were frustrated by the refusal of the Turkish Cypriot leadership to take up these grants on offer. All EU initiatives foundered on the recognition issue. Grants offered directly to the TRNC would have been accepted with alacrity as implying recognition. This the Commission could not do, because the Protocol had been signed with the recognised government, which had to agree to any disbursement. The Commission accepted the Government's lack of interest in promoting the EU to the Turkish Cypriot side if this meant any recognition of the legitimacy of their regime. For its part, the TRNC would have nothing to do with grants which implied its acceptance of the legitimacy at once of the Greek Cypriot claim to be the government of the whole island, and of the legitimacy of its accession process (Axt & Brey, 1997:82). In private, Commission officials are as one in putting the blame on the intransigence of Mr Denktaş.

Sponsoring Turkish Cypriot participation

Both the Government of Cyprus and the Turkish Cypriot Government were adamantly opposed to any Turkish Cypriot participation in the accession talks. Nevertheless the larger states of the EU took the issue of Turkish Cypriot participation so seriously that it was the subject of a series of major rows in the Council, some of which are in the public domain. To understand the EU position on a possible settlement of the Cyprus question, some explanation of this apparently fruitless and frustrating campaign has to be found.

One explanation is that the larger member states did not grasp the subtlety of the Greek and Greek Cypriot position on participation. In March 1993, Mr Michaelides as the new Greek Cypriot Minister of Foreign Affairs, found on his first visit to Brussels that what was stopping progress on the Cypriot application of 1990 was 'the continuation of the Cyprus problem' (Michaelides, 1996: 7). He argued in Brussels that Cyprus' European Orientation had two parts. As well as accession and harmonisation, there was 'the activation of the European factor in the efforts to find a solution to the Cyprus problem'. Beginning accession talks would constitute 'an invitation to the Turkish Cypriots to join together with us on the great venture'. What his listeners may have understood by this was that the Greek Cypriots wanted the Turkish Cypriots to join with them in the accession process, thereby making the process a means to a settlement. Indeed, Mr Clerides had offered a series of concessions to this end, including the offer of a revolving presidency so that Mr Denktaş would not always be the junior in a federation. However, the condition was that Mr Denktaş accept the legitimacy of the 1990 application. Mr Clerides knew that Mr Denktaş was unlikely to concur that the Greek Cypriot Government spoke for all Cyprus in 1990, or to participate on any basis which did not recognise communal equality or at least a legally enforceable right of veto for the Turkish Cypriot side. France, Britain, Germany and Italy, however, took the rather different position that the Greek Cypriot Government must include Turkish Cypriots in the Cypriot negotiating team. In June 1995 at the Cyprus Association meeting, the French Presidency threatened to interpret Cypriot accession as meaning the accession of a future Federation of Cyprus, after a settlement with the Turkish Cypriots. At the structured dialogue meetings in June and November 1996 the foreign ministers of the larger states demanded that Turkish Cypriots be included once the formal negotiation process got under way *(EC Bulletin* 5-1996 and 11-1996).

When the Netherlands took over the Presidency for the first six months of 1997, the State Secretary for Foreign Affairs, Mr Michael Patijn, said both that 'We have a commitment to the accession of Cyprus' and that 'When negotiations begin, we have to make sure that they are conducted on behalf of both communities'. On 25 February 1997 a structured dialogue meeting, scheduled simultaneously with an Association Council meeting, had to be postponed. The Member States could not reach agreement on a common position on Turkish Cypriot participation in the forthcoming accession talks. *The Financial Times* reported that same day:

> The German-led move, supported by France, [to involve the Turkish community] reflects pressures for a more even-handed approach to membership talks, to tie EU accession unequivocally to a peace settlement between the Greek and Turkish communities.

The Greek Foreign Minister, Mr Pangalos, complained that Germany, France and the UK were 'acting like lords' and that to insist on consulting Turkish Cypriots in political dialogue on EU external policy was 'criminal and foolish' *(The Times,* 28 February). At its eleventh meeting on 18-19 March 1997 the EU-Cyprus Joint Parliamentary Committee expressed the Cypriot Government line that accession was not dependent on a prior settlement *(EU News, the Newsletter of the Commission Delegation* 3/97: 4). In April 1997

Mr Pangalos agreed at an informal Gymnich-style meeting of the General Affairs Council at Apeldoorn that he would use his influence in Nicosia to obtain a compromise on Turkish Cypriot participation. The wording of the Conclusions of a General Affairs Council held on 15 September 1997 suggested a compromise had been reached. On the one hand the Council rejected 'any link between the [intercommunal] talks and the start of EU accession negotiations with Cyprus'. On the other hand, it welcomed the new 'willingness of the Government of Cyprus to include representatives of the Turkish Cypriot community in the accession negotiating delegation'. On 25 September *European Voice* reported that Nicosia was now ready to include representatives of the Turkish Cypriot community on an individual basis. On 16 December 1997 the *Cyprus Mail* reported that France, backed by Portugal and the Netherlands, had opposed including Cyprus in enlargement talks to be officially opened on 30 March 1998 until there was a political settlement and Turkish Cypriot participation. It quoted Cypriot Foreign Minister, Kasoulides as saying, 'This gives us a taste of what is to come'. In February 1998 the British Presidency negotiated another compromise announced at the European Council of Heads of Government at Edinburgh. The Greek Cypriot proposal was not made public, but may well have been to include up to seven Turkish Cypriots without any power of veto. The French Government let it be known that the compromise was unsatisfactory.

Some insight is given into the thinking of the Council by an interview given to the *Turkish Daily News* by the Foreign Minister of Norway, a state outside the European Union. On 28 April 1998 Mr Knut Vollebaek confirmed the differences among his EU colleagues:

> I know that there is a disagreement and different views among the EU countries on the process... I discussed this issue with the French Foreign Minister in Paris recently. They see this as a process and they hope that by starting negotiations with Cyprus there should always be a possibility of finding a solution. They also look at the economic interests of both sides in Cyprus. As you know, they had seminars with the businessmen from both sides on Cyprus and they hope at least that there could be a possibility,

> *even without finding a political solution at the outset,* you can find
> mechanisms where both sides could come together. Through these
> mechanisms and through this process you could also find a
> political solution. [my italics]

The disagreement has a consistent pattern in which France and the
larger states confront Greece and some of the smaller states. The
most likely explanation is that the French Presidency believed that
agreeing to open accession without a prior settlement would remove
the Turkish Cypriot veto but would nevertheless be followed by a
serious Greek-sponsored attempt to bring the Turkish Cypriots on
board. Furious at finding that the Republic of Cyprus was happy to
exclude Turkish Cypriots, at least until after their own position had
been strengthened by accession, the French attempted to use
'participation' as a lever either to enforce a Greek Cypriot opening to
the Turkish Cypriot side or to justify not taking on the problems of
Cyprus as a divided island. The French position was undermined by
the absurdity of battling for Turkish Cypriot participation when Mr
Denktaş had opted for non-co-operation. It was also inadequate as a
lever for persuading either Greece or Greek Cyprus to switch from
treating their Turkish and Turkish Cypriot counterparts as occupiers
of Greek lands, not to be appeased.

However, the accession of a Cyprus sympathetic to Serbia and
implacably hostile to Turkey had unwelcome implications for those
trying to develop an intergovernmental common foreign and security
policy. The issue of Turkish Cypriot participation becomes
overshadowed by the more serious division on whether the
membership of a divided Cyprus was in the European interest.
France again expressed doubts in public before the first substantive
negotiations at ministerial level scheduled for 10 November 1998.
The debate within the General Affairs Council is reflected in the
long press release after the meeting on 5 October 1998:

> With regard to Cyprus, the Council noted that because of the
> political situation the Commission's analytical examination of the
> '*acquis*' (screening) could not cover Cyprus as a whole and that
> the invitation of the Cyprus government to include representatives

of the Turkish Cypriot community in the negotiations had so far not been taken up. It regretted that it had not been possible to achieve a political solution to the continuing division of Cyprus in time for the accession negotiations. The Union believes that Cyprus's accession to the EU should benefit all communities, including the Turkish Cypriot community, and help to bring about civil peace and reconciliation on the island. In that context its objective remains a bi-communal, bi-zonal federation on the basis of a comprehensive political settlement in accordance with UN Security Council Resolutions. A political settlement would allow the provisions of the Accession Treaty to be implemented throughout the island. Progress towards accession and towards a just and viable solution to the Cyprus problem will naturally reinforce each other. The Union reaffirms its full support for the search for a solution under the aegis of the UN (Paragraph 6).

In *The Financial Times* of 6 October 1998 Quentin Peel reported that, in view of Greek threats should Cyprus be excluded from ministerial negotiations, the French Foreign Minister, Hubert Vedrine had 'agreed to proceed in order to be constructive'. His statement was balanced by a simultaneous threat from Pierre Muscovici, the French Minister for Europe that 'There can be no automatic membership for a divided island'. Peel was told that the French attitude was, less publicly, shared by other states, including Germany. This was borne out by a declaration tabled at the General Affairs Council on 9 November, the day before the opening of ministerial sessions with applicant countries. France, Germany and the Netherlands, with Italian support, put down a warning marker:

> Full membership negotiations between the Greek Cypriot side and the EU will be problematic unless the Cyprus question reaches a peaceful solution. The course of the process of negotiations will give rise to a series of problems...They draw, in particular, attention to the fact that the division of the island poses fundamental problems for the operation and coherence of the Common Foreign and Security Policy.

This attitude had already been denounced in October by Mr Pangalos. He said it was immoral that the victim, Cyprus, should be left to the mercy of the victimiser, Turkey.

The EU and Turkey

It had been agreed on 6 March 1995 that the troika of foreign ministers from the present, past and future presidencies should visit Ankara on 29 March together with Commissioner van den Broek. Their mandate was to seek progress on the issues that might influence the European Parliament to assent to the Customs Union —human rights and democracy, the fierce campaign waged by the Turkish state against the PKK rebellion in the Kurdish Southeast of Turkey, the dispute with Greece over the extent of territorial rights in the Aegean sea and its airspace. Van den Broek stayed on for an extra day to discuss the Cyprus issue.

At the Madrid Council in December 1995, the EU Heads of State gave the clearest possible indication that Turkey's eligibility for membership did not mean that Turkey would be included for the foreseeable future in the enlargement process. Turkey is listed in the Conclusions among the neighbours of the enlarged Union, in the same category as the Ukraine and the Russian Federation. At a celebration in 1996 of the fifteenth year of the European Institute of Public Administration, attended only by Eurocrats, the Deputy Secretary-General of the Commission was less dismissive but also factual and uncontroversial when he said, 'If we leave aside Turkey and Malta, whose requests for accession have been put on hold, there is the perspective of eleven countries joining the European Union' (Trojan, 1996: 6).

By the time he made this speech, it was already obvious that the economic potential of the Customs Union was not sufficient to produce a stable political relationship with Turkey. As we have seen above, the Greek Government had contested the linkage whereby the inclusion of Cyprus in the first wave of applicants entailed that Greece should join other member states in promoting good relations with Turkey. Greece still refused to appease the occupier of an Hellenic island by lifting its veto on the payments legally due to Turkey under the Fourth Protocol of the Association Agreement. The near-war over Imia/Kardak had provided unstable governments in both Turkey and Greece with irresistible opportunities to invoke nationalist and populist support for national sovereignty. Unlike the Parliament, the EU foreign ministers did not give much support to the Greek thesis of enmity with the Turks, but then neither could they altogether restrain their fellow member. The situation did not change until a stronger Simitis government in 1999 was able to dismiss Pangalos during the Öcalan affair, face down popular agitation on behalf of the Serbs in Kosovo, and then magnanimously deliver aid to the victims of an earthquake in Istanbul. This initiative was reciprocated by the Turkish Government, enabling both sides to attempt neighbourly relations which might go beyond the coexistence of the Venizelos-Atatürk tradition and restore the co-operation on Cyprus established in 1959 by Averoff and Zorlu.

In the five years after 1995, Turkey pursued a dual policy on Europe which confirmed the Member States' view that its membership was not an immediate option. In 1996 an unexpected coalition came to power in Turkey led by Mr Erbakan of Refah, the Islamic party. On the one hand Mrs Çiller, now Foreign Minister, continued the line reaffirmed by Murat Karayalçın on 6 March, 1995. Invited to a dinner for foreign ministers at the Dublin summit in December 1996, she put the case for membership with characteristically ill-advised emphasis on Turkey's prominent position in NATO. On the other hand, the new Prime Minister, Mr Erbakan, did not visit any Western capitals, preferring to emphasise his alternative policy of identification with the Muslim world. While Mrs Çiller was not welcome in the TRNC, Mr Erbakan in July went to Cyprus to express his solidarity. The European Parliament felt deceived by this outcome, having been persuaded to accept the Customs Union on arguments which included the claim that a vote for the Customs Union would preclude the Islamists coming to power in Turkey. The 'civilisation' question also came out in the open in EU circles. The Christian Democrat prime ministers in March 1997, through the Belgian leader, Mr Wilfried Martens, issued a (swiftly retracted) statement which encapsulated a lot of the underlying feeling on the pragmatic political Right against Turkish membership. Turkey, they said, was not part of the civilisation of

Western Christendom on which the EU was based. This had the unexpected effect of bringing not only condemnation from the European socialist coalition but also a strong statement from Mr Pangalos. He objected to the exclusion of Orthodox Christendom, Greece, Bulgaria, Serbia, Russia and Cyprus from the civilisation on which the EU was based. In Washington on 6 March 1997, he said, 'Turkey of course belongs to Europe. If Turkey is not part of European history, then Greece is not part of European history' (*Agence Europe*, 7 March, 1997).

He reiterated this surprising solidarity reminiscent of the historic Greek preference for the turban over the papal tiara in Istanbul on 9 June, 1998: 'Greece has always supported the European identity of Turkey...as Greece is against the limitation of the European Union due to religious and historical traditions' (*Anadolu Agency*).

After Mr Erbakan had been forced out of office by pressure from the army in the interests of a secular republic, the new German-speaking Prime Minister, Mr Yilmaz, began a serious campaign for membership of the EU in 1997. All fourteen EU capitals other than Athens were visited by either Mr Yilmaz or Mr Ecevit, his deputy Prime Minister, well known as the Prime Minister who had ordered the 1974 landings on Cyprus. The European foreign ministers responded with a series of separate communiqués of which the ambiguity is epitomised by the statement of the Luxembourg Prime Minister, who held the Presidency of the EU in the second half of 1997. On 30 October 1997, M. Jacques Poos told the European Parliament, in reply to a question from Panayotis Lambirias, 'Turkey will be a full member of the EU sooner or later. We have given a promise in this respect and all EU members confirmed this. Nobody opposed'.

According to Ali Birand, the well-informed and influential Turkish journalist, a more serious misinterpretation of the European vagueness on the timing of Turkish membership was made by Mr Yilmaz. He thought that Chancellor Kohl's offer to reaffirm Turkish candidature meant that Turkey would be included in the second wave of countries negotiating full membership. The mistake was perhaps understandable as more than wishful thinking in that Mr Yilmaz' tour for the first time convinced many EU insiders that Turkish membership sooner rather than later might be to the benefit of both sides. Nevertheless, the die had already been cast. The German position remained that Turkish membership could not be taken on at the same time as Eastern enlargement and that in any case Turkey had first itself to remove some obstacles such as the Cyprus question. On 1 October 1997, German Foreign Minister Klaus Kinkel had clearly signalled Germany's position. *The Turkish Daily News* translated his remarks as:

> The Turkish train remains on the rail line to Europe, but the path to full membership goes via the human rights situation, the Kurdish situation, relations with Greece, the Cyprus situation and naturally over several economic problems.

The Heads of State at the Luxembourg Council on 12-13 December 1997 rejected Mr Yılmaz' bid for a place in the second wave in a manner which was so unnecessarily undiplomatic in both presentation and content that all Turkish public opinion was alienated from the European Union. The content was bad enough. Turks could not accept that Slovakia was regarded as being more democratic, or that the Bulgarian economy with its three-digit inflation was stronger than that of Turkey. What made it worse was the inept way in which the Council presented its rejection of Turkey's European credentials. It did try. The Conclusions unenthusiastically reaffirmed that Turkey was 'eligible for accession'. The Conclusions instructed the Commission to draw up another 'European strategy' to prepare Turkey for membership, as it had done after postponing Turkish membership in 1989. On 4 March 1998 the Commission produced a 'Strategy for Relations Between Turkey and the EU'. Meanwhile, the EU offered to recognise Turkey's importance by inviting it to a hastily invented annual 'European conference' to include all European states willing to commit themselves to 'respect for the integrity and inviolability of external borders and the principles of international law and a commitment to the settlement of territorial disputes by peaceful means, in particular through the International Court of Justice at the Hague'.

To Turks this seemed to repeat the one-sided Conclusions of the previous 1990 Luxembourg summit. If the Law of the Sea criteria were applied to the Greek islands, ninety per cent of the Aegean would come under Greek sovereignty. The European Council advised Turkey to reform itself on human rights without mentioning PKK terrorism. The Luxembourg Prime Minister added fuel to the flames by remarking that the personal responsibility of Turkey's leaders for torture separated Turkey from the other applicants. On Cyprus, Turkey was asked to support the UN sponsored negotiations on the basis of UN resolutions, and to respond to the offer to include Turkish Cypriots in the negotiations for an accession which all Turks regarded as illegitimate in international law. Under American pressure, the European Council at the Cardiff summit was able to put a better gloss on Turkey's status by requesting regular reports on Turkey's progress towards accession on the basis of Association. With the possible exception of the Italian Mr Dini, (*Agence France Presse*, 27 October 1997) most members of the Council were unconcerned about the Conclusions on Turkey which they saw as no change in a longstanding and correct decision.

Mr Yılmaz called the rebuff a 'historic mistake'. He set off for Moscow to make the point that Turkey was the only NATO member which could reverse its alliance commitments. He then went to Washington, which publicly supported the Turkish right to EU candidature. He rejected the invitation to attend the 26 March European Conference, refusing to engage in further political dialogue with the European Union. In particular, he refused to discuss with EU representatives human rights, relations with Greece, or the Cyprus problem. At the start of the UK Presidency in 1998 Sir David Hannay had to re-badge himself as Mr Tony Blair's personal representative before he was received in Ankara. Supported by Turkish opinion, Mr Yılmaz announced that the Association between Turkey and the TRNC outlined in July would be implemented in step with moves to include Greek Cyprus in the European Union. Further economic integration leading to eventual union between Northern Cyprus and Turkey was the opposite of what the EU foreign ministers had intended in 1995.

Assured of this level of solidarity from Turkey, Mr Denktaş

repeatedly told the UN, American and European special representatives that there was no point to direct intercommunal negotiations. Mr Clerides was equally determined not to delay accession by either negotiating derogations on behalf of the Turkish Cypriots with the EU or negotiating any compromise dividing Cyprus into two or three sectors. Mr Clerides' purchase of Italian and Russian missiles emphasised military security in union with Greece. He may have calculated that international diplomacy might secure a withdrawal of Turkish troops in return for Greece deploying the Russian missiles in Crete.

The EU was heavily involved in the international diplomacy which culminated in the first involvement of the G8 in calling for a settlement in Cyprus at their Cologne summit on 20 June 1999. G8 meetings are attended by the Presidents of the EU Commission and Council, and by the leaders of the seven richest industrial nations, excluding China, but including the Russian Federation. On 10 June a preparatory meeting of G8 foreign ministers called for intercommunal talks under the auspices of the UN Secretary General at the instance of the UN Security Council. Appended to the forty-nine Conclusions of the Summit Conclusions on 20 June is a statement on regional issues. In seventh or last place are three paragraphs on Cyprus. The significance of the G8 invitation from the EU perspective is twofold. If Turkey maintained its objections to the Turkish Cypriots taking up the UN invitation, then internal opposition by some member states to admitting the Greek Cypriot Republic of Cyprus would dissipate. If Turkey agreed to persuade Mr Denktaş to go to New York, then the pressure on those member states who opposed a fundamental shift towards EU acceptance of Turkish EU candidature would increase. The Turkish reply was discussed for two and a half hours at a meeting in Ankara on 16 September 1999 attended by all the Turkish and Turkish Cypriot politicians, officials and generals who had responsibilities related to the Cyprus question. The day after this meeting, Mr Denktaş signalled the impending shift of position by saying, 'Once Turkey is a candidate, the EU will have more say on Turkey and the Cyprus Issue than it has now. Now it has none' (*AA*, *News*, 17 September). He went to New York.

The Helsinki Conclusions

> We Europeans are dedicated to promoting a new, exemplary harmony between peoples of the three religions of Jerusalem. A resounding 'No' to the clash of civilisations' (Romano Prodi in his first speech as President of the Commission to the European Parliament, September 1999).

The Helsinki summit of 10-11 December 1999 agreed that Turkey and Malta should be added to the existing eleven countries within the single framework of the enlargement process (Paragraph 4). The Maltese application, dormant since the election of a Labour Government in October 1996, had been reactivated in October 1998. Already on 22 March 1999, the General Affairs Council had authorised its inclusion in the screening process of new applicants. Now the Helsinki Conclusions listed Malta with Romania, Slovakia, Latvia, Lithuania, and Bulgaria in the second wave of countries, the Helsinki Six, with whom negotiations could begin.

Turkey was persuaded to agree that its status as a candidate was assured even though its progress towards meeting the Copenhagen criteria was not sufficient for the immediate opening of negotiations. Paragraph 12 provided for an immediate reopening of political dialogue, an Accession Partnership, an analytical examination of the differences between European and Turkish law and financial aid. The EU expectation that Turkey's membership was conditional on its goodwill in backing a settlement in Cyprus was clearly, if diplomatically, expressed as 'the issues referred to in Paragraphs 4 and 9(a)'. Paragraph 4 envisaged that before 2004 candidates would settle all border disputes either by diplomacy or by reference to the International Court of Justice in the Hague. If Turkey is held responsible by the EU for the establishment and continuation of the *de facto* border in Cyprus, which is implicit in the European refusal to recognise the TRNC, then the Cypriot as well as Aegean dispute must be settled prior to membership.

Paragraph 9 refers specifically to Cyprus:

> (a) The European Council welcomes the launch of talks aimed at a comprehensive settlement of the Cyprus problem on 3 December in New York and expresses its strong support for the UN Secretary-General's efforts to bring the process to a successful conclusion.
>
> (b) The European Council underlines that a political settlement will facilitate the accession of Cyprus to the European Union. If no settlement has been reached by the completion of accession negotiations, the Council's decision on accession will be made without the above being a precondition. In this the Council will take account of all relevant factors.

The final sentence qualifies the commitment to accession without a settlement, presumably to leave the Council some leverage if they judge that the Greek Cypriot Government has not compromised sufficiently. As in Eastern Europe and Africa, the concept of conditionality has been developed to make membership or aid conditional on the applicants' behaviour. With respect to Cyprus, the conditionality is asymmetrical. Greek sponsorship of the Republic of Cyprus will bring accession without a settlement provided this can be blamed on Turkish Cypriot intransigence. Turkish membership, however, is conditional on either diplomatic or judicial settlement of the Aegean dispute with Greece and, by implication, the disputed frontier in Cyprus. In the EU view, a settlement in Cyprus depends most on decisions to be taken by Turkey in the interests of developing a satisfactory relationship between Turkey and Greece, and Turkey and the European Union.

At Helsinki, the EU15 took the decision to treat Turkey as a normal state and potentially a welcome addition to the Union. This shift from its 1995 perspective showed an increased commitment to a multicultural as well as reunified Europe. At a stroke the danger of the Cypriot frontier becoming even more dangerous as a frontier between civilisations, or between Turkey and Greece, was reduced. However, the EU does not see itself as having either the duty or the personnel to impose a settlement. The EU15 still regards the Cyprus dispute as a matter to be settled between the parties themselves.

| 4 |

Greek Cypriot and Greek Initiatives

'Cyprus is nothing but an outpost of Hellenism guarding the Thermopylae of the South'(President Clerides, 31 August 1998).

1. Introduction

The content and context of this sentence illustrate the three subjects of this chapter. The first question concerns the present and past relationship of the two Greek states, and the implications for the European Union when both are members. The allegiance to Hellenism, and the pride in accepting Athens as the centre of a world of which Cyprus is a colonial outpost, is a much more powerful emotion than, say, Scandinavian identity. By invoking Thermopylae, President Clerides patriotically identifies Cyprus with a Greece extending back over more than two and a half millennia. De Gaulle could only invoke 1400 years of French history, Churchill 1000 years of British history, while Hitler's 1000 year Reich had to be projected forwards in time. To pride and passion is added the adrenalin of fear and the whiff of treachery. King Leonidas had only a thousand men defending the pass against the far greater number of Xerxes' Persians; Mr Clerides has a National Guard of 10,000 Greek Cypriots facing over 30,000 Turkish troops protected by the overwhelming air superiority of the Turkish air force. The Persians were victorious at Thermopylae because treachery enabled them to get behind the Spartans and their more numerous Thespian allies. In the next sentence of his speech, Clerides half-promises that this time there will be no defeat because of Cyprus' strategic importance to Greece itself. 'The world will never hear "Cyprus has fallen" because, if Cyprus falls, the whole of the Aegean Sea will come under threat'.

The speech was made in direct response to Mr Denktaş' assertion on 18 August 1998 that the only basis for future intercommunal talks had to be Greek Cypriot acceptance of equality with the Turkish Cypriots in a confederation. The second subject of this chapter is the wide spectrum of Greek Cypriot views on 'a just and lasting settlement', and the more difficult question of what could be given up in intercommunal negotiations with the Turkish Cypriots. The European Union and its member states in international fora regularly call for the two parties to reach a settlement between themselves. They consistently support the view of both parties that this time a settlement must not be imposed from outside. Ideally a settlement should be reached before the end of the accession process. However, the immediate difficulty is whether serious negotiations can take place on the basis of each side recognising that the other has been elected by its own community. From the Greek Cypriot perspective to be explored in this chapter, the Turkish Cypriots are a secessionist minority who have welcomed the Turkish army on to an Hellenic island, and subordinated themselves to Turkish control. They are therefore more of an enemy than when they were supporting British rule, or when they could be coldly categorised by President Makarios as '*to synoikon stoicheion*, the element which inhabits the island jointly with us' (Stavrinides in Dodd, ed. 1999: 94). Moreover the remarkable consensus behind the European Orientation in Southern Cyprus seems to be based on a patriotic belief that membership will strengthen the Republic in the face of the Turkish occupation. In comparison with Malta, the economic interests likely to be harmed by accession and left-wing hostility to the ideas represented by the European Union have been repressed. Pan-Cypriot sentiment that the accession process would undermine efforts at reconciliation with the Turkish Cypriots has been downplayed. Cypriot nationalists have not joined in with the anti-European sentiments of other nationalists in the EU, a silence all the more surprising in view of Slav and Orthodox solidarity with Serbia.

The context in which Mr Clerides delivered his speech was a meeting in South Africa of the Non-Aligned Movement, in the presence of UN Secretary General Kofi Annan. The internationalisation of the Cyprus dispute balances the military might of Turkey with the diplomatic weight of world and European opinion. The third topic to be discussed in this chapter is the place of Cyprus' European orientation in this major theme of internationalisation against Turkey. When President Clerides on 28 February, 1998 inaugurated his second elected term as President of the Republic of Cyprus, he promised to continue the policy implemented after his victory over Vassiliou in 1993:

> The lynchpin of this strategy is well known, namely: mobilising the international community, effectively exploiting the international factor and exerting intensive efforts to achieve a mutually acceptable solution through talks. Proceeding towards the European Union and utilising the dynamics created by following this course to reunify Cyprus. Building our defence and implementing the Cyprus-Greece Joint Defence Doctrine. Co-operating closely with the Greek government and the political leadership of Greece (Quoted by Stavrinides in Dodd, ed, 1999: 56).

In so far as increases in defence forces and the mobilisation of the international community are targeted on Turkey, this joint Greek and Greek Cypriot strategy is incompatible with the alternative approach of seeking a solution by agreement between Greece and Turkey. This approach had brought independence to Cyprus in 1959/60. 'Bilateral Graeco-Turkish talks, without the participation of the Republic of Cyprus, took place in a number of contexts' between 1964 and 1967 (Polyviou 1976: 70). Between then and 1974 the Junta made several attempts under NATO auspices to make a deal directly with Turkey (See Chapter 6).

Thermopylae also resonates in European culture. Hellenism, and especially the association with Periclean democracy, brings with it a cultural identification with things Greek. Nineteenth century Greek independence was the consequence of the first European intervention on behalf of a national liberation movement. 'The Greek myth did not arise from contemplation of ruins, but was almost entirely the product of Western European modernity' (Tsoukalis, 1991: 8). Nineteenth century European imperialism is associated with a sense of cultural superiority over the Orient derived from identification with Ancient Greece. This identification still gives Greeks an edge in the capitals of Europe. When the Council overrode the negative Commission Opinion on the Greek application for membership of the European Communities in 1980, it helped that President Giscard d'Estaing and German Foreign Minister Genscher were themselves Hellenophiles.

The wholesale Greek reception of nineteenth century European ideas of nationalism and modernity has led to two problems affecting Greek Cypriots today. The first stems from the nationalist assertion that Greeks are different from other groups, in particular all those that they had been living with for centuries. As the British left education in Cyprus to the communities, modernising Greek teachers from the mainland came to Cyprus to teach the new reinvented history and language, which emphasised separation and superiority. Now that post-imperial Western Europe has adopted the North American discourse of multiculturalism, Hellenistic rhetoric sounds suddenly discordant to other European ears.

The second problem is the cultural clash in Greece between West and East. The long-standing tension between the 'Olympic' ideal celebrating the human body, democracy and scientific enquiry, and the Greek Orthodox ideal of concealing the human body, ritual and deference, has taken on a novel political significance. Before 1989, the Greek Orthodox Church supported identification with nationalism and Western Europe to such an extent that the 'liberation' of Cyprus was led by right-wing groups. After 1989, Orthodox identification with Slav peoples in Eastern Europe and Russia has been at odds with both Greek Governments' commitment to the EU. During the Kosovo crisis the Greek Government resisted popular feeling in favour of Serbia to a greater extent than would have been the case if Greece had not been a member state. It was the Republic of Cyprus that took on the task of representing Serb interests in London—fellow Slavs with their backs to the wall before defeat in their Thermopylae.

2. Greece as Motherland

'It is Greece that will determine when Cyprus will join the European Union' (Greek Foreign Minister, Theodoros Pangalos, *Athens News Agency*, 12 September 1997).

Greek sponsorship of Cyprus has changed its meaning since 1954. Then a White Paper drawn up by the Greek Foreign Ministry on 'The question of Cyprus' envisaged its liberation as part of the process of national unification. Greece aspired to incorporate all 'islands whose population was mainly or wholly Greek... the Ionian islands, Crete, the Aegean islands of the Eastern Mediterranean, the Dodecanese, Cyprus' (Şakir Alemdar in Dodd, 1993: 77). Today, both Greece and the Republic of Cyprus are at one that Greece is sponsoring the membership of Cyprus as a separate and independent state in the European Union, entitled as a nation-state to membership of all the EU institutions in its own right.

Despite this fundamental change, the bilateral constitutional, military and political links between the two Greek states remain strong. The Constitution of 1960 allows for the Greek flag to be flown on official buildings, and for Greece to intervene at will to maintain the state of affairs established by the Constitution. Militarily, the Constitution entitles Greece to maintain 950 troops in Cyprus. In 1993, the two states agreed that Cyprus should be part of one Greek unified defence space. In addition to joint military exercises, a co-ordinated rearmament programme has paid for a big naval and air base at Paphos, new tanks, aircraft, and Italian and French missiles. The extent of co-operation was demonstrated in 1998-9 during the crisis over the intended deployment of S-300 Russian missiles in the Troodos mountains. Whether the purpose was military in countering Turkish air superiority, or a diplomatic counter to be withdrawn in return for the evacuation of Turkish troops from Cyprus, the outcome was deployment instead in the Greek island of Crete.

Political relations between the two Greek states have ranged from total dependence and attempted union by armed intervention to the present close co-operation on the aim of accession to the EU, a common aim which allows for occasional disagreements on tactics. For example, the independence of Cyprus was initially negotiated in 1959 unilaterally by the Greek Foreign Minister. The renunciation of *enosis* was accepted by Archbishop Makarios in London after long telephone consultation with the Greek royal family. In 1963 President Makarios was able to propose his thirteen amendments, emphasising the unitary over the bi-communal character of the Constitution, only after Mr George Papandreou had replaced Mr Karamanlis as Greek Prime Minister. Between 1964 and 1967 Mr Papandeou and the Junta gradually infiltrated 10,000 troops to work with the National Guard under General George Grivas in an abortive attempt to realise *enosis* (Kyrrhis, 1996: 382). Relations between the Greek Junta and President Makarios were tense after the abdication of King Constantine. In 1967 the Junta infiltrated 8000 Greek troops into Cyprus to work with EOKA-B in an abortive attempt to realise *enosis*. President Makarios' desire for integrating Cyprus into Greece is also contentious. Whether or not Michael Attalides is correct in explaining President Makarios' public enthusiasm as necessary equivocation to preserve Cypriot independence from the NATO-backed Junta, his speeches leave no doubt about the expectations of his public. For example, on 14 March 1971 he said of his own rule in Cyprus; 'Greek and undivided we have taken it over. Greek and undivided we shall preserve it. Greek and undivided we shall deliver it to Greece' (Attalides, 1979: 73).

Actions speak louder than words. The coup by Greek officers in 1974 was backed by Athens in order to win popularity for the Junta in Greece by overthrowing Makarios and forcefully uniting Cyprus with Greece. The initial bloodshed in Cyprus was between Greek Cypriot supporters and opponents of the refugee President. The threatened *enosis* alarmed the Turkish Cypriots whose enclaves in South Cyprus and Paphos were attacked by the National Guard (Kyrrhis, 1996: 401).This brought about Turkish military intervention. After the resignation of Nicos Sampson, installed as President by the Junta, the Greek Cypriots were reunited under the leadership of the President of the House of Representatives, Mr Clerides. After the fall of the Junta, the Greek and Greek Cypriot delegations worked in tandem at the

Geneva Conference. However, the Greek side did not support Mr Clerides' suggestion of renewing the fight, despite the odds, in the hope of provoking Soviet intervention and American mediation (Polyviou, 1976: 352, 364).

After 1974, claims to enosis were dropped by both the Greek and the Greek Cypriot Governments as incompatible with the mobilising of international opinion against the *de facto* partition of the island by Turkey. The incoming Karamanlis government in Greece enunciated a new slogan appropriate to the policy of close cooperation between sovereign states, 'Cyprus decides, Greece supports'. The Cypriot Government emphasised the geographic distance and historical differences between independent states. Larnaca is 360 km from Rhodes, 380 km from Crete, and 949 km from Athens. Cyprus is different from Greece in that it did not have a long civil war against a strong communist party; it also inherited the legacy of British colonial administration. There are now vested interests in Cypriot independence of Greece. The wide spectrum in Cyprus of attitudes to Turkish Cypriots is not analogous to the attitudes of mainland Greeks to Turks. Moreover, in Greece there are conflicting opinions about the merits of Greek Cypriots (Pettifer, 1994: 196). The first visit of a Greek Prime Minister to Cyprus did not take place until 1982. When the Greek Prime Minister, Andreas Papandreou, during that visit called the Cypriot problem a 'national issue', he meant the Greek commitment to the reunification of Cyprus, not a return to the aspiration of uniting Cyprus with Greece.

Nevertheless the links between Greece and the Republic of Cyprus are closer than those between any other member states. Greek Cypriot schools follow the Greek national curriculum. Five fibre optic cables have been laid between Cyprus and Greece. In November 1990 a compulsory surcharge was levied on Cypriot electricity bills to pay for the television link between Cyprus and ET-1, the first channel of the Greek national network. The right-wing parties in Cyprus, which have won all the elections on the Greek Cypriot electoral roll since 1960, celebrate the national holidays of Greece. Their allegiance to the Greek flag has both a patriotic and an ideological content. Allegiance to Motherland Greece is like the Ulsterman's allegiance to the Union Jack. It expresses a willingness to fight on ethnic lines, if necessary against fellow Cypriots. It sets the Hellenocentric parties in Cyprus against the left-wing parties, who celebrate the October Revolution and May Day. The left-wing parties are more inclined to identify on a pan-Cypriot ideological basis with the trade unions and left-wing parties on the Turkish Cypriot side.

These close political and cultural ties raise an obvious question about the future relationship between Cyprus and Greece in the European Union. If it is the case that in 1960 and 1974 the majority in Cyprus accepted sovereign independence of Greece for pragmatic reasons, as second best to their preference for union, then if the fear of Turkish intervention is removed, would not the majority go back to their first preference? This would have the advantage from a European Union perspective of removing the problem of accommodating a sovereign state arguably too small to run the Presidency. In 1995 a book by four retired Greek ambassadors included double *enosis* as one of the options that might be in the national interest of Greece (Theodhoropoulos et al, 1995 quoted by Zambouras in Dodd, ed., 1999: 118). However, this idea of uniting Southern Cyprus with Greece is not within the realm of practical politics. The consensus among Greek Cypriots backs the Government in looking forward to an eventual pan-Cypriot settlement with Turkish Cypriots, which implies that the Republic of Cyprus will remain an independent sovereign state within the European Union.

3. The Greek Cypriot consensus on the European orientation

The Government's drive to prepare Cyprus for membership has received full and consistent backing from the wide spectrum of opinion among Greek Cypriots. The European orientation of Mr Clerides' 'Democratic Rally' party, DESY, was supported first by Mr Lyssarides' socialists, EDEK, and then by the hitherto strongly anti-European communists of AKEL. In the Presidential elections of 1993 and 1998 the leading candidates were all in favour of the European orientation. The Government has gone to great lengths to demonstrate its European credentials. In 1990 it set up an independent Competition Authority. In 1991 Cyprus signed the European Charter on Energy. In 1992 the Central Bank pegged the Cyprus pound to the ECU. It established a new monetary framework for regulating the money supply to the Government, the public enterprises and the commercial banks; it attacked money laundering by requiring explanation of all transactions over $10,000. In 1993 a special European division of the Ministry of Foreign Affairs established twenty sectoral groups to prepare for harmonisation of Cypriot law with the European *acquis*, and trained over 600 officials in relevant European law. It took every opportunity to align Cyprus with the EU in international organisations and, after 1995, with EU statements on foreign affairs. Once the negotiations on accession got under way, the Government sought to avoid reserving its position or asking for derogations that might delay the process and permit the unraveling of the domestic consensus.

The depth of the present political commitment of Greek Cypriots to accession to the EU can be illustrated by contrasting Cyprus with Malta. Cyprus is like Malta in being an ex-British colonial base in the Mediterranean with a strong leftist political tradition. In Brussels, Cyprus and Malta have long been coupled together as Mediterranean Associates. Malta became an Associate in 1970 and applied for full membership in 1990. The same unit in the Commission deals with both countries and Turkey. The Commission Report on Malta of June 1993 was issued at the same time as that of Cyprus, and in March 1995 the Commission proposed that the date for opening negotiations on membership should also be within six months of the close of the inter-governmental conference. Commission President Jacques Delors called them the 'orphans' of the Community. This was not a reference to parentage—Cyprus has two motherlands and Italy has seen itself since 1987 as the sponsor of the Maltese application. Delors meant that Brussels saw them as micro-states that might not be able to emulate Luxembourg in discharging the functions of the Council Presidency, for example. Whereas the EFTA states were actively encouraged to get involved in the debate over institutions before they became members, Cyprus and Malta were barred from any such involvement (Pace, 1995: 18). The other common difficulty is that both Malta and Cyprus are 'non-aligned' states; Malta additionally claims neutral status by virtue of its Constitution, a neutrality guaranteed by the 1980 Treaty with Italy. Despite these similarities, membership of the EU was sufficiently disputed within Malta for its application to be withdrawn by the Labour Government elected to power between 1996 and 1999. If opposition from left-wing parties and sectoral interest groups was so strong in Malta, the absence of similar effective protest in Cyprus has to be explained.

Since 1974, Cyprus has established itself as the successor to Beirut as an unregulated centre of capitalist enterprise in the Mediterranean. In 1998 it boasted 25,000 offshore banking enterprises, 3000 of them linked to the Russian Federation and Eastern Europe (*Cyprus Mail*, 10 May 1998). The Cypriot 'flag of convenience' had attracted 2,641 ships constituting a quarter of world tonnage in 1995 (ROC, 1997: 51). Yet sectoral opposition to EU regulation from banking, shipping, and ocean fishing interests remains muted. Secondly, small manufacturers did not protest the loss of subsidies, tariff protection and the 49 per cent ceiling on foreign ownership which required foreign investors to work with Cypriot entrepreneurs. Farmers and fishermen will have to balance further loss of production of uncompetitive agriculture and fisheries against the hope that the EU will compensate them through agricultural and regional subsidies despite the costs to the CAP of enlargement to Eastern Europe. Thirdly, one might have expected the deeply entrenched public sector in Cyprus to resent the greater competition implicit in the Single Market's bias towards privatisation of public enterprises in aviation, water, and especially in telecommunications. Cypriot Parliamentarians will lose their authority, and patronage, over a range of sectors from fertilisers to telecommunications, and will be unable to incur spending going over the strict Maastricht criteria on budget deficits and public debt. Fourthly, all individuals will be affected by the rise in food prices on items subject to European price-fixing. The unpopular Value Added Tax introduced to compensate the Government for loss of tariff revenue is likely to rise on entry from 8 percent to 10 per cent. Meeting European environmental standards for water and air will also require more taxation. The attempted removal of the 9 per cent ceiling on interest rates, dating from British protection of farmers against moneylenders and now incompatible with EU capital liberalisation, stands out as the issue on which popular protest has been uniquely effective.

The Government's chief negotiator on entry, former President

Vassiliou, has been able to counter these considerable threats to specific interests with very unspecific arguments on the economic benefits of membership. He has justified accession as the necessary response to a general change towards globalisation and information technology. Cypriots have to accept that traditional exports of citrus and potatoes, fish and minerals are in decline, and that the Arab market which proved so profitable after the oil price rise of 1973 is no longer as attractive as the EU, which accounts for nearly half of Cypriot exports and imports. EU membership is to bring in foreign direct investment as policies of privatisation and liberalisation replace protection and import substitution.

In terms of party politics also, much stronger opposition to the European Union might have been anticipated in Cyprus than in Malta. The Cypriot communist party, AKEL, has a tradition of militancy, backed by secret arms caches, which cannot be matched by the Maltese Labour Party. The dominant nationalist parties have a more militant and strident tradition in opposition to Western liberalism and NATO involvement than the Maltese National Party or the anti-EU nationalist parties of Western Europe. The propertied Orthodox Church in Cyprus is much more influential in politics than the much poorer Catholic Church in Malta. Yet even Cypriot demonstrations against the NATO intervention in Kosovo have not brought the Church and the communist party, AKEL, to unite against the European Union.

What made the political consensus behind accession in Cyprus so much stronger than in Malta was neither economic calculation nor the sudden discovery of a longstanding European identity. The consensus was based on patriotism. The explanation lies entirely with the Greek Cypriot perception of its problem with Turkey and the Turkish Cypriots. In 1990 the EU became the favoured vehicle for mobilising the international factor in the containment of Turkey. Militarily, Greek Cypriots could feel more secure from Turkey if they were an EU member state. The principal exception to the Government's model behaviour as a candidate was that it allowed the budgetary deficit to rise. The rise in arms spending accounted for the deficit, despite the Government's attempt to put the blame on lower tariff revenues. The exception proves the rule. What motivated Mr Clerides, and explains his re-election, was the dominance of security concerns now that the end of the Cold War gave Turkey more freedom of manoeuvre. While the Greek Cypriot consensus on the European orientation had a lot to do with making the Republic of Cyprus more secure against Turkey, the leadership was much less clear on the question whether the predictable damage to relations with Turkish Cypriots would be outweighed by the benefits.

Greek Cypriots vs. Turkish Cypriots

> We still have not understood that satisfactory solutions of problems like ours can only be the result of two people learning to walk together the path of co-existence and co-operation for the common benefit of both, instead of facing each other with pointed guns and looking at each other through gun-sights (Clerides, 1991: Epilogue).

It has already been said that Cypriot President Vassiliou refused to allow Greek Prime Minister Papandreou to use the Greek Presidency of the EU in 1988 to initiate an application for membership from Cyprus that predated the collapse of communism in Eastern Europe. He thought an application would make it more difficult to achieve the aim to which he gave priority—negotiating a settlement with the Turkish Cypriots in the framework of the United Nations (Zervakis in Axt and Brey, 1997: 144). The same source goes on to say that when in 1990 President Vassiliou changed his position and agreed to submit an application on behalf of the whole island of Cyprus, 'the newly elected Greek government of Constantine Mitsotakis concurred... that an EC membership for Cyprus should also entail tangible benefits for the Turkish Cypriots'. In defending the right of the Government to speak for Cyprus, Greek Cypriot ministers usually express the hope that the accession process will itself stimulate the Turkish Cypriots to accept a settlement (See Michaelides, 1996).

However, while the Greek Cypriot Government might hope for 'a just and lasting settlement', it did not expect Mr Denktaş to support their application. In economic terms, the 'tangible benefits' on offer were EU subsidies to add to the far more important potential economic benefits which had so far failed to impress the Turkish Cypriots—the lifting of sanctions, the more stable Cyprus pound, and the increased wealth from allowing Greek Cypriot entrepreneurs to develop the coastline and resources. In political terms, Mr Clerides' offer to accept a more cantonal interpretation of a future Federation and to talk about a revolving presidency if the Turkish leadership would accept the legitimacy of the 1990 application, was unlikely to be enough to bring the Turkish Cypriots to accept Mr Clerides' right to speak and act on their behalf.

The priority for the Greek Cypriot Government was to prevent any delay in the accession process due to the Turkish Cypriot factor. The only criticism that the Greek Cypriot Foreign Minister made of the Commission's 1993 Opinion was its suggestion that a political settlement should precede the opening of negotiations. During the negotiations, the Government fought alongside the Greek Government to prevent the inclusion of Turkish Cypriots in its team if this implied either a Turkish Cypriot veto or recognition of the regime or of a separate entity in the North. The Government did not ask for the derogations on freedom of movement for persons or capital that the Turkish Cypriots needed. Such a request would have risked the political consensus in the South. Unilateral concessions by the Government would have been unacceptable to many nationalists. Delay might encourage the mobilisation of economic sectors opposed to accession. Moreover, the Cypriot Government did not ask the EU to fund a costed settlement package to be put to both communities. The priority was enhanced international legitimacy, not local legitimacy. Membership of the EU would better enable Cyprus either to keep Turkey outside Europe, or to make the withdrawal of its troops the price of Turkish entry. Some hoped that Mr Denktaş' authority might be undermined as Turkish Cypriot businessmen counted the costs of non-membership, or of the reduction of Turkish Cypriot living standards to those of Anatolia.

This lack of concern that the accession process must drive the North into further integration with Turkey has three possible explanations. The first is the nationalist view that Turkish Cyprus is already a province of Turkey. The second is that many Greek Cypriots have got used to the status quo or at least do not expect any change. The third explanation compatible with either position is that one day

Anatolian Turks and the Turkish army will leave Northern Cyprus, as the Russians and Russian army unexpectedly left East Germany. Turkish Cypriots could then become more prosperous as individuals by reintegrating with the richer economy of the South.

This leads us on to the vexed question of whether the Greek Cypriots want the bi-zonal, bi-communal federal settlement with the Turkish Cypriots which the European Union would like ideally to precede accession, or to follow as soon afterwards as possible. Oliver Richmond contrasts international and local opinion thus:

> Greek Cypriot negotiating tactics have been balanced between the need to pander to international opinion which supports the bi-communal, b-izonal framework, and local opinion which tends to support a return to the pre-1974 positions, on the part of the nationalists, or simply a continuation of the status quo (Richmond, 1999: 14).

By way of introduction to a description of the Greek Cypriot view of a possible settlement in terms of culture, politics and law, it may be useful to begin with the apparently factual question of the relative population size of the two communities.

Population

At independence in 1960 the numbers in each community were precisely known because Cyprus differed from the European norm in having separate voting lists for Christians and Muslims. 442,138 Greek Cypriots constituted 77.1 per cent of the population (Kyle, 1997: 5). A few thousand Maronites, Armenians and Latins chose to be added to the 'Greek' voting lists. In every town there was a Greek quarter and a separate Turkish quarter. Of the 629 villages, 392 were purely Greek and 123 purely Turkish. The decline by a third of the number of mixed villages since 1890 to the 114 'mixed' villages of 1960 is an indicator of the slow rise of nationalist sentiment, a process accelerated after 1950.

Since 1974, the numbers in each community have become difficult to establish precisely. One reason is that the size of the unusually large diaspora from both communities is difficult to determine. Figures for

Britain range from 200-250,000, and there are large Cypriot populations in Australia, the United States and Canada. Many of these emigrants are still entitled to vote in Cyprus, and frequently return to the island on a temporary basis. A more important reason is political. Thus in 1999 the Government reported to the Council of Europe that in 1996 621,800 Greek Cypriots constituted 83.9 per cent of the population and 89,200 Turkish Cypriots constituted 12 per cent. [The Official Overview of the Republic of Cyprus for 1997 estimated the Greek Cypriot population at 623,200 constituting 84.7 per cent of the population. The Turkish Cypriot population is estimated at 90,600 or 12.3 per cent of the population.] This result is obtained by estimating the net emigration of Turkish Cypriots at 47,000 between 1974 and 1995 and by not including approximately 109,000 immigrants from Anatolia, as being illegal colonists lacking authorisation from the internationally recognised Government. [The 1997 Overview gives a figure for 1994 of 88,000. See also Council of Europe, 1992, Doc. 6589]. The Government does not publish the precise number of an estimated 10,000 Turkish Cypriots who have obtained ROC passports while abroad, in defiance of the regulations of the Turkish Republic of Northern Cyprus. Official statistics, which give the percentage of Turkish Cypriot population at 12 per cent and falling, when an estimate of 30 per cent and rising would be nearer the truth, are bound to mislead Greek Cypriots themselves as to the nature of the problem, and are understandable only as weapons in a war of words.

Culture
Different languages, religions and histories have contributed to a sense of deep racial and cultural division between Greek and Turk, Orthodox Christians and Muslims. Divisions have been exacerbated by separate educational systems which do not teach their children the language of the other community. It has to be said that Greek Cypriots believe that they are culturally superior to Turkish Cypriots, more prosperous because they are more urbanised, better educated, better at commerce, finance and diplomacy. On the other hand, despite this divergence, both communities were able to live together up to 1954 unaffected by the 1923 exchange of populations between Greece and Turkey (Zurcher, 1993; 248). In the diaspora, some Cypriots from

these contrasting backgrounds can recognise that they are culturally closer to each other than to Scandinavians or Sinhalese in multicultural Europe. They have much in common with each other by way, for example, of cuisine and lifestyle, racial prejudice against Africans, and absence of missionary zeal in religion.

However, allegiance to one's own community defined by race, language, religion and culture has not been broken down by urbanisation and the like in Cyprus. As in Ulster and the Balkans, profound economic and political changes, produced by outside forces, have reinforced loyalties to separately educated communities. This has been allowed to become self-reinforcing according to the logic of any security dilemma. What promotes one's own security against another is perceived by the other as threatening, and hence requiring additional measures in a spiral based on, and reinforcing, mutual distrust. The dominant community must bear the most responsibility for inducing mutual insecurity. A Greek Cypriot minister who would not appoint three accountants after 1960 because that would require giving a job to a Turkish Cypriot is discriminating on the same ethnic grounds as the official who became angry at being tricked into giving a job on the Christmas post to a Greek-speaking Turkish Cypriot. The 1960 Constitution envisaged the integration of a police force and army drawn from both communities. Instead, the pattern of separate, ethnically homogeneous forces established for unofficial armed groups like EOKA was continued in the regular forces of the new Republic. As each Cypriot community is too small to be militarily viable on its own, each has contributed to the spiral of fear by getting help on a kith and kin basis from its cultural motherland. The other community becomes necessarily the focus of distrust and is accused of building up its arsenals, to which the only realist response is to build up one's own defences. On a wider perspective, such ethnic security dilemmas are not uncritically self-reproducing. French and German schools no longer teach that each nation is the hereditary enemy of the other. The Religious Wars of the early seventeenth century were followed by eighteenth century religious tolerance. Glasgow and Liverpool are no longer riven by religious differences leading to perpetual conflict. The long history of Cyprus contains more evidence for the view that religious coexistence between two non-proselytising religions is the norm than it does for Huntington's view of religious conflict inevitably replacing the ideological divide. In a secure Continent, differences can be mutually beneficial, as in a North American multicultural dialogue. Greek Cypriots, however, are not into the language of identity. They operate in terms of allegiance to one's own people or leader in the patriotic sense of being willing to fight for rights and boundaries.

Politics

The Greek Cypriots justify their right to rule the whole of Cyprus on the basis of the internationally accepted post-war doctrine that the self-determination of peoples entitles them to replace colonial rule. They won the war of liberation against the forces of the British Empire and its Turkish Cypriot police. They constitute the clear majority in a democracy. The Constitution was imposed on them even though they voted for President Makarios rather than John Clerides, the father of Glafcos, who campaigned against the 1960 settlement because it gave a disproportionate share of jobs in the civil service and police to the Turkish Cypriots. In 1963 the treasonable retreat of the Turkish Cypriots to their municipal enclaves gave the Government no alternative but to make the Constitution work. It may have been a mistake to press the Turkish Cypriots so hard between 1963 and 1974, but the refusal of the minority to allow government officials access to their enclaves made it impossible to implement the promises on human rights made to the UN. The disaster of 1974 was due to outside intervention. The coup attempted on behalf of the Greek Junta gave Turkey an excuse to carry out their long-planned partition. The Greek Cypriots see themselves as the victims, having to cope with 160-200,000 refugees, losing 37 per cent of the island, 51 per cent of the coastline, the best tourist spots and the most productive mines to the secessionist Turkish Cypriots.

The Greek Cypriot view of justice

The Greek Cypriot side which, on common admission, has an unshakable case in law and morality alike, now faces bankruptcy and the stark prospect of a partitioned island with all that that implies (Polyviou, 1976 : ix).

Polyvios Polyviou stands out among Greek Cypriot lawyers for the deliberate care with which he describes the Turkish Cypriot case in the intercommunal negotiations before 1974. The fact that all Greek Cypriots believe their own case to be unshakable in law and morality is an essential aspect of any explanation of the difficulty of intercommunal negotiations.

In terms of constitutional law, the Greek Cypriots believe that the unitary state created by the 1960 Constitution was deficient. The sovereign power of a people to give itself by majority decision a new Constitution was absurdly limited by internal and external constraints incompatible with the principle of self-determination. The 1960 Constitution proved unworkable in that potential secession was being prepared in the municipal enclaves. Unintegrated Turkish Cypriot police and army units were arming themselves with weapons obtained from Turkey. The necessary amendments were passed in the Assembly after the Turkish Cypriots had rejected them at Turkey's instance. When the Turkish Cypriots removed themselves from the offices and jobs they held, the Greek Cypriots 'of necessity' had to carry on the business of government without the participation of the minority community. The attempted secession of the Turkish enclaves, the partition of the island, and the successive declarations of a Federated State and then a Turkish Republic were all illegal under the terms of the founding treaties of the Republic which the Turkish side themselves acknowledge are still valid. The Republic has taken great care to respect the property rights of Turkish Cypriot citizens who chose to flee. In international law, the recognition of the sovereignty of the Republic of Cyprus has two particular implications for other states and for Turkey. Other states have to respect the embargo imposed by the Republic of Cyprus on all dealings with the illegal entity in the North. Turkey is responsible for taking the territory of another sovereign state by a military intervention and occupation which went well beyond its right to restore the state of affairs established by the founding treaties. Turkey is therefore responsible for all war crimes, for damage to the cultural heritage of Byzantium, for failing to provide information about the 'missing', for depriving Greek Cypriots of their rights of property and free movement in the zone under its military occupation, and for imposing a puppet government on the Republic's Turkish Cypriot citizens.

In terms of morality, an ideally just settlement in the eyes of virtually all Greek Cypriots means the restoration of an Hellenic island in its entirety to democratic rule. The majority will respect its Turkish Cypriot citizens both as individuals and as a minority group entitled to autonomy in educational and other cultural matters. The meaning of a lasting settlement is more ambiguous. As a minimum, Greek Cypriots want a normality that cannot be upset by outside intervention. Turkish colonists and the Turkish army of occupation have no right to be on the island beyond the 650 troops permitted after independence. Greek Cypriots mostly take care not to condemn Turkish Cypriots as traitors to Cyprus who have invited in the aggressor. Most Greek Cypriots are willing to speak well of some of their former neighbours or employees, as individuals. For example, Mr Clerides arranged that the remains of Mr Denktaş' close relatives be transferred from Paphos to the North in 1997. On the one hand, this bodes well for future co-existence. On the other hand, it indicates how strong is the communitarian, or ethnic, as against civic, understanding of national allegiance—the good that it is right to promote is the good of the Greek Cypriot community. This utilitarian approach is standard. No Greek Cypriot politician speaks in social contract terms of what he would be prepared to accept as a just and lasting settlement if he had been born a Turkish Cypriot. Nor is there any suggestion of Truth Commissions to establish the facts of wrongdoing in the inner-Greek fighting of 1974, or against the Turkish community before 1974, or against the Turkish Cypriots who felt too afraid to live in the South after 1974. For Cypriots of both sides, history is a club for beating the other side.

The spectrum of Greek Cypriot opinion on negotiating a settlement

Just as the Greek Cypriot preoccupation was that Cyprus should be a Greek Cypriot state with a protected Turkish Cypriot minority, the Turkish pre-occupation was to defeat any such effort and to maintain the partnership concept which in their opinion the Zurich Agreement created between the two communities. The conflict therefore was a conflict of principle and for that principle both sides were prepared to go on arguing and even if need be to fight rather than compromise. The same principle is still in conflict even today, though a federal solution has been accepted and though a federation is nothing more than a constitutional partnership of the component states, provinces or cantons which make up the federation (Clerides, 1991, vol. 3: 105).

The spectrum of opinion in Greek Cyprus is wider than on the Turkish side. Some are more Cyprocentric, looking for an accommodation between the two Cypriot communities which will distance Cyprus from dependence on Turkey or Greece (Stavrinides in Dodd, ed., 1999). Cyprocentrics tend to be on the political left, where trade union and political activity on ideological lines provided a basis for co-operation going beyond coexistence. The majority, who have always won the elections, are more Hellenocentric. The majority, however, can also be divided between those who accept the need for a political compromise and those who reject any appeasement of Turkish aggression. The High-Level Agreement between Makarios and Denktaş of 1977 sketched out the lines of compromise, regaining some of the lost territory in exchange for recognition of Turkish autonomy in a bi-zonal federation. The harder line rejecting federation was articulated by Archbishop Chrysostomos as Mr Clerides prepared in 1999 for exploratory talks at the United Nations. The Archbishop and House Speaker Kyprianou argue that any settlement should be negotiated exclusively between Cypriots, thus giving preponderance to the more numerous and richer Greek Cypriot side:

> A federation is a violation of human rights, because people are forced to leave their ancestral homes. A federation in Cyprus involves three Governments and four Parliaments...Cyprus is too small to be a federation...Any solution must be made exclusively between Turkish and Greek Cypriots.

Disagreement about the nature of an acceptable federation is one reason why very little detail is discussed in public. It would disrupt the consensus behind the European orientation to little immediate purpose. The Greek Cypriots favour a 'strong' federation, with federal taxation, a federal police to assure the freedoms of movement and of property throughout both zones, a federal central bank to manage the currency, and a bicameral legislature with a Greek Cypriot majority in the Lower House (see Theophanous, 1996). They also assume that, as is normal with federations, the central government should manage foreign policy. This makes some sense in relations with the EU, but none at all in the Eastern Mediterranean so long as Greece and Greek Cyprus remain hostile on all fronts to Turkey.

Before turning to this most important question of Greek and Greek Cypriot attitudes to Turkey, three additional remarks are apposite. The first is that another reason for the paucity of Greek Cypriot debate on federalism is that there is no enthusiasm for it either for its own sake or as a positive solution to the Cyprus problem. A poll in April 2000 found that 80 per cent of Greek Cypriots would not live in a Turkish Cypriot canton. The Greek Cypriot majority on the island regards itself as entitled to enjoy a version of the dominant model of the liberal democratic state—that of a polity belonging to a people, in sovereign possession of a clearly bounded territory. They do not identify with the Swiss Federation as an exception that proves the rule in that several peoples can be drawn together to preserve each part against external aggression. Legislation is difficult to pass in Switzerland precisely because it requires consensus between communities, protecting the minority cantons from being overruled by a majority.

The second remark is that the European Union is not yet regarded as an alternative to the sovereignty model outlined above.The European flag, like the Cypriot flag, is more a logo to be recognised than a national flag of allegiance or a medieval banner of local identity. European law is intended to preclude discrimination in favour of one's own people, a European version of American pluralism and multiculturalism over a Continent. Its institutions have restrained the individual states of France, Germany and Greece from unilateral aid to their protégés in the Balkans. Its troops are increasingly justified as professional resources for humanitarian intervention than as citizens in arms defending lands. The Member States worry more about foreign immigrants than about hostile armies. However, the attraction of Europe to Greek Cypriots is not that it is a new form of polity within which communitarian antagonisms can be subsumed; the attraction is to strengthen the Republic of Cyprus against its local enemies.

The third remark is that the Greek Cypriots necessarily have little enthusiasm for the confidence-building measures recommended by the international community as a step-by-step approach towards making a federal solution negotiable between the two communities. The international embargo on Northern Cyprus which the Greek Cypriots have successfully upheld for a quarter of a century is in power political terms their equivalent of the Turkish army. The embargo is predicated on non-recognition of the Turkish Cypriots as a legitimate actor. The Greek Cypriots could not bring themselves to allow the derelict international airport of Nicosia to be used by both sides in return for their being able to develop the derelict border resort of Varosha. They did not want to accord any measure of recognition of the illegal regime or to lift the embargo on direct tourist flights to Northern Cyprus.

The recognition weapon therefore makes a step-by-step approach too difficult. Negotiators have to deliver a complete package. Yet any negotiations are necessarily impeded by the second consequence of the recognition weapon. Serious negotiations between the parties themselves are inevitably blighted by the inability of both sides to accept the status claimed by the other. The Government side cannot recognise the equal status claimed by the Turkish Cypriots as the Government of the North; the Turkish Cypriots cannot recognise the right of the wholly Greek Cypriot Government to apply on their behalf for membership of the European Union. Mr Boutros Ghali had therefore to draw up a package to be put to the two communities talking separately to the UN as third party. In negotiations about imperial withdrawal, the difficulty for the imperial Government to recognise rebels as a future government has been less serious in that the occupying imperial power intends to leave the country. In Cyprus, both communities intend to stay put, and both communities are adamant that the Cypriot problem and its settlement are primarily a matter for themselves. The view of the majority Greek Cypriot side has not wavered from the claim expressed in 1975 thus:

> The Constitutional conflict in Cyprus is basically a conflict between the two Communities, and must be so presented. It is true, of course, that a delicate network of other national and

international interests involving Greece, Turkey, NATO, the United States and the Soviet Union, Great Britain and the European Community cannot but be taken into account in any final settlement; yet, in the final analysis, the problem of Cyprus must be solved by the Greek and Turkish Cypriots themselves, without outside interference (Polyviou, 1975: 97).

4. International Problem or Greek-Turkish problem?

The Greek Government and the wholly Greek Cypriot Government of the Republic of Cyprus insisted that the Association Council of 12 June 1995 should explicitly conclude that there was 'no junction' between the date fixed for beginning negotiations on Cypriot accession and the Customs Union with Turkey. In 1995 the Greek strategy was to further internationalise the Cyprus problem through the deeper involvement of the European Union. The 6 March compromise can be seen as the fifth act in the internationalisation saga, linked to the preceding acts by the invocation of resolutions of the United Nations. Neither Greek state wanted to deal directly with its Turkish counterpart, historically the alternative route to a settlement.

In the first phase of internationalisation, Greek sponsorship of the Greek Cypriot cause had been directed in the United Nations against the apparently superior power of the British, a permanent member of the Security Council. This campaign achieved a partial success in the General Assembly of the United Nations. The armed insurrection led by EOKA, with the support of the Greek State, eventually tied up 40,000 British troops in Cyprus; it also brought in Turkey and the Turkish Cypriot guerrillas, the TMT, as determined opponents of union with Greece. However, Cypriot independence was not won on the floor of the General Assembly. It was achieved by unexpected direct negotiations between the Greek and Turkish Foreign Ministers following the initial friendly overture by Mr Zorlu to Mr Averoff after a meeting in December 1958 of the General Assembly's Political Committee in New York (James, 1999: 13). The leader of the Greek Cypriot community, Archbishop Makarios, was credited with alterations of detail, including the limiting of the British sovereign base areas to less than three figures, ninety-nine square miles.

It was Archbishop Makarios who then gradually began the second phase of the internationalisation of the Cyprus problem. He asserted himself on the international stage by overcoming British resistance to full membership of the Commonwealth. He adopted a high profile in the Non-Aligned Movement which obviated the Gentleman's Agreement between Greece and Turkey to bring Cyprus into NATO. Both moves associated Makarios with the leaders of the UN General Assembly, alongside Nehru, Nasser and Tito. The Third World majority in the General Assembly emphasised the rights of democratic majority rule, unfettered sovereign independence and territorial integrity. In domestic terms, Makarios' linkage with Tito and Nasser brought him some support from the strong Greek Cypriot communist party. This domestic consensus among Greek Cypriots emboldened President Makarios to propose in 1963 thirteen amendments to what he claimed was the imposed and unworkable bi-communal Constitution of the Republic.

Greek Foreign Minister Averoff protested that these amendments would harm Greek relations with Turks whereas, with good relations, all matters could be arranged. The viability of this Greek-Turkish alternative to internationalisation is supported by a passage in Glafcos Clerides' Memoirs. He tells how the Turkish Ambassador advised Dr Küçük not to use his veto to prevent Cyprus joining the Non-Aligned Movement:

> The decision of the Council of Ministers that Cyprus should follow a Non-Aligned policy, which, of course, was in conformity with the views of President Makarios and out of line with those of the Vice-President, Dr Kutchuk, began to show symptoms of a looming political crisis, which was avoided by Turkey advising Dr Kutchuk not to exercise his veto on the decision of the Council of Ministers and not to proceed with his recourse to the Constitutional Court (Clerides, 1991, 1: 126).

However, in 1963, Averoff ceased to be Greek Foreign Minister. The new government, led by the populist George Papandreou, encouraged Makarios in his policy of confrontation.

In the crisis, Makarios was able to insist in 1964 that a UN peacekeeping force rather than a NATO force be despatched to separate the combatant communities. The UN Security Council Resolution 186 of 4 March 1964 refers four times to the 'Government of Cyprus'. The UN thus provided sufficient international recognition of the now wholly Greek Cypriot Government, despite the Council of Europe's contemporary refusal to accept the credentials of wholly Greek Cypriot delegations. The UN mediator, Galo Plaza, in 1965 supported the Cypriot Government in rejecting the plans to divide Cyprus between Greece and Turkey (double *enosis*) commended by American Secretary of State, Dean Acheson, to Galo Plaza's predecessor, Mr Tuomioja (Polyviou, 1976: 70). On 18 December 1965 the UN General Assembly in Resolution 2077 supported the UN mediation effort, noting the Cypriot Government's Declaration of Intent to fully apply human rights and support minority rights. The Assembly helped Makarios by calling upon all states to 'respect the sovereignty, unity, independence and territorial integrity of the Republic of Cyprus, and to refrain from any intervention directed against it'.

The alternative route to a solution through a Greek-Turkish understanding took on comic opera proportions during the American-backed Junta rule in Greece. On the one hand, the Junta precipitated the 1967 crisis, expecting Turkey to accept the loss of Cyprus in return for a base, the formula of a succession of NATO plans to meet the perceived political and military needs of both Allies. Prime Minister Demirel was told by Colonel George Papadopoulos that Turkey had enough land, 'Give us Cyprus and we will give you a base'. On the other hand, after the Greeks had been forced to withdraw their troops in 1967, the Junta's foreign minister, Panayiotis Pipinelis bluntly told the Cypriot Government that 'it was most unlikely that *enosis* would ever become possible without the agreement of Turkey or without important reciprocal Greek concessions'. Wrapping himself in the mantle of Venizelos' pragmatic attitude to Turkey, he insisted that 'the basis of Greek foreign policy had to be friendship with Turkey'. Cyprus could not be defended against the Turkish air force. Even a successful war against Turkey would not bring *enosis*, but only a disrupted Greek economy and over-extended supply lines. Prophetically his memo made it clear that

'America would do nothing...in case Turkey invaded Cyprus' (Polyviou, 1976: 89-90).

After 1974, the basis of Greek policy could not possibly be 'friendship with Turkey'. Occasional gestures like the talks between Constantine Karamanlis and Süleyman Demirel, or the Davos meeting between Turgut Özal and Andreas Papandreou in 1988, or the Quadripartite initiative of 1991/2 involving President Özal and Prime Minister Mitsotakis, could not begin to resolve the Cyprus problem.

Internationalisation of the Cyprus problem now became the major weapon of Greece and Greek Cyprus in attempting to assert their right to rule over of the richest third of an Hellenic island. No appeasement could be entertained until Turkey gave up its conquest in a 'just and lasting settlement'. In this third phase of internationalisation, Greek and Cypriot diplomacy strove to isolate Turkey as a 'non-European, semi-civilised country' (Polyviou, 1975: 96), and Turkish Cyprus as an illegal regime. With the aid of a sophisticated diaspora, their arguments received an immediately sympathetic response in international organisations and, after two decades, some considerable successes in international courts. The third prong of a sustained campaign for public opinion was also effectively organised. For example, tourists coming to the South were informed of the fate of the 160,000 refugees, of the harsh treatment which had reduced 20,000 enclaved Greek Cypriots to 600, of the 1,619 'missing' who had not received a Christian burial, of the careless treatment of historic sites, of the colonists from Turkey who had replaced the 80,000 Turkish Cypriots who could not accept foreign Turkish rule.

International Organisations

For ten years, the United Nations, the Council of Europe, the Commonwealth, the Non-Aligned Movement, and the institutions of the European Community passed resolutions demanding the withdrawal of 'foreign' troops, respect for the sovereignty of Cyprus, and rejecting the unilateral declarations of Turkish Cypriot statehood in 1975 and 1983 (see especially UNSC 541/83). The indictment of Turkey was not just a reflection of the justice of the Greek Cypriot case and the hostility of sovereign states to secessionist claims. It was aided by the restoration of democracy in Greece, by Mr Karamanlis' correct stance on the independence of the Republic of Cyprus, and by Greek membership of the European Union after 1980. The isolation of Turkey at the United Nations and in the Council of Europe after 1975 was reinforced by the instability of the Turkish Republic leading to direct military rule from 1980 to 1983. The even more isolated Turkish Cypriot leadership did not help their own claim to independent statehood by emphasising their Turkish allegiance in calling themselves 'Turkish Federated State' in 1975 and the 'Turkish Republic' in 1983. The international non-recognition of the secession of Northern Cyprus effectively limited sea and air links with the North.

After ten years, however, the Greek and Greek Cypriot Governments became increasingly disenchanted with the unwillingness of the international community to implement their resolutions and persuade Turkey to withdraw its troops. At the United Nations, Greek diplomats could no longer marshal support for strongly worded resolutions. The restoration of democracy in Turkey had been accompanied by a diplomatic drive to win international backing. Turkey became a leading member of the Organisation of Islamic Countries and gave aid to over ninety states. After 1984 Turkey actively sought membership of the European Community. In January 1990 Turkey accepted the right of individuals to petition the European Court of Human Rights. In the NATO context, Turkey was much more important to the United States than Greece.

In these circumstances, Greek Prime Minister Andreas Papandreou began the fourth phase of the international campaign, this time trying to use the European Community against Turkey. This was all the easier because at the time of Greek accession in 1980, the military coup in Turkey had pre-empted the Council's intention to balance Greek accession with a deepening of the Association Agreement with Turkey. At the Turkish Association Council of 5 February 1980 (*EC Bulletin* 2/1980 points 1.3.1-1.3.5) the Member States did promise Turkey that Greek accession would not affect EC relations with Turkey. However, at the time of accession Greece offered only verbal assurances that it would not veto a Turkish application (Redmond, 1993: 40). Greece was free in all other respects to isolate Turkey from Europe and to inflict damage in retaliation for its policies in Cyprus and the Aegean. Greece avoided signing the protocol binding it to the Association Agreement with Turkey until April 1988. Greece cited the Cyprus issue as its justification for repeatedly blocking EC financial aid to Turkey under the Fourth Financial Aid Protocol of 1981 (*Agence Europe*: 5759, June 1992). In 1986 Greece excluded itself 'on grounds of national security' from EC proposals permitting the free movement of Turkish workers who were already domiciled in the Community. In 1987 it voted in the Council against asking the Commission for an Opinion on the Turkish application for membership. Greece did not lift its veto on assistance to Turkey under the revised EU Mediterranean programme (MEDA) until the other Member States had confirmed their support for the UN resolutions on Cypriot sovereignty in a Declaration of June 1992 (*Agence Europe*: 5767). The Member States could therefore be in no doubt that, from the Greek perspective, the application from Cyprus in 1990 and the compromise of March 1995 were further steps in the mobilisation of a reluctant international community against Turkey. This European phase of the internationalisation of the Cyprus problem also brought the Greek Cypriots some belated success in international courts.

International law
The Cyprus problem might be a case study to show the inadequacy of the rule of law. Within any European state, the claim that one competing group had monopolised all government jobs in breach of the Constitution, or that another group had seized the lands of the first group by bringing in foreign troops to terrorise the rightful owners, could be tested in a Court. In 1974 the Greek Cypriots were frustrated by the lack of any international or European court of law competent to decide such large issues. The EC Court of Justice in Luxembourg was inward looking and trade oriented. The Human Rights Commission in Strasbourg could not receive individual complaints unless the states concerned, in this case Turkey, had agreed to allow such petitions, and was inclined to avoid questions affecting sovereignty in its referrals to the Committee of Ministers or to the part-time Court of Human Rights. The International Court of Justice at The Hague heard very few cases as it needed the prior agreement of all parties before it

could take on a case. If all the parties did assent, there would be a further problem of implementation if the verdict proved unacceptable to any party. Nevertheless, Greek Cypriot persistence, and the increasing confidence of European tribunals in their own jurisdiction, brought them some success in the two European Courts. Meanwhile, Greece also received the backing of other member states in appeals to Turkey to allow its disputes to be brought before the International Court of Justice at The Hague.

Queen v. the Minister of Agriculture, ex-parte Anastasiou

The Anastasiou firm appealed to the British High Court disputing the right of the British authorities to accept certification issued on behalf of Turkish Cypriots. The British Court asked for a preliminary ruling from the Court of Justice of the Communities on whether the British practice was permissible in European Law under the Association Agreement of 1972 and the most recent Council directive on certification, 77/93/EEC. On July 5 1994, the Court decided in favour of the Greek Government and S.P.Anastasiou, Ltd, the firm which brought the action, and against the British Government and the Commission. Closing this loophole in the embargo on Turkish Cypriot trade confirmed the Greek Cypriots in thinking that the EU was on their side, despite the position taken by the Commission. This success was welcome, even at the price of setting back any prospect of Turkish Cypriot agreement to a Cypriot federation.

Loizidou v. Turkey (Merits)

The Cypriot Government has been even more successful in the three judicial organs of the Council of Europe, an organisation wholly separate from the European Union and with a larger membership. Several separate cases were the subject of petitions to the Commission, including one from Archbishop Chrysostomos. Mrs Titina Loizidou's complaints against Turkey received the most attention. Her case was the subject of a Report in September 1993 by the Commission of Human Rights to the Ministerial Council of the Council of Europe. It was referred for adjudication by the Court of Human Rights sitting in Strasbourg. The Court's Judgement of 18 December 1996 denied the validity of the TRNC appropriation of her property in Kyrenia. It found that Turkey exercised overall control in Northern Cyprus and was therefore responsible for the actions of the TRNC after 1990, the date when Turkey recognised the jurisdiction of the Court. As the occupying power, Turkey was liable for the damages suffered by Mrs Loizidou, including psychological damage. The Court reserved its position on the question whether it should adjudicate under Article 50 of the Convention, which permits the Court to afford just satisfaction to an injured party where the internal procedures of the State in breach of its obligations have failed to produce adequate compensation. By taking the view that the Turkish Government was responsible for the harms suffered by Mrs Loizidou, and by extension to all other refugees, the Court put severe pressure on Turkey. Whether it was correct in law to attribute the blame for the continuing partition of Cyprus entirely to Turkey as one of the parties, and to attribute blame to Turkish troops in a situation where they had no direct involvement with Mrs Loizidou or her property in 1985 is a debatable matter. The Commission in its 8 July 1993 report on the admissibility of her claim had chosen not to rule on the status of the Turkish Republic of Northern Cyprus. Once again the pleasure of the Greek Cypriot camp was matched by Turkish Cypriot hostility to European interference that harmed the intercommunal political negotiations.

The International Court of Justice

The Luxembourg Conclusions of 1997 and, more pointedly, the Helsinki Conclusions of 1999, expressed the European Council's agreement with the Greek view that Turkey should submit its disputes to adjudication by the International Court of the Hague if they could not be resolved by diplomacy. It is possible that the two disputants will be able to agree on a panel of judges and terms of reference for the dispute over territorial jurisdiction in the Aegean. If such adjudication is successful in giving legal form to the diplomatic compromise implicit in defining the terms of the remit to the Court, then it is remotely possible that the Cyprus dispute could be the subject of legal adjudication rather than diplomatic negotiations.

Greek - Turkish diplomacy again

Even in democracies, the feelings of peoples about their neighbours are not the only guide to the national interest. After 1945 in Western Europe an elite-driven policy of reconciliation between warring neighbours overcame feelings of revenge and punishment of the 1918 ilk. In Eastern Europe, where anti-German feeling was given its head, the communist parties repressed the expression of national grievances felt by Hungarians and Romanians, or the communal grievances of Serbs, Croats and Muslims. Greece has a choice between the policy of excluding Turkey from Europe and the policy of treating Turkey as a potential fellow member of the European Union.

In 1995, the four retired Greek ambassadors mentioned above (p.148) put the case for coexistence, invoking Venizelos. They questioned the policy of internationalisation from two directions. They questioned the 'political dependence on European Community solidarity'. They questioned the Greek national interest in the integrity of Cyprus. Instead of treating Turkey as an enemy outside the pale, they suggested resolving or putting aside some disputes to concentrate on more critical issues. As Cyprus was then the focus of Greek diplomacy, this implied that the Balkans and the Aegean were more important national concerns of Greece. The ambassadors thought that Greece could live with either a Cyprus of two states or the incorporation of Greek Cyprus into Greece and the incorporation of Turkish Cyprus into Turkey (Zambouras in Dodd 1995: 118). The resulting border between Greece and Turkey in Cyprus would be different from other Graeco-Turkish borders only in that it ran through an island and would be indefensible in the event of war.

The ambassadors' contribution was periodically dismissed by Greek ministers on visits to Cyprus, one claiming in April 1998 that the EU wanted a united Cyprus as its 'castle in the Eastern Mediterranean'. However, there were strong pressures from outside as well as from inside Greece for a policy going beyond co-existence to co-operation between the two Mediterranean neighbours. After the near-war over Imia/Kardak, Prime Minister Simitis on a visit to Larnaca committed Greece to the 'peaceful method' in resolving the Cyprus problem. In July 1997, the United States brokered the Madrid accord in which Prime Minister Simitis and President Demirel acknowledged that both had legitimate vital interests in the Aegean. As NATO approached its fiftieth anniversary, the Americans were anxious that enlargement to the East should not be undermined by discord in the South. As we have seen, the European Union promoted the Customs Union in 1995 and the prospect of candidature in 1999 because it wanted to improve relations with Europe's second largest state.

The Helsinki Conclusions of December 1999 were particularly significant because Greece accepted Turkish candidature without, as in 1995, requiring other member states to pay a price for Greek acquiescence. The Greek Government's humanitarian assistance after the Istanbul earthquake had not only been reciprocated by the Turkish Government after the Athens earthquake; both governments had gone out of their way to change populist perceptions about the inimical nature of the other. The Canadian-educated Foreign Minister of Greece, George Papandreou, and the Turkish Foreign Minister, İsmail Cem, acted as if it would be in the interests of both Greece and Turkey if the nationalist and fundamentalist wings of Turkish politics were subordinated to a pro-European stable government which could reassure the army while carrying through reforms to protect the human rights of all Turkish citizens. Businessmen in Greece publicised their willingness to expand their existing co-operation and to invest in the expanding and privatising Turkish economy. Although both foreign ministers reiterated their incompatible positions on the status of the TRNC, and hinted that the Aegean issue was both separate and riper for discussion, the Greek shift from rhetorically battering Turkey to diplomacy with Turkey had implications for the Cyprus problem. After Foreign Minister Cem had returned from discussions with his Greek counterpart in New York in September 1999, there was a meeting in Ankara of the Turkish and Turkish Cypriot officials with responsibilities for Cyprus. It is time to look at the problem from their perspective.

| 5 |

Turkish Cypriot and Turkish Reactions

I am told, very plainly, by the representatives of countries that count, 'If you continue to object to the entry of the island into the EU because Turkey is not yet a member, you will be isolated in the world' (Rauf Denktaş in Doğramacı, ed., 1997: 20).

1. Introduction

Isolation in the world has been the condition of the Turkish Cypriots since 1963. Mr Denktaş can take as much pride in being a beleaguered outpost of the Turkish nation as can Mr Clerides in invoking Thermopylae. While he may lack the international recognition accorded to Mr Clerides, his personal standing in Turkish politics has brought Turkish Cypriots more powerful support from nearby Turkey than Mr Clerides has been able to command from distant Greece. Turkey supplied arms to the anti-EOKA 'Turkish Resistance Organisation'. On behalf of the Turkish Cypriots, Turkish diplomats negotiated the favourable terms of the 1960 Constitution. Turkish material assistance enabled the Turkish Cypriots to resist Greek Cypriot pressure for *enosis*, and to establish a separate territorial zone in the North in defiance of UN Resolutions.

Any settlement of the Cyprus problem has to take into account both Turkish Cypriot self-determination and Turkey's longstanding commitment to their cause. The TRNC has a democratically elected parliament which chooses the Prime Minister, an independent judiciary and an electedpresident. However, every week the electedPresident also meets with three Turkish citizens, the Turkish ambassador, the Turkish Commander of some 30,000 Turkish troops, and the Turkish Commander of some 4,000 Turkish Cypriot troops. He can do little in Northern Cyprus without the support of the democratically elected representatives and of Turkey. This duality in the foundations of government has proved workable for two reasons. Turkish Cypriots have repeatedly re-elected Mr Denktaş as a president prepared to work closely with Turkey. Ankara has generally resisted international pressure to bring Turkish Cypriots to accept a settlement that would restore Greek Cypriot influence in the North.

The first two sections of this chapter therefore describe Turkish Cypriot self-government and its relationship to the Turkish motherland. The first section concentrates on what is constant in the successive claims of the Turkish Cypriots to be a community equal in status to the Greek Cypriot majority, a separate people and yet part of the Turkish nation. It sets out the successive expressions of this self-determination in the Turkish Cypriot communal chamber, in the territorial enclaves, in the establishment of what was intended to be a canton in a federal state, in the proclamation of an independent sovereign state, in proposals for a confederation and in the threat to turn *de facto* integration into *de jure* integration. The focus of the second section is on Turkey, where popular identification with the Turkish Cypriots, and the state's security concerns with Greece, have undermined Atatürk's doctrine that the Republic should take no responsibility for Turks or Moslems outside its borders. Both the Turkish Cypriot cause and the response of Turkey have been influenced by four decades of change in the international milieu. For example, the 'countries that count' took action to counter the oppression of Moslems in Bosnia and Kosovo. Since 1989 nearly a dozen unrecognised communities claiming statehood have come into existence (Bartmann: 1989: 39). Self-determination in United Nations parlance is no longer restricted to decolonisation from European empires. The enlargement of the European Union has generally reduced the saliency of sovereignty as an issue.

The question of Cypriot membership of the European Union means that the third section, on a possible settlement, is also inextricably linked with the final section, on Turkish Cypriot hostility to the European Union. Turkish Cypriots hold differing views on whether the end of their isolation requires some modification of the status quo by agreement with the Greek Cypriot majority on the island who have orchestrated that isolation. Any settlement would now have to take into account that the Greek Cypriot side has made substantial progress towards accession. Turkish Cypriot views on the existence of a pan-Cypriot identity, the meaning of security, the extent of their territorial zone, and the resolution of property claims are bound up with their views on the form of any joint rule with Greek Cypriots. Turkish Cypriot legal and political objections would doubtless be reduced if the Turkish Government manages to sustain its own accession process in the face of nationalist and fundamentalist alternatives. The timing of Turkey's possible accession process has become crucial. If Turkish membership can be negotiated within a decade on the Spanish model of a long subsequent transition period, then the Turkish Cypriot leadership would have seriously to weigh up the economic costs and benefits of membership against those of remaining outside, like Switzerland. Accession for the Turkish Cypriots would require answers to questions about participation in institutions and policies that would very much depend on timetabling. The answers would be different in the three possible scenarios of entry in the first wave by participation in the present process, of later entry after a harmonisation process between the two sides in Cyprus, or of the entry of Northern Cyprus simultaneously with Turkey, either as a separate state or as an integrated province of Turkey.

2. Turkish Cypriot self-determination

The two constants over four decades of Turkish Cypriot aspirations to self-rule have been a demand for equality of status with the Greek Cypriot majority, and the presence of Turkish troops on Cyprus to guarantee that status. A short history may help to demonstrate the flexibility of the Turkish Cypriot leadership with respect to the constitutional forms in which self-determination may be realised. In the words of Ergün Olgun, the Under-Secretary to the TRNC President, 'The TRNC is not an end in itself for the Turkish Cypriots' (Olgun, 2000: 33).

Population

There are very few Turkish Cypriots. In 1960 there were 103,822 Turkish Cypriots constituting 18.13 per cent of the population (ROC 1997: 8).

The figures for today's population are disputed. The European Commission Report of November 1998 cites a figure of 89,000. This figure agrees with the 89,200 reported by the Republic of Cyprus to the Council of Europe for the end of 1996 (ROC, 1999: 5). The first full census of the population in the Turkish Republic of Northern Cyprus was undertaken on 15 December 1996. It reported that the total population was 200,587. Of these 164,460 (81.99 per cent) were nationals of the TRNC, 137,398 having been born on the island. Nationals of the Turkish Republic numbered 31,977 (15.94 per cent) of whom 8,287 were students, 12,922 migrant workers who have not needed a visa since 1991, and 1,327 unemployed. Turkish troops were not included in the census. In the same year the UN Secretary-General reported that there were 343 Turkish Cypriots in the South (UNSC, 1996: 5); Turkish Cypriots in the South are not registered to vote in the South but are entitled to registration on the Turkish Cypriot communal list. The number of adult citizens can be gauged from the figure of 126,674 entitled to vote at the presidential election of 15 April 2000.

The discrepancy between the ROC and TRNC figures is mainly due to the Greek Cypriot Government's refusal to include in its estimates the 'blackbeards' from the Black Sea and Anatolia who have settled on the island since 1974. The ROC does not include children born on the island if their parents came from Turkey. The discrepancy is also partly due to the doctrine that Turkish Cypriots are, according to the TRNC Constitution, part of the Turkish nation. On this criterion, the 1996 census counted the Turks in Northern Cyprus as 197,264 (98.34 per cent), taking Turkish Cypriot and Turkish citizens together.

In addition to the census of inhabitants, the number of Turkish Cypriots might also be taken to include emigrants, many of whom retain ties to Cyprus. Between 1955 and 1974 17,106 Turkish Cypriots emigrated (Olgun, 1993: 271). Since 1974, 47,000 have emigrated from the North (1997 ROC Overview: 9). Some 90 per cent of the 400,000 tourists who visit Northern Cyprus each year are from Turkey. Also the student population is expanding rapidly towards a target of 40,000; in

1998 Turkish students numbered about 12,000 out of a total student population of 17,000.

The total population of the North is thus demonstrably greater than the figure given by the ROC Government and used by the European Commission. Instead of concluding that the proportion of Turkish Cypriots has fallen to just over a tenth (12.3 per cent) of the total population, a more realistic view would be that about a quarter of the population of Cyprus lives in the North.

A community

Whether their number is 100,000 or 200,000, the Turkish Cypriots insist that they are not a minority in the sense applicable to Maronites, Armenians, Latins, Romanies or foreigners. Fearful of subordination to the dominant Greek Cypriot community, they demanded equality of status within the new Republic, rather as Flemings in Belgium and Nationalists in Ulster have demanded equality of status as a condition of participation in the polity. In retrospect, Mr Denktaş' comparison of Cyprus with Yugoslavia makes the case that in some countries allowing majorities to have their way must lead to the dissolution of the stateOn 16 June 1978 he prophetically told the UN Security Council:

> If minorities and majorities are going to play an important part in the future of Cyprus, then Yugoslavia must break up into minority-majority groups and must cease to be a federal system composed of equal members irrespective of numerical composition (Moran, 1997: 158).

In the same speech he told the Council that their recognition of the wholly Greek Cypriot Government in 1964 had been interpreted as giving them authority to 'cleanse Cyprus of the Turkish Cypriots' (Moran, 1997: 152).

Turkish Cypriots can claim to be different from both Greek Cypriots and Anatolian Turks. For over 400 years there has been a Muslim community in Cyprus. Sorbonne Professor Dr Mehlike Kaşgarlı has found evidence of their presence before the Ottoman conquest of 1571, an event that itself pre-dates the landing of the Pilgrims in Massachusetts. In that some of the locals adopted Muslim ways during the centuries of Ottoman rule, there is no necessary racial difference between the Greek and Turkish communities. Moreover, during British rule, the legal system of both communities became differentiated from that of their respective motherlands through the influence of English common law. Nevertheless, the two communities maintained distinct systems of civil law for marriage and property. They financed and to a considerable extent controlled their own schools. The Treaty of Lausanne gave Cypriots the right until 1927 to claim Turkish citizenship; most of the 5000 Turkish Cypriots who left are said to have returned shortly to the island. Although the reception of Turkish nationalist ideas was slower among Muslims than the reception of Greek nationalist ideas among Greek Cypriots, after 1929 Islamic judges could no longer resist the appointment of secular judges on the Turkish model.

The bi-communal Constitution of 1960 emphasised the differences between the two main communities. Turkish had equal status with Greek and English as an official language. The flag of the Turkish Republic could be flown from public buildings. Turkish Cypriots had their own judges. They had separate electoral voting lists to elect a communal assembly, a third of the members of the House of Representatives, and a Vice-President with powers to veto some acts of the Executive and Legislature. Turkish Cypriots were entitled to a third of representatives in the Assembly, a third of the Judiciary, a third of all Government jobs and 40 per cent of army posts. Unfortunately, within three years what was then the novel principle of bi-communality had been fatally undermined. The embedding of the Constitution in three international treaties had not succeeded in persuading the UN that the bi-communality of Cyprus was part of the public law of Europe, deserving as much respect as the neutrality of Switzerland.

Enclaves

Between 1964 and 1974 about 60 percent of the Turkish Cypriots ruled themselves in their 39 enclaves. According to C.P. Ioannides, (1991: 131) 'While the Turkish Cypriots in the areas of mixed population were technically under the authority of the Cypriot Government, their political allegiance was to the leadership in the Turkish sector of Nicosia, whose orders they obeyed'. Their elected representatives from the Communal Assembly and the House of Representatives constituted the Turkish Cypriot Legislative Assembly. The Vice-President, and the three former

Turkish ministers of the 1963 Cabinet, formed the executive 'General Committee'. The Turkish Cypriot inhabitants of 103 villages left them for the greater safety of the Turkish quarters of the towns. These enclaves were protected by UNFICYP troops, encircled in their turn by Greek Cypriot military or paramilitary units. The Turkish Cypriot economy was virtually separate from that of the remaining 96 per cent of Cyprus. After 1967 they established a 'Provisional Turkish Cypriot Administration' to negotiate after 1968 a return to communal rule in an independent unitary state (Polyviou, 1976: 82). The qualification of 'provisional' was dropped in 1971 after a legislative assembly had been elected the previous year. Turkish Cypriot authors note that the three Guarantor Powers in July 1974 jointly referred to the existence in practice of 'two autonomous administrations, that of the Greek Community and that of the Turkish Cypriot Community' (Dodd, 1999: 10). At the Geneva Conference, before the second stage of Turkish military intervention, the Turkish Foreign Minister, Mr Güneş, suggested that the enclaves become the basis of separate territorial rule in one large canton in the North and five other smaller cantons, amounting to 34 per cent of the island (Polyviou, 1976: 351).

Federation

After 1 October 1974 an 'Autonomous Turkish Cypriot Administration' ruled the northern third of Cyprus. In February 1975 it was renamed the 'Turkish Federated State of Northern Cyprus', legitimised on 8 June by a referendum in the North. The name implied a communal and territorial identity as a canton but also a willingness to unite on the new bizonal basis in a federation with the South. On 16 June 1978, President Denktaş told the UN Security Council that 'we have not asked to be recognised as a separate State' (Moran, 1997: 157). The High-Level negotiations with the Greek Cypriot side after 1977 were based on the premise of a reduction of the territory controlled by the North in return for recognition of their right to rule their zone in a state constituted on the federal principle of equality of status for the constituent parts. The Turkish Cypriot side emphasised the powers of the regional governments, wanting a weak federal government. In support Mr Denktaş cited Article 3 of the Swiss Constitution, 'The federated states are sovereign in so far as their sovereignty is not limited by the sovereignty of the federal state'. The idea of federation was pursued in negotiations under the aegis of the UN even after the TRNC declaration of its own sovereignty. While consolidating their exclusive rule in the North, the dominant Nationalist Right supported Mr Denktaş in asserting that the self-ruling Turkish Cypriots were now more than a community. Mr Denktaş habitually refers to Turkish Cypriots as 'my people', a part of the great Turkish nation, views provocative to the pan-Cypriot opposition parties of the Left. He does not make any distinction between a 'people', as ethnically united through common ancestors, and a 'nation', culturally united by sharing a common history. In an 'Explanatory Note to the UN Secretary General' of 13 April 1978, he asserted that, 'There is not, and never has been, a Cypriot nation.' As evidence, he cited Archbishop Makarios, 'The Agreements have created a state but not a nation' (*Cyprus Mail*, 28 March 1963). On 17 June 1983 the Turkish Cypriot Assembly prepared the way for claiming sovereignty by resolving that the Turkish Cypriot 'people', in exercising the right of self-determination, was one of two equal peoples in Cyprus (Dodd, 1993: 126).

Sovereign statehood
On 15 November 1983 the Turkish Cypriot Assembly approved unanimously a Declaration of Independence and the proclamation of the Turkish Republic of Northern Cyprus. The TRNC has its own flag. Where the ROC flag displays only the geographical outline of the island, the TRNC flag asserts its kinship with, and difference from, Turkey. Where the Turkish flag displays a white crescent and star on a red background, the TRNC has a red Turkish crescent and star on a white background within two protective red horizontal bands. The choice of the awkward name of 'the Turkish Republic of Northern Cyprus' seems to have been intended as reassurance to both their Greek Cypriot neighbours and Turkey. Where the simpler formulation of the 'Republic of Kıbrıs' might imply a claim to the whole island, the limitation to Northern Cyprus renounced such an aim without going as far as to recognise the legitimacy of Greek Cypriot rule in the South. The qualification of republic by 'Turkish' may have been intended to reassure the unenthusiastic new civilian regime in Ankara of the continued loyalty of the new state. It is similar to the use of 'Hellenic'

for the Republic of Greece. However, this assertion of the Turkish character of the new state, coupled with internal criticisms that writing a new Constitution got around the limitations on the re-election of President Denktaş to a third term, did not help the TRNC to be recognised internationally as independent of Turkey. On 5 May 1985 the Constitution was approved by 70.18 per cent of those voting in a referendum. In asserting their right to self-determination as a sovereign micro-republic, Turkish Cypriot nationalists have a strong moral case, perhaps stronger than the legal arguments on which they prefer to rely.

Morally, their case is most analogous to the creation of Bangladesh. The Bengalis, a separate community oppressed by the Pakistani majority, were willing to risk their lives to create a new state with the help of the Indian army. Bangladesh would have recognised the TRNC if the USA had not intervened to prevent them. The Bangladesh case, however, is different from that of Northern Cyprus in two respects. Pakistan quickly accepted the loss of East Bengal, and the Indian army did not provide the Bengalis with new lands. The Bangladeshis, therefore, unlike the Turkish Cypriots, did not find themselves up against the Stimson doctrine inhibiting international recognition of territory acquired by force. Since 1974 Turkish Cypriots have emphasised that the Turkish Peace Operation achieved peace, by which they mean that individuals are not in constant fear of sectarian attack. This argument that peace is a good cannot be dismissed as propaganda, comparable to Hitler's aim of establishing European peace. However, the moral strength of the Turkish Cypriot case is weakened by their own treatment of Greeks in the North as potential traitors. Greek Cypriots could not travel freely in the North, nor bequeath property to anyone resident in the South. If Greek Cypriots lost legitimacy by oppressing Turkish Cypriots, Turkish Cypriots also became oppressors in meting out the same treatment to Greek Cypriots. Point 11 of the TRNC Declaration of Independence bases itself on non-discrimination as being a good in itself:

> 11. The Greek Cypriot leadership, who wishes (sic) to subjugate the Turkish Cypriots to alien domination, has in fact displayed one of the most flagrant examples of discrimination based on race, national origin, language and religion.

Just as international recognition of the wholly Greek Cypriot government in 1963 implied that the denial to Muslims of their constitutional rights was then acceptable as an internal affair of Cyprus, so recognition of the separate statehood of the present TRNC implies acceptance that Turkish Cypriot ethnic discrimination was legitimate. To put the same point another way, it would be easier for a multicultural Europe to recognise a state that comprised both communities, with institutional means for protecting Cypriot freedom to travel and trade in both zones.

Legally, the Turkish Cypriots argue that no wholly Greek Cypriot Government has the right to make laws applicable to Turkish Cypriots or to represent them in international fora. In a speech to the United Nations Security Council on 28 February 1964, 1997: 139) Mr Denktaş said that 'no Constitution is in effect'. However, a year later in the same forum, on 5 August 1965, he claimed that the 'harassed but unbeaten Turkish (sic) community...is clinging to the Constitution'. Turkish Cypriot judges attended the courts until 2 June 1966 (Necatigil, 1996: 62-3). Some inconsistency of position is inevitable in denying recognition to an adversary with whom one is also from time to time negotiating. In general, Turkish Cypriot lawyers maintain retrospectively that the Constitution has been defunct since December 1963. All three Guarantor Powers, in their joint Declaration of 30 July 1974, recognised the illegitimacy of Nicos Sampson's coup and implicitly of all Cypriot Governments since 1963. The British, Greek and Turkish governments called for 'an immediate return to constitutional legitimacy, the Vice-President assuming the functions provided for under the 1960 Constitution'. The Turkish Cypriots therefore claim the right to give themselves a new Constitution without incurring the charge of secession from the Republic of Cyprus.

The 1960 treaties, however, remain valid. Both Turkish states invoke the general rule of international law that all signatories are obliged unless all have agreed to changes, and overlook the rule that parties cannot rely on treaties that they have themselves broken. The Treaty of Guarantee is of particular sensitivity. Turkey's Guarantor status justifies its military intervention in 1974, if not its subsequent partition of the island. Guarantor status is also the foundation of Turkey's claimed right to maintain military forces in the North well in excess of the 650 troops permitted by the Constitution. Understandably, most Turkish Cypriots are at one with their Government in wishing to maintain a Turkish military presence, which they see as the only reliable protection against the Greek Cypriot majority on the island. In the North, the Turkish army is not regarded as an alien army of occupation akin to the Russian 'liberators' of East Germany or the European Protectorates of colonial times.

Recognition is not crucial to sovereignty. The People's Republic of China ruled its vast territory with no interference from Taiwan, the seat of the internationally recognised exile Government. Mr Denktaş takes the view that the recognition accorded by Turkey is enough. The TRNC fulfils three of the four criteria postulated by the 1933 Montevideo Convention on the Rights and Duties of States:

- It has a permanent population. The Turkish Cypriots call the 1975 agreement in Vienna to facilitate movement across the Green Line an 'Exchange of Populations Agreement' to make their point that separate populations imply the existence of two states in Cyprus.
- The TRNC has a defined territory in that the cease-fire line has to be respected by the authorities on both sides.
- It has an effective government.
- The fourth criterion is capacity to enter into relations with other states. Mümtaz Soysal (1999: 63) argues that the existence of TRNC missions in London and Washington shows that the TRNC has this capacity. The capacity is difficult to exercise only because other states do not recognise realities. Since 1997 Turkish Cypriots have been included in Turkish diplomatic delegations where Cyprus is on the agenda.

Moreover, in so far as it is the case that democratic credentials have become by usage an additional fifth criterion of assessing claims to statehood, the TRNC has held regular and fair elections to the Presidency and the Assembly, and referenda of the whole people.

On the other hand, Turkish recognition of the sovereignty of the TRNC has one unusual feature. President Denktaş on his frequent visits to

Turkey is not usually treated with the protocol accorded to a visiting head of state.

Integration with Turkey

On 28 April 1998, Prime Minister Ecevit visited Cyprus. As usual, he took pride in saying that 'in 1974 peace, prosperity, democracy, and freedom came to Cyprus after the Operation'. He then spoke of Turkey and the TRNC as being already 'integrated economically and politically', immediately qualifying this strong claim by describing them as still separate entities. 'The TRNC is the guarantee of Turkey. It is out of the question that these two countries will be separated from each other.' President Denktaş replied that he was 'proud to be Anatolian'.

The threat to integrate part of Cyprus into Turkey had been used before 1960 to deter Greek ambitions to incorporate Cyprus. After 1964 *double enosis* was invoked to counter Greek Cypriot pressure on the enclaves. However, the renewal of this threat after 1990 meant a further deepening of the unnecessary divide between Turkey and the European Union. To the Turkish Cypriots it was a necessary retaliation for the pressure exerted against them by the EU at the instance of the Greeks and Greek Cypriots. For example, after the considerable tightening of economic sanctions by the European Court of Justice in its 'Anastasiou' judgement of 1994, the TRNC Assembly revoked previous resolutions favouring federation and pronounced the need for economic integration with Turkey (Dodd, 1998: 68). Mr Denktaş proposed that the North become an 'autonomous region' of Turkey. This did him no harm in the 1995 election where he received 62 per cent of the votes.

On 20 July 1997, the two Turkish governments reacted to the European Union's decision to open formal negotiations under *Agenda 2000* with the Greek Cypriot Government. They outlined a programme of retaliatory and proportional integration of the TRNC into Turkey. They said it was:

> necessary to implement, step by step, and in parallel to the full membership process between the Greek Cypriot administration of South Cyprus and the EU, the following measures towards economic and financial integration, as well as partial integration via partnership in security, defence and foreign policy:

- Until the TRNC is officially recognised by the international community... a special relationship will be established in the sphere of foreign policy...
- An Association Council will be created between the two states with the participation of the two Parliaments and the relevant ministries...
- The TRNC will be included in Turkey's priority, regional development macro-economic master plans...
- Water requirements of the TRNC will be met...
- Every structural co-operation and harmonisation measure to be initiated between the Greek Cypriot administration of Southern Cyprus and the EU will be similarly implemented between the TRNC and Turkey.'

In consequence a variety of economic agreements have been signed in the framework of annual meetings of a Partnership Council. In addition to meeting the costs of its army in Cyprus, Turkey pays for special projects like the provision of water through balloons. Nearly half the regular income of the TRNC budget comes in subsidies and loans from Turkey. In 1998, of the total budget of 93,600m Turkish lira, 41,800m Tl came from Turkey. A Turkish official in every spending ministry supervises the use to which the Turkish contribution is put. To avoid the charge that this amounted to political integration and a change of borders that could not be justified as retaliation for Greek Cypriot membership of the EU, Foreign Minister Cem had to state on 10 November 1997 that 'Turkey's initiatives and support for the TRNC were primarily in the economic field'. This degree of dependency makes it difficult to inhibit corruption and clientilism. In 1995, and again in 2000, the Turkish Government itself put the TRNC under heavy pressure to impose austerity by withholding the open-ended subsidies that make the TRNC richer than it would be if it became fully integrated with Turkey.

Confederation

Although this term has fallen into disuse, the idea of a 'Union of States' by treaty jointly deciding foreign policy and possibly defence, or jointly regulating aspects of domestic policy, like agriculture and commercial competition, is a respectable way of understanding the European Union. A paper from the Centre for European Policy Studies (CEPS) in Brussels acknowledged the potential of confederation in Cyprus as 'an initial step towards a settlement' and a way of including the Turkish Cypriots as 'a political equal in accession negotiations and ultimately within the Union' (Tocci, 2000: 24,30). This route to finding a workable structure for joint rule of the two zones of Cyprus was proposed by President Denktaş on 31 August 1998. It was this speech that provoked President Clerides to invoke his analogy with Thermopylae.

The proposal consists of five points. The first point suggests a special arrangement between the TRNC and Turkey. The second point allows for similar arrangements on the Greek side. The 'establishment of a Cyprus Confederation between the TRNC and the GCA' to be negotiated between the two states appears as the third point. Besides the dismissive reference to 'the Greek Cypriot Administration', participation in these negotiations would mean, from the beginning and irrespective of a successful conclusion, recognition that 'Greek and Turkish sides are two sovereign and equal states'. The fourth point suggests that the '1960 Guarantee system' will continue. The final point allows for the possibility, if the parties jointly agree, of pursuing a policy of accession to the European Union. This possibility is then qualified by a demand for Turkish participation in EU matters relating to Cyprus which demonstrates conclusively how little thought has been given to the European Union in the Office of the TRNC President:

> Until Turkey's full membership to the EU, a special arrangement will provide Turkey with the full rights and obligations of an EU member with regard to the Cyprus Confederation.

One can only imagine that the intention is to give Turkey the right to monitor and veto changes in Cypriot laws in the same way that, as a Guarantor Power, it was entitled in international law to intervene unilaterally to protect the state of affairs established by the Constitution. In EU terms it makes no sense. The full rights include membership of all the institutions. Is Turkey to elect every five years some ninety members of the European Parliament to vote only on resolutions affecting Cyprus? Is it to appoint a judge to participate only in cases involving Cyprus, and to be paid per diem? Is Turkey to appoint a member of the European Investment bank for the sole purpose of considering loans to Cyprus? It might be possible for member states in the Council to agree informally that Turkey be invited to attend without a vote on agenda items specifically concerning Cyprus, but the TRNC proposal is not limited to this achievable end.

The full obligations include the obligation to transfer all customs revenues less a charge for collection, payment of VAT at a rate up to 1.78 per cent, and a further payment proportional to national GNP. How this is to be determined for matters relating to that proportion of the budget relating to expenditure and commitments to Cyprus is not explained. The only possible conclusion is that the Presidency of the TRNC was so hostile to the European Union that it did not need to find out more while Turkish membership remained only a remote possibility.

2. Turkey as Motherland

Turkey will continue to be politically and legally opposed to EU membership for Cyprus, in whole or in part, before her own accession to the EU as a full member like the other Guarantor Powers. Turkey disagrees with the decision taken by the Council on the membership negotiations of Cyprus. The Council's decision on the membership of Cyprus is an unfortunate step, which could lead to the permanent division of the island. The opening of accession negotiations, before a negotiated settlement is reached, will lead to the conduct of talks exclusively with the Greek Cypriot side. In such an undesirable eventuality, Turkey will be left with no option but to take steps towards achieving a similar integration with the Turkish Republic of Northern Cyprus... Turkey's support to the negotiating process, henceforth, will to a large extent depend on the willingness of the Greek Cypriot side for a solution and on the degree of support which Greece will display (Murat Karayalçın, 6 March 1995).

The first sentence of this blunt but carefully worded statement fully supports Turkish Cypriot objections to the accession requested by Greek Cyprus, and reiterates Turkey's right to membership. In deciding that it was in Turkey's national interest to complete the Customs Union with the EU, Mrs Çiller's Government had to respond to two serious charges that it was betraying that national interest. The first was that Turkey was accepting the Customs Union as an alternative to the full membership to which Turkey, as a pluralist democracy with a capitalist economy, was more entitled than the Eastern European countries. The second charge was that Turkey was betraying the cause of its kith and kin in Turkish Cyprus and endangering Turkish security interests by allowing the Republic of Cyprus to strengthen its international position through membership.

In the autumn of 1995 the Turkish Grand National Assembly held a secret session on the Cyprus issue, a most unusual event. In October 1995 President Demirel categorised Cyprus as 'a national issue' (Dodd, 1998: 67). On 28 December 1995 the two Turkish states jointly declared that 'the full and effective guarantee of Turkey will continue under the Treaty of Guarantee and Alliance of 1960 following a final political settlement'. On visiting Cyprus shortly after becoming Prime Minister, the fundamentalist leader, Mr Erbakan repeated the assurance that Cyprus was a 'national issue'. He would not accept any change 'posing a threat to the interests of our brethren in Cyprus'. On 20 January 1997 the two Presidents reacted to the announcement that Russian missiles would be bought by the Republic of Cyprus by declaring that any attack on the TRNC would be an attack on Turkey. A joint military concept between Turkey and the TRNC would be established (Dodd, 1998: 186). On 27 January 1997, after an address by His Excellency Mr Denktaş, the Turkish National Assembly Resolution concluded:

> The world must know the fact that the Turkish Grand National Assembly and the Turkish nation are in a full unity on this national cause (Dodd, 1998: 189).

Kith and Kin

The Turkish Republic's identification with Turkish Cyprus as a 'national cause' has to be explained. Concern for the Turks actually expelled from Bulgaria in 1987, or for the Moslems of Bosnia and Kosovo, has not led to the assumption by Turkey of a duty of permanent military intervention. Atatürk's slogan of 'Peace abroad' meant that Turkey was no threat to its neighbours because it had no responsibility for Turks or Moslems outside its borders unless they were already citizens. 'Peace at home' meant the French concept of citizenship as civic and secular, not ethnic or religious. Those who invoke Atatürk in support of Turkish identification with Cyprus have to make do with a remark to army officers that they must remember Cyprus, whose turn will come.

Yet Turkish popular sympathy for kith and kin in Cyprus appears to be more widespread than Greek sympathy for Greek Cypriots. Mr Denktaş' status as a national hero dates back to his four years of exile in Turkey after speaking to the United Nations in 1964. So far from being a puppet of Ankara, he used his personal influence in the Turkish National Assembly to resist President Özal's support for the 'Set of Ideas' in 1992 and to attack Mrs Çiller's compromise in 1995. The obvious reason for the public's identification with Turkish Cyprus is that in Cyprus the enemy are Greeks—the anti-Greek riots in Istanbul and Izmir in 1955 were ignited by events in Cyprus. It may be that ethnic hostilities are basic to the creation of nation states. Atatürk's civic ideology only partly restrained Turks keen to take over Greek and Armenian property as rightfully belonging to Turks in the new republic. On this view, the state's willingness to adopt an ethnic identification as the basis of policy in Cyprus might be the precursor of a return to Turanian identification with the Turks of Central Asia. Internally, this shift of ideology would imply a cultural tolerance of Kurds and fundamentalists, no longer forced to adopt the national language and style of dress that Atatürk thought appropriate to the equal citizens of a secular republic.

Civic ideology was certainly perverted to justify in modernist democratic terms the extension of Turkey's borders to incorporate the Syrian province of Hatay in 1939, a precedent of some relevance to Cyprus. In 1937 the French allowed the Turkish community in their Syrian province of Hatay the right to use Turkish as their official language, proclaiming that Hatay was in future to be autonomous within Syria. In July 1938 the French allowed Turkey to share the policing of Hatay as joint guarantors of its autonomy. As a Guarantor, Turkey built on a Turkish community constituting 40 per cent of the population to produce a rigged majority supporting the proclamation of Hatay as an independent republic. Hatay proclaimed its union with Turkey in June 1939 (Hitchens, 1997: 153). Although presented in terms of self-determination, the state's security interest in controlling the port of

İskenderun was probably the major motivation during this period before the Second World War.

Security interests

According to Mr Ecevit, it is Turkey that owes Northern Cyprus a debt for contributing to the security of the Turkish mainland. To President Özal's complaint that Cyprus was costing Turkey $200m per annum, Mr Ecevit replied that the gains were cheap at the price. Fighting to establish control of Cyprus might well have broken out if the bellicose crises between Greece and Turkey in 1996, 1987, 1974, 1967 and 1964 had led to war. The Turkish Government had long expressed its preference for partitioning the island to preclude full Greek control, a preference it renounced in 1959 in return for the Greeks abandoning *Enosis*. Ten years before the Peace Operation, in May 1964, Turkey proposed to NATO a Northern zone extending over 36.2 per cent of the island, which it said would preserve the 'equilibrium of territorial interests in the Eastern Mediterranean'. Turkey put the same plan to the UN Mediator in 1965. Since 1974, Greece has been unable to build offensive military and naval bases in Northern Cyprus. After its 1974 experience of impotence in Cyprus, Greece breached its treaty commitments to keep the Eastern Aegean islands demilitarised; it is a military axiom that islands are easier to defend than other territories provided that defences are built in advance of war. The Turkish occupation of Northern Cyprus is said to be essential to the protection of the oil route to the projected Turkish terminal at Ceyhan, through which Caspian oil will flow to Western Europe and the USA. Again, the Turkish bases are an asset to their American and Israeli allies. American reinforcements for their several purposes can be more reliably sent through bases in Cyprus controlled by Turkey than would be the case if the Greek Cypriots controlled the North and the two British bases

This posture would be different if Turkey and Greece were not enemies. The 41 miles between Turkey and Cyprus are twice the 20 miles between Dover and Calais. Moreover, even on the assumption that Greece is an enemy, Turkey's emphasis on military security may be criticised as unnecessary and counter-productive. There is no way that Greece could successfully attack the Turkish mainland from Cyprus. The present disparity in population is in the ratio of six Turks to one Greek.

If the naval forces have some equivalence, the size of the Turkish army cannot be matched by greater Greek spending per soldier. The withdrawal of the Turkish Aegean army, like the withdrawal of the army on the Bulgarian border, is more likely to reassure Turkey's smaller neighbours. Similarly, keeping 30,000 troops in Cyprus may give the local commander the immediate 3:1 superiority needed to deter any surprise attack. But by provoking the Greek enlargement of its Paphos base and countervailing missile deployment, the effect on Turkish Cypriot security may be judged counter-productive.

Moreover, Turkish military doctrine has changed in ways that have been affected by, and in turn affect, its involvement in the Cyprus dispute. In 1964 Turkey did not have sufficient landing craft to move its troops from Iskenderun in Hatay province to the beaches of Northern Cyprus. Turkey was limited to Atatürk's concept of security, whereby troops would be moved up by railway to defend the land frontiers of the Republic, and no further. After 1964 Turkey built its own landing craft in defiance of American embargoes. Today, Turkey has helicopters, naval and air forces whose modernisation is scheduled to cost $150bn over twenty-five years. All army units have been trained in the mobile warfare relevant to Cyprus by being sent in rotation to the mountainous terrain within south-east Turkey. Unless it were seriously endangered on another frontier, Turkey could now quickly send forces from the mainland to Cyprus with much greater confidence than was the case in 1974.

International pressure

> 'The Cyprus question is a national case for Turks, and friendly countries should not bring up this question when dealing with bilateral relations with Turkey' President Demirel, 8 May 1999 (*Anadolu News*, 10 May).

President Demirel in May 1999 included the European Union among such friendly countries, saying in the same month that it was not in Turkey's national interest to remain in an emotional state about Europe. Nevertheless, this unilateral attempt to exclude the Cyprus issue from any agenda cannot remove all the costs of supporting the TRNC in an unsympathetic international environment. Turkey's relations with the

USA, and the conservatively minded Organisation of Islamic Countries are all made more difficult by its identification with Northern Cyprus. In relations with the European Union and Greece, the Cyprus issue can at best be postponed. The timetabling of EU membership of the Republic of Cyprus and of Turkish negotiations for accession will considerably reduce the option of postponement. Already the Customs Union negotiations have provided an interesting illustration of the pervasiveness of the difficulty. With issues as important as the Customs Union or Turkish membership, Ankara's sympathy for Turkish Cyprus cannot translate into giving the objections of the Turkish Cypriot leadership absolute priority where other friendly countries are concerned.

The detail of the 1995 Customs Union Agreement required Turkey to reluctantly recognise the Republic of Cyprus. In Article 16 Turkey promised to progressively align itself over five years with the Community's preferential customs agreements with third countries. The Republic of Cyprus is listed in the appendix to the Agreement as a third country to which preferential tariffs apply. There was no way that the fifteen Member States and the European Parliament could accommodate omitting an Associated country. A statement appended to the Agreement shows that the Turkish Government knew what it was doing. Turkey would give priority to all other countries listed in the appendix before aligning itself with EU tariffs on goods from the Republic of Cyprus (Bıçak, 1997: 250). Another detail is also relevant. The Association Agreement between the EU and Turkey does not specify which Court should be chosen to adjudicate any dispute. In 1995 Turkey agreed in Article 64 that the decisions of the Court of Justice of the European Communities would apply in resolving differences of interpretation over the application of the Customs Union Agreement. This raises two questions that have never been tested. The first is whether the Court's decision of 5 July 1994 invalidating TRNC certification requires Turkey to implement restrictions on its imports from Northern Cyprus. The second concerns the legality of exports to the EU of TRNC produce that has been certificated in Turkey.

Not surprisingly, there have been other instances of Turkey bending before international pressures over Cyprus. İsmet İnönü, having criticised Adnan Menderes for accepting the 1959 compromise renouncing partition, himself accepted the UN Resolution in 1964. He judged it better to get a UN intervention force protecting Turkish Cypriots into Cyprus at the price of recognising the credentials of the wholly Greek Cypriot Government, rather than risk unilateral intervention by sea. Later in the same year, he again decided against intervention when Lyndon Johnson threatened that the USA would not honour NATO commitments to defend Turkey in the event of a counter-intervention from the Soviet Union. As Prime Minister, Süleyman Demirel was prepared to accept minority rights in 1965 on behalf of the Turkish Cypriots. Turgut Özal, having reluctantly recognised the TRNC during the first days of Turkey's transition from military rule, was willing to go along with pressure from President Bush to improve relations with Greek Prime Minister Mitsotakis by getting the TRNC to discuss the UN 'Set of Ideas' (US State Dept, 1991, 2 August).

Since the Helsinki Conclusions of December 1999, the question has become whether Turkey will be prepared to renounce its threat of integrating the TRNC, and reduce its open-ended financial and military commitment to the TRNC, in response to pressure from the European Union. On 11 April 2000 the first meeting of the EU-Turkey Association Council since 29 April 1997 discussed Cyprus, EU financial obligations, the inclusion of 'services' in the Customs Union, and eight sub-committees to screen the compatibility of Turkish legislation with the *acquis.* In July 2000, Mesut Yılmaz became deputy prime minister with responsibility for Turkey's EU candidature. Cyprus was one of the four items on which Commissioner Günther Verheugen wanted change before presenting his promised paper on the content and timetable of the pre-negotiations stage of Turkey's candidature. The nationalist and fundamentalist opponents of Turkey's EU candidature and of co-existence with Greece are bound to focus on the Cyprus issue as a means of stirring populist discontent against Turkey's alignment with Europe and against neighbourly relations with Greece.

3. Turkish Cypriots and a settlement

The international empowerment of the Turkish Cypriot side is the only way to motivate the Greek Cypriots to share power (Mümtaz Soysal, 1999: 65).

Since 1974, Turkish Cypriot nationalists, with the backing of the Turkish army, have felt able to resist outside pressure. The status quo has much to recommend it. Within their zone they enjoy being masters in their own house. After the divorce of 1963-1974, the physical separation from Greek Cypriots has become more pronounced. Individual acts of kindness to Greek Cypriots have never extended to any organised attempts to encourage Greek Cypriots to remain in the North as equal citizens. Schools in the North have not started to teach Greek to Turkish Cypriot children. It is true that the other side do not teach Turkish, and have deprecated any fraternisation by Greek Cypriots with the illegal regime. But language teaching in particular is a litmus test that shows whether parents expect, or desire, reconciliation and normal relations with the other community. The majority votes at Assembly and Presidential elections have supported variations of the Nationalist thesis giving priority to relations with Turkey over reconciliation with the South. Mr Denktaş has been demonstrably a popular president. He has been re-elected as leader each time he has stood. He is able to move about without guards.

Nevertheless, doubts about the longevity of the present complete separation can be shown on three levels. About 10,000 individual Turkish Cypriots, according to Greek Cypriot sources, have taken the precaution on trips abroad of applying for Republic of Cyprus passports, available at all Greek Cypriot embassies to Turkish Cypriots born before 1974. Secondly, a minority associated with the trade union and internationalist Left prioritises its pan-Cypriot identification with Cypriots in the South over its loyalty to motherland Turkey. However, the European Union's courting of Opposition politicians is unlikely to produce a change of leadership. Over four decades the parties of the Left, taken together, have not won an election. Some of their leaders are willing to work with the nationalist Right. Four months after the Helsinki Conclusions had opened the way to Turkish membership, electoral support for the leaders of the two major left-wing parties in the Presidential elections held on 16 April 2000 amounted to a combined total of 21.73 per cent of the votes cast. Thirdly, the Government itself would like the rest of the world to recognise the reality of Turkish Cypriot sovereignty in the North, and lift the embargoes on trade and air travel.

The Nationalist majority is divided and uncertain about what, if any, concessions to the status quo might be made to gain recognition from the international community and the Greek Cypriots. The default position is to await recognition first, arguing that only on the basis of equality of status can a mutually satisfactory settlement be envisaged. Such a settlement has to be agreed by separate referenda prior to opening negotiations for accession to the European Union. As the strongest card of the Greek Cypriot side is their successful denial over decades of this recognition, and as EU harmonisation and accession negotiations have now proceeded so far that EU accession is inextricably part of any settlement, the default position means that no serious negotiations on an islanders-only basis can be expected.

Nevertheless, two changes are always possible that might quite suddenly make a settlement desirable to enough of the Nationalist majority in the North. The first would be a cessation of the Greek Cypriot point scoring designed to portray their neighbours as enemies, law-breakers, or inferiors. The second would be a decision in Ankara that a settlement between Turkish and Greek Cypriots is preferable to a unilateral entry by a Greek Cypriot government bent on making difficulties for Turkey's ambitions in European markets, European defence and European political decision-making. In this light, it is worth setting out likely Turkish Cypriot views on the three major substantive issues of any settlement—their security, territory, and property that would have to be resolved in any negotiations on the constitutional issue.

Security

The contrast between their insecurity as individuals and as a community before 1974 and the security they have felt since 1974 makes this issue the priority for Turkish Cypriots. Most Turkish Cypriots insist that Turkish troops remain in the North without any specific time limit. As individuals, they do not expect to be safe in the South for the foreseeable future. Few would welcome the presence of Greek Cypriot police or the National Guard. If a Greek Cypriot were to come to the North with his friends, and demand the return of a family home, there would have to be some effective Turkish Cypriot police and international supervisory force to prevent violence.

In the event of a settlement, the UNFICYP mandate is unlikely to be renewed. Moreover, to continue accepting payment for such a force from the Greek Cypriot side only, or even a federal Government, would induce Turkish Cypriot distrust. The Europeans will have to provide even-handed police monitors able to move quickly to all parts of the island. Military support might be cheaply available if Cyprus became a training base for troops deploying in support of international monitors in the Balkans, and other WEU combined joint task force exercises.

Territory

Article 2/1 of the TRNC Constitution proclaims 'an indivisible whole with its territory and people'. This defiant assertion indicates how reluctant the Turkish Cypriot side would be to give over to Greek Cypriot present control Gazimağusa (Famagusta) and Güzelyurt (Morphou). On balance, the idea of giving up control of more land to an internationally controlled buffer zone is even less attractive. The reopening of Nicosia airport, thereby opening the door to tourism in North Cyprus, has to be balanced against opening the door to Greek Cypriot land purchases. On the other hand, proposals to reduce the 37 per cent of the island controlled by Turkish Cypriots to some 29 per cent were left on the table, reluctantly, after the UN in 1992 presented its non-map to a very dismissive TRNC. Boutros Ghali saw the UN as fleshing out the 1977 'High-level Agreement' between the two Cypriot sides that Cyprus would in future be bi-zonal.

Property

Land registers in Cyprus have been meticulously administered in the past, although some were taken in 1974 to the South by fleeing Greek Cypriots. The Turkish Cypriot idea is that each side should establish an agency to compensate individuals for loss of property left behind in the zone of the other. The model of public expropriation is suggested. Turkish Cypriots are particularly indignant at the *Loizidou* decision by the European Court of Human Rights that Turkey, not the TRNC, is responsible for protecting Greek Cypriot property in the North. Talks with the Greek Cypriots are at risk in consequence. President Denktaş struck a more conciliatory note on 17 December 1999. He said that, with a Turkish guarantee on land, the state and sovereignty, we can 'in this way realise the unification with the Greek Cypriots in the EU'.

4. Turkish Cypriot perspectives on the European Union

I was disappointed to learn that the European Council has taken a decision on 6 March 1995 with regard to setting a time-frame for the opening of accession negotiations with the Greek Cypriot Administration which passes itself off as 'The Government of Cyprus'... Nobody should expect the Turkish Cypriot authorities to give support to an illegal and void unilateral application made by the Greek Cypriot side, which the Turkish Cypriot side has been strongly and vehemently opposing ever since the illegal application was made on 3 July 1990 (Rauf Denktaş in identical letters to M. Alain Juppé, President of the Council, and M. Jacques Santer, President of the Commission, March 9,1995).

Economic advantages
European Commission officials think that Turkish Cypriots in general are much more open than their intransigent leadership to the economic advantages of accession. Spending on seminars for businessmen by the USA and the EU estimated at $15m was designed to point up the wealth creation possible once the frontier is dismantled. The biggest incentive is the prospect of foreign direct investment to build up the tourist industry in the North. The European Investment Bank would be able to lend money for promoting economic development and preparing accession. Northern Cyprus would be eligible for aid from the structural funds to compensate for the loss of agricultural and mineral production that has happened for economic reasons totally unconnected to the politics of Cyprus. In so far as agriculture remains, it would be eligible for the subsidies on income support and modernisation if not for the direct subsidies compensating Western European farmers who have lost subsidised exports to the rest of the world. Individual Turkish Cypriots could apply for jobs in the EU institutions. EU publications in Cyprus routinely cite the relative disparity in wealth between the two communities as a reason why Turkish Cypriots should be more favourable than they are to membership of the European Union, and to a settlement that would end the embargo.

In 1996 the per capita GDP income share of Turkish Cypriots was estimated at $4,222 in comparison with an average income of $13,600 for Greek Cypriots. This raw comparison has to be qualified to understand why it has had so little political impact in the North. Bıçak estimates that in terms of purchasing power parities, and taking into account a black economy amounting to 60 per cent of the total economy, Turkish Cypriots earn on average nearly $7000, which makes them already about half as rich as Greek Cypriots (Doğramacı, 1997: 268). Unemployment at 1.2 per cent conceals under-employment in family businesses but is agreeably low. Turkish Cypriots enjoy a higher standard of living than they did in the past, and a higher standard than the $2,078 earned (GDP per capita) in 1999 by Turks on the mainland.

However, the Turkish Cypriot preference for economic, as distinct from political, integration with Turkey over the potential gains and dangers of integration with Greek Cyprus in the EU is not just a passing resentment at the punishing embargo imposed by the EU at the instance of the Greeks. Historical memory of disasters laid at the door of their Greek Cypriot neighbours is an important component of Turkish Cypriot suspicion. Under British rule, Turkish Cypriots were not much poorer than the Greek Cypriot majority. Constituting 18 per cent of the population, they owned 16 per cent of motor vehicles. Government jobs in the police and forestry service were given disproportionately to Turkish Cypriots.

When the Turkish Cypriots took over control after 1963, Turkish Cypriots had to abandon 4000 jobs. Their per capita GDP income fell from $500 per annum in 1963 to $130 in 1964 (Brey in Baier-Allen, ed., 1998: 94). It was Turkey that stepped in to pay some part of the salaries and pensions due.

In the crisis of 1974-75, the proportion of the Turkish Cypriot population that fled the North was greater than the proportion of the Greek Cypriot population that fled the North. Yet in per capita terms the European Community through its four Financial Protocols contributed 44 ECU to each Turkish Cypriot and 3 17 ECU to each Greek Cypriot (Bıçak, 1997: 256). The Turkish Cypriots complain that projects submitted by them had to be bi-communal, whereas this condition was not applied to projects submittted by the Government side. As for trade, although the Turkish Cypriot side reduced their duties on imports from the EC by 15 per cent, and wanted to participate in the talks on a Customs Union, 'they could only succeed in having informal meetings with EC officials' (Bıçak, 1997: 246). Their request to have a representative on the Trade and Economic Co-operation Committee established in 1987 was turned down.

The impact of the 1994 *Anastasiou* case has been more serious. The sudden end of exports of citrus and potatoes to the EU is attributed by Turkish Cypriots to the malignity of its institutions, at the instance of the Greek Cypriot Government. In 1991, 80 per cent of Turkish Cypriot exports went to the EU, 13.9 per cent to Turkey (Olgun in Dodd, ed 1993: 293). In 1996, 48 per cent of TRNC exports went to Turkey, 35 per cent to the EU (Tahiroğlu in Baier-Allen, 1998: 115). Moreover, Turkey supplies without charge the additional water that is vital if the island is to be economically viable through tourism and agriculture. Lowering the water table allows in seawater, bringing permanent salination. Turkish Cypriots' experience thus gives them some reason to prefer the certainties of Turkish support to exposing their businesses and properties to the laws of a Federal Republic and the competition laws of the European Union. 'The discriminatory attitude of the EU does not leave any options to the Turkish Cypriots but to have economic integration with Turkey for their economic development' (Hasan Bıçak, 1997: 257).

Nevertheless, European officials can point as evidence for their optimism about Turkish Cypriot views on accession to a poll by COMAR in *Kıbrıs* of 23 November 1997. It found that 94.5 per cent of respondents were willing to consider accession of Northern Cyprus to the European Union. Only 1.5 per cent were totally opposed, and only 3.6 per cent in this highly politicised community had no opinion. However, this apparent approval rating is misleading. Only 10 per cent wanted to join unconditionally. 42 per cent of COMAR's respondents were willing to begin talks with the EU only after a settlement with the South had been agreed. Another 41.7 per cent of COMAR's respondents were willing to join only after Turkey had become a member. This breakdown is entirely consistent with analysis of the electoral results of political leaders. The only political leader in the North to advocate unconditional membership, Arif Hasan Tahsin of the YBH, received no significant support in the first and only round of presidential elections held on 15 April 2000. His party, the New Cyprus party, has no members in the Assembly. Mehmet Ali Talat, leader of the left-leaning Republican Turkish Party and sympathetic to AKEL, advocates accession after a settlement. In the same presidential elections he received 9,834 votes, 10.03 per cent of the votes cast. Mustafa Akıncı, leader of the Communal Liberation Party, favours accession only after Turkey has been accepted for EU membership and a settlement with the Greek Cypriots has been agreed. As deputy Prime Minister he is prepared to work with the Nationalist leadership. He received 11,469 votes, 11.70 per cent. At least 80 per cent of the Turkish Cypriot voters can therefore be assumed to support the leadership in its refusal to participate in the negotiations undertaken by the Republic of Cyprus on behalf of the whole island.

Political objections
The Turkish Cypriots and Turks have two principal objections to the accession process initiated by the Republic of Cyprus. The first is that the wholly Greek Cypriot Government has no right to speak on behalf of Cyprus as a whole and of the Turkish Cypriot North in particular. On this question of the authority of the Greek Cypriot Government, the TRNC Memorandum asking the Presidents of the European Council and Commission not to consider the 1990 application from the South is particularly subtle. Accepting that the Republic of Cyprus had established itself internationally, however illegitimately, the author argued that even so it was not constitutionally entitled 'to represent the whole of Cyprus in so fundamental a development as the acquisition of membership of the European Communities, or at all'. In 1991 Turkey joined with the TRNC in stating that there was no legitimate government of Cyprus (Dodd, 1999: 138).

A corollary of this objection is that a settlement must precede a legitimate application. The 1990 application should be withdrawn as being provocative as well as illegitimate. Knowing that an application to the EU was imminent, UNSC Resolution 649 of March 12 1990 called on 'the parties concerned to refrain from any action that could aggravate the situation'. A second corollary for the Turkish Cypriots is that each community must have the authority to hold its own referendum on the terms of accession, lest the enthusiastic majority community outvote the Turkish Cypriot minority and undermine its separate right to self-determination (Necatigil 1993: 65). Paragraph 92 of the 1992 'Set of Ideas', which Mr Denktaş later said had been agreed with President Vassiliou, reads:

> Matters related to the membership of the Federal Republic in the European Economic Community [the pre-Maastricht designation] will be discussed and agreed to, and will be submitted for the approval of the two communities in separate referendums.

This commitment would enable the North to reject any accession project that did not meet its approval.

At the same time, Mr Denktaş' willingness to submit EU accession to a referendum implies that Cypriot accession to the Union might be lawful after a settlement, a possibility that he habitually rejects as absolutely illegal under the terms of the Treaty of Guarantee. Part of the Turkish Cypriot case that the Cyprus Government does not have the authority to apply for EU membership is that by the first Article of the Treaty of Guarantee, echoed in Article 185 of the Constitution, the Republic of Cyprus unconditionally 'undertakes not to participate, in whole or in part, in any political or economic union with any State whatsoever'. The intention of the drafters was to rule out union with Greece. Turkish Cypriot and Turkish authors are unanimous that this will happen if Cyprus as well as Greece becomes a member state of the EU. Also, in so far as the EU is a state in the making, the wording rules out union also with the EU. In so far as the EU is an organisation, the objection has always been less absolute. The Constitution gives a power of veto to the President and Vice-President of the Republic in the event of the House of Representatives approving Cypriot membership of any international organisation that does not include both Turkey and Greece as members. Turkish Cypriot lawyers argue that, although the Constitution is defunct, because the EU and the Greek Cypriot Administration regard the Constitution as still valid, they should not entertain the idea of an application to an organisation of which Turkey is not a member. The EU Council and Mr Vassiliou should honourably refuse to negotiate accession because the veto to which the Turkish Cypriots are entitled cannot be applied in the absence of a Vice-President.

The second principal objection concerns the rights of Turkey. The Turkish Guarantee might be undermined by an accession that would mean that any Turkish exercise of its rights of intervention would in future directly confront the whole European Union.

More critically, membership could weaken the Treaty of Guarantee, since the guarantor powers could hardly intervene in a European Union member state. A decision by the Union to open entry negotiations with the Greek Cypriot side could escalate the sharp reaction in North Cyprus, as the European Court ruling of 5 July 1994 did. In a hostile world the Turkish Cypriots would see no alternative to closer integration with Turkey, a process which has already begun (Necatigil, 1995: 29).

The political importance of the Turkish factor was illustrated by the enthusiasm with which the TRNC joined with Turkey in boycotting all dealings with the EU and with the Greek Cypriot community in the aftermath of the Luxembourg Conclusions. On 16 December 1997, President Denktaş showed no regret in announcing that 'Anouil's mission in the TRNC is over. The Cyprus problem cannot be discussed with the European Union'.

Moreover, Turkey would not be able to match Greek support for Greek Cypriot interests within the EU unless Turkey itself became a full member.

Related to this second objection is a corollary about the paucity of Turkish Cypriot representation in the institutions of the European Union. Professor Haluk Kabaalioğlu pointed out that, with its small population, the TRNC would not be entitled to a Commissioner, or Council member, or judge, and might or might not be represented on the European Parliament depending on the formula for over-representing small countries. Membership of the Committee of Regions, a large but impotent body attended only by half its membership on average, would be all that was on offer:

> Turkish Cypriot interests would not be represented in the Community institutions even if the Turkish Republic of Northern Cyprus joined as a full state... This issue can only be solved when both Turkey and the TRNC join the European Union jointly' (Doğramacı 1997: 224).

The implication is also true, that Turkish Cypriots would not be represented if they entered as a zone of the Republic of Cyprus. In each case representation would depend on the willingness of either Turkey or the ROC to treat the Turkish Cypriots as what are becoming known as 'intermediate authorities'. Bavaria and Wallonia, Ulster and Catalonia often send representatives to committee or Council meetings on the basis of *ad hoc* formulae agreed for particular policy sectors with particular institutions. In general, it is not obvious how any degree of representation would enable such a tiny community to influence the content of EU legislation.

Eventual membership?

The Nationalist leadership has generally been careful to refer politely to the possibility of eventual accession after a prior settlement and after Turkish membership. Point 19 of the Turkish Cypriot memorandum to the EU Council of Ministers on 12 July 1990 cited above, p.71, reads:

> The TRNC does not wish to create the impression that it is opposed to the eventual membership of the European Communities by a State of Cyprus restored to legality and stability by a settlement freely negotiated between parties of equal standing.

On 20 January 1995 President Denktaş in a 14-point peace initiative contemplated EU membership of the future Federal Republic of Cyprus within the framework foreseen in the UN 'Set of Ideas'. First an agreement had to be reached on a bi-communal bizonal federal solution of the Cyprus problem that respected the equal political status of the two peoples. Speaking in 1996 to a Turkish Cypriot audience on the illegitimacy of the Greek Cypriot application, Necati Munir Ertekün, Q.C. nevertheless balanced his criticisms by saying that:

> As part of Europe, the Turkish Cypriot side fully shares the European vision of democracy, secularism, human rights, and free enterprise, but it also needs to know a) what the parameters will finally be of an overall settlement in Cyprus, and b) what its status will be in the EU (Doğramacı, ed., 1997: 241).

Although the same author in his 1990 memorandum had criticised the Greek Cypriot application on the ground that 'a prospective member of the EU, which has not got an integrated economy within itself, can hardly be expected to integrate with the economy of the EU', he was optimistic that the economic problems of the North constituted no insurmountable obstacle:

> Regarding the economic implications of EU membership, let me say that I do not see insurmountable problems on this front, and believe that if a political breakthrough is realised and the necessary steps taken to align the Turkish Cypriot economy to the EU, it will be easy to work out arrangements that will provide for the mutual benefit and prosperity of both communities.

However, not ruling out accession in unlikely circumstances is not the same as supporting either a settlement involving substantial changes from the status quo, or expecting Turkish entry in the foreseeable future. For the ten years since 1990 the Turkish Cypriot leadership has been as unenthusiastic about membership of the European Union as the Greek Cypriots have been enthusiastic. They have been reactive where the Greek Cypriots have been proactive. Complaints about exclusion from negotiations are in part expressions of frustration at the consequences of lack of recognition, partly point-scoring to no practical purpose. For example, in 1995 Attorney-General Zaim Necatigil gave voice to this persistent complaint at the exclusion of North Cypriots from negotiations:

> The Turkish Cypriot view is that the European Union should not exclude the Turkish community from negotiations for a Customs Union, because, supposing that the Union is relying on the 1960 Constitution, it should not fail to note that conclusion of international treaties, conventions and agreements is a matter that, under the Constitution, requires the consent of both communities. Article 50 of that Constitution is explicit on this issue (Necatigil, 1995: 25).

The Turkish Cypriot leadership is unanimous that participation without prior recognition of their equality of status with the Greek Cypriots would mean either surrender or subordination. They choose not to achieve recognition by exploiting their total control of the North. They would offer to provide accurate information and to consider adaptations to laws and institutions which only they could deliver. As the Helsinki Conclusions have increased the pressure on the Greek Cypriot side to be more accommodating to the Turkish Cypriots (see below) as a condition of Cypriot accession, Greek Cypriot negotiators could not demand that a settlement precede participation. Participation in formal meetings and through informal discussions on the telephone would implicitly and continuously constitute recognition of the reality of Turkish Cypriot control of the North. Meanwhile the Helsinki Conclusions have opened up three possibilities for timetabling Cypriot accession to the European Union.

The first would be to keep to the Commission's promise to the Greek Cypriots that non-members like Turkey and the unrecognised North of Cyprus will have no veto on the accession of the Republic of Cyprus. This would mean ROC entry in the first wave of accession anticipated at the end of 2002 without the northern zone. For the Turkish Cypriots to enter in 2002, which the EU spokespersons have always maintained is their first preference, immense enthusiasm on everybody's part would be needed in three sets of negotiations. Hostile communities would have to agree a settlement of the constitutional and other issues. The leaders of the North of Cyprus would have to adapt institutions and legislation to show that they could implement the *acquis*. The European Union would have to negotiate the terms of a more complicated accession treaty to include derogations on an unusually long time-scale to protect the North of Cyprus from being bought up by Greek Cypriots. What might be possible is a series of declaratory commitments on the part of the EU Council, Commission and Parliament on the one hand, and of the Republic of Cyprus on the other, that the Northern zone is being prepared for membership of the EU on terms that protect its autonomy as a community policing its own zone.

The second possibility is for the timing of Northern Cyprus' accession to be related to the pace of their separate harmonisation process. It might be possible for Northern Cypriots themselves to choose whether to apply as a separate state, as part of a confederation, or as part of a federation as outlined in an agreement. The possibilities would be limited by the need for approval from the Republic of Cyprus, which would be by then itself a member state. If entry were in 2005, Turkish

Cypriot entry would be as an advance party preparing the way for Turkey.

The third possibility would depend more closely on the success of Turkey's own accession process. If this was going well, Turkish Cyprus would enter the Union at the same time as Turkey. With Turkey and Greece both members, a return to the state of affairs in 1960, with the considerable modification of zones occupied by distinct populations, would be the best imaginable option. For Turkey to enter with the North of Cyprus as an integrated province would be difficult for several member states to accept.

5. Conclusion

The Turkish Cypriots and the Greek Cypriots both state repeatedly that this time a settlement must not be imposed on them from outside. By this they mean different things. In the last chapter we saw that the Greek Cypriots mean that last time external pressure forced the Greek Cypriot majority to accept undemocratic and unworkable arrangements with the Turkish Cypriots as the price of independence. This time, once outside interference in the form of the Turkish army of occupation has removed itself, a federal Constitution can be agreed with flexible leaders of the Turkish Cypriots that will give them autonomy within the framework of the European Union. The Turkish Cypriots mean that the external pressures of the embargoes imposed by the international community and especially the European Union will be lifted. Equality of status, once recognised, will enable talks with the Greek Cypriot leaders under the aegis of the United Nations to agree on a Confederation with weak powers to manage inter-island relations between its two owners.

> In conclusion, it could be said that international and regional organisations, such as the EU, should not be involved with the Cyprus question in such a way as to interfere with the efforts and initiatives of the UN Secretary-General, but only to complement such a process (Necatigil, 1995: 29).

The contradictions evident in the Cyprus issue can be summarised in three pairs.

- Turkish Cypriots want Turkey in; Greek Cypriots want Turkey out.
- Turkish Cypriots want equality; Greek Cypriots want democracy.
- Turkish Cypriots do not want membership of the European Union; Greek Cypriots do.

A reconciliation of these three pairs of contradictions is conceivable.

If Turkey was also a member of the European Union, it would be no more of a threat to Greek Cypriots than is contemporary Greece to Turkish Cypriots. Both motherlands would be restrained by the need to explain themselves in the European Council and Parliament; the pursuit of national interests by professionals within the institutional framework is reassuringly mundane. Secondly, the European Union, through derogations on the free movement of capital, could become the protector of Turkish Cypriot owners in the North, making the presence of the Turkish army less important in the scenarios. Thirdly, establishing equality between the zones would have different meanings depending on whether the zones were constituted as separate states, a federation or a confederation. If the TRNC were recognised as a separate micro-state, it would be formally equal in the EU and in Cyprus as a sovereign state. However its consequent influence in the EU and in Cyprus would be so small as to be discountable in a world where sovereign rights are exercised jointly. In a federation, zonal equality could be reconciled with majoritarian democracy within each zone, and there would be a greater say for the majority community in the Central Bank's dealings with the Eurozone and in the Foreign Office contribution to European political dialogue. In a confederation, much the same would be true in practice. The European Union's calls for a settlement between the two communities also regularly repeat the mantra that it does not seek to impose its will. From the EU perspective, a settlement between the Turkish and Greek Cypriots would remove German, French, Italian and Dutch doubts about the wisdom of taking on the problems of a divided island. Therefore the 'countries that count' have put heavy pressure on the Turkish Cypriot leaders and their Turkish mentors both directly and indirectly through the United Nations, the Group of Eight industrialised countries and the European Union.

Also the Greek Cypriots understand by the Helsinki Conclusions that the Council's decision on their accession, taking 'account of all relevant factors', requires them to be more accommodating to the Turkish Cypriots in the UN proximity talks (McDonald, 2000: 8).

The EU's self-contradiction between heavy pressure to reach a settlement and not imposing a settlement is more difficult to reconcile. It might be said that the pressure is being applied to bring the Turkish and Greek Cypriots to reach a mutually acceptable settlement, not to 'impose' a settlement. In practice we have a slow and multilateral version of what in 1959 was a remarkably quick bilateral diplomatic exercise. The end or purpose is a complete draft package of measures that might be acceptable to all parties. The means are proximity talks in which each side talks to a UN facilitator on acceptable terms for face to face negotiations, in which the leaders of each community sign up to this prepared package so that they can recommend it to their own voters. The role of the Internationals is the subject of the next chapter.

| 6 |

The Internationals
and
The European Union

'It is very important for the EU and the US to co-operate between them, and with the UN, so as to achieve a political solution of the Cyprus issue.' Commissioner van den Broek, 14 November 1997 (*Athens News Agency*, 16 November 1997).

1. Introduction

During the Bosnian war, journalists coined the collective noun, 'The Internationals' to describe all the personnel from international organisations and concerned states who had involved themselves in Balkan disputes after the end of the Cold War. The European Community, renaming itself as the Union, became suddenly a principal among these inexperienced international actors in Eastern, Central and South-East Europe. Delors likened the EU to a magnet surrounded by iron filings, an image that captures the size and passivity of the EU in its external relations.

In retrospect, the 1990 membership application from the Republic of Cyprus to the European Community was the harbinger of a wave of applications from the East. Other Europe-focused governmental organisations also enlarged their membership and took on new responsibilities in the Balkans, filling the vacuum left by the collapse of the USSR and the reduction of American forc es in Europe to fewer than

100,000 personnel. The European Union found itself working more closely with NATO, the Council of Europe, the rebadged Organisation for Security and Co-operation in Europe, and a host of financial, humanitarian and sectoral agencies. The influx of 'Internationals' precluded the return of pre-1939 Great Power rivalries, between Germany, France, Poland and Russia.

However, just as the shift from the superpowers to the European Union was incomplete, so was the shift in the new international agenda. Before 1990, every international development had a Cold War aspect. The creation of Cyprus and the European Community were important not just in their own terms, but also in terms of strengthening the Western bloc against Communist subversion. At the same time, the Member States of the European Communities did not expect their institutions to concern themselves with questions of air power or ground forces. As former empires, they saw deliberate non-involvement in the internal affairs of Cyprus (Stephanou & Tsardanidis, 1991: 207-30) and Eastern Europe as new virtues, limiting themselves to the pursuit of purely national interests.

After 1990, the militarily secure and rich West European states no longer had to fear the Red Army. However, to choose to do nothing when individuals or groups were being attacked for being of the wrong religion was incompatible with a vision of Europe committed to protect individual rights. Moreover, disputes between ethnic communities of differing religions, fanned by rivalry between neighbouring motherlands, were likely to cause cross-border migrations and disputes involving secession from, or annexation to, existing sovereign states. The dissolution of the USSR, Czechoslovakia, Ethiopia and most of Yugoslavia brought over twenty new recognised states and as many unrecognised states, like Abkhazia and Chechnya, into the international system. As Mr Denktaş pointed out, the Europeans were now prepared to take the kind of action to protect Muslim Kosovars within Serbia that they had earlier refused to take to protect the Turkish Cypriot community in Cyprus.

However, the new European willingness to take responsibility for promoting individual and minority rights had considerable limitations. The EU provision of a few advisers, some hard currency and the prospect of accession, was relatively successful in Hungary. In a region where 3.5 million Hungarians live in the seven surrounding states, Hungary welcomed the EU conditions requiring them to respect existing borders and articulate rights that would reassure Hungarian minorities elsewhere and Rumanians in Hungary. On the other hand, in the new state of Bosnia, the fall of Srbenica tragically symbolised the EU's incapacity or unwillingness to prevent the Serbian version of ethnic cleansing. To stop Serbian aggression required the more decisive intervention of the United States in arming Croats and using NATO air power. In Kosovo, American air power combined with ground troops from European states exemplified a post-1990 version of the Cold War formula of deterrence from a distance. In trying to settle the Cyprus dispute, the EU had to keep itself in line with the other concerned Internationals, especially with the United States and the United Nations.

2. The United States

Under American pressure, the European Union approved a controversial but important Customs Union with Turkey in the spring of 1995, and moved Cyprus into the first tier of countries to be considered for future membership (Holbrooke, 1998: 61).

Until the archives are open, Richard Holbrooke's claim that American pressure during a French Presidency caused the member states to do what they would not have done otherwise is a matter for conjecture. Holbrooke at the time was Assistant Secretary of State for relations with Europe and Canada. He was one of the high officials on both sides of the Atlantic who were determined in early 1995 to improve relations. According to Horst Krenzler, the Commission's Director-General for external economic relations, 'EU-US relations were characterised by a certain malaise in 1994 and early 1995. Some thought that the relationship had not been as bad in decades' (Krenzler & Schomaker, 1996: 10).

One underlying issue was whether the end of the Cold War would mean an economic struggle between the USA, Japan and Europe. The EU rejected renewed American proposals for an Atlantic free trade area. It refused the American request for a treaty giving American officials the kind of active role in EU external decision-making that they enjoyed in

NATO. A related issue was whether American dominance of the security agenda was being undermined by the alignment of WEU membership with that of the EU and its Associates, thereby excluding the USA and Canada. Horst Krenzler modestly recognized the inadequacy of the EU and argued for joint action.

> The EU's failure in former Yugoslavia highlighted the importance of a continued US presence in Europe and underscored NATO's validity. Where the EU and the USA acted in agreement, as demonstrated by their joint support for the Bosnian-Croat Federation, it has been possible to contain the conflict (Krenzler & Schomaker, 1996: 12).

The malaise had a procedural aspect. Unlike trade discussions like the Uruguay round where the Commission controlled effective policy-making procedures, the USA complained that consultations on foreign policy were mere exchanges of views (Krenzler & Schomaker, 1996: 12). To an extent, the Americans could exploit the reluctance of member states to accept a common secretariat. Informed in advance of the agenda in foreign policy discussions, Washington could lean on Germany, Britain and the Netherlands to promote American views. The 1990 EU-US Declaration provided a pragmatic basis for managing relations in the new era under the umbrella of one summit meeting during each EU Presidency term. On a mandate from the EU-US summit of 14 June 1995, senior officials drew up the interlinked New Transatlantic Agenda and joint Action Plan, which were adopted at the EU-US summit on 3 December 1995 (*Agence Europe* documents 1970, 1971 of 12 & 13 January 1996). This Executive-level agreement with the Council and Commission institutionalised the previous high-level co-operation as it had developed during the Bush and first Clinton Administrations.

In Brussels all branches of the US Government consistently advocated Turkey's cause. Completing the Customs Union meant lower tariffs in Turkey, and protection of US patents in sectors like pharmaceuticals. Washington consistently supported Turkey's bid for membership, publicly regretting the Luxembourg Conclusions that excluded Turkey. Strobe Talbott, State Department Deputy Secretary, on 15 October 1998 in a memorial lecture for Turgut Özal, said that an EU declaration reserving a place for Turkey 'will be the best guarantee for

Turkish progress on human rights and other issues that have prevented the EU from accepting Turkey as a member'. The State Department argued that a European Turkey was less likely to take the fundamentalist or nationalist alternatives. Permanent exclusion might lead Turkey to leave the Customs Union and the Council of Europe, redefining its military relationship with the USA outside NATO, thus damaging transatlantic relations (Kramer, 1997b: 29). Caspian oil, piped through Turkey to its terminal being built on the Mediterranean Bay of Ceyhan, links American interests in Europe, the Middle East and Eurasia.

American support for Cypriot membership of the EU was less solid. Former US special co-ordinator for Cyprus, Ambassador Nelson Ledsky, told the *Turkish Daily News* on 6 June 1995:

> My own experience over the Cyprus issue suggests that the question of membership inside Europe for Cyprus is a divisive issue rather than a unifying one. In the past it has been a source of misunderstanding between the two communities, not a source of understanding.

Also some policy differences over the future of the Mediterranean remained. The Americans were not invited to observe the Barcelona conference in November 1995 in which the EU launched its Euro-Mediterranean Partnership Initiative, the low-key assistance programme to compensate twelve non-member Southern countries, including Malta and Cyprus, for not being allowed to compete by price in the EU's agricultural markets. The Americans continued to oppose any EU political involvement in the Israel-Palestine conflict. By 1998 EU aid mostly to the Palestinians had totalled $2bn (Joffe, 1998: 2), a far greater contribution than the Council envisaged for peacemaking in Cyprus. Moreover, the Americans drew the conclusion during the 1995 Dayton Process, and again during the Imia/Kardak crisis in 1996, that the Europeans could not co-ordinate timely action in military crises unless the reins were firmly held by their transatlantic superpower. At Dayton in Ohio, the EU Representative in former Yugoslavia, Carl Bildt, was shown every consideration, but Richard Holbrooke played the decisive role.

The United States' role in Cyprus

> America has a role in the tragic events of Cyprus, that's why we're here... America's role in the region in the mid-sixties and in the 1974's has been shameful (Richard Holbrooke, 12 November 1997, Ledra Palace).

The US has had communications facilities in Cyprus since before its independence (Attalides, 1979: 13). Since 1960, America's leading role in Cyprus can be illustrated in different ways. For the three years after independence, American aid to the new republic amounted to $20 million (Attalides, 1979:14). From 1964 to 1995 it supplied $234 million in military and financial aid to the Greek Cypriots, and $305 million in humanitarian aid to both communities through the UNHCR and the Red Cross. The United States contributed nearly half the budgetary costs of UNFICYP peacekeeping (US State Department, 1997: 6).

The 'shameful' actions in the mid-sixties must include CIA support for the Greek Junta and hence for EOKA-B against the Makarios government. American fears that Makarios was a clerical Castro (Attalides, 1979:18) caused Secretary Dean Acheson to promote detailed plans to partition this sovereign member of the United Nations. American plans for uniting most of Cyprus to Greece were balanced by 'the cession to Turkey either in perpetuity or on long lease of a large base in the Karpasia area of Cyprus; three cantons with some form of local autonomy to be established for the Turkish Cypriots; and the cession of the Greek Aegean island of Kastellorizon to Turkey' (Attalides, 1979:18). In 1965 the USA voted with Albania, Iran, Pakistan and Turkey against the UNGA resolution reaffirming Cypriot sovereignty. Whether or not American actions in stopping a Turkish intervention in 1964 and a Greek intervention in 1967 were shameful is more debatable. In 1964 President Johnson prevented Turkish action in defence of the Turkish Cypriots by bluntly threatening not to fulfil his commitments under the North Atlantic Treaty should the Soviet Union attack. In 1967 his envoy Cyrus Vance was equally decisive in demanding the removal of 12,000 Greek troops from Cyprus to prevent a Turkish intervention that President Johnson feared would lead to an irreversible Soviet intrusion (Attalides, 1979: 99). These examples of Superpower pressure give all sides reason to be suspicious of the 'Internationals'.

The 'shameful' role attributed by Holbrooke to America's stance in 1974 is different in that Secretary Henry Kissinger did not intervene. He did not put a stop to plans for the coup against Makarios or for handing Cyprus over to a fascist Junta. He did not order the American fleet to impede the Turkish intervention or prevent the forcible partition of Cyprus. Kissinger's non-intervention policy was not however based on respect for the sovereignty of Cyprus. He had supported discussions begun at the Lisbon NATO summit in 1971 between the Junta and Turkey to unite Cyprus with Greece while moving Turkish Cypriots into cantons protected by a Turkish base (Hitchens, 1997: 72). In 1967, at a Harvard seminar he had raised the question whether Greece and Turkey would tone down their hostile rhetoric if America left them to confront actual war over Cyprus. He may have miscalculated; Cyprus does not figure prominently as a success in his own memoirs. It is also possible that the American wish for peace between NATO allies and on the island itself is moderated by the leverage which a 'no war, no peace' partition gives to a bloc leader courted by both Greece and Turkey. The October war of 1973 had demonstrated that a reliable base near Israel was desirable. Makarios had tried to stop the Americans using the British bases to supply Israel (Attalides, 1979: 160). Since 1974, neither the Greek nor Turkish Cypriots have offered any impediment to the British willingness to provide storage, landing or communications facilities to the Americans.

Nevertheless, Holbrooke's thesis that America has a duty to redress the past wrongs it has inflicted seems genuine in the light of his experience of ethnic conflict and territorial division in Bosnia. After Bosnia, Holbrooke could wield the kind of plain speaking authority enjoyed by Harry Hopkins, Roosevelt's wartime emissary to Churchill and Stalin. A Cypriot solution may well depend on the right combination of circumstances and of an individual's determination to succeed, as with Monnet in Upper Silesia or Kurt Waldheim in the Tyrol. At the beginning of 1996, the circumstances seemed favourable. An impending presidential election in the USA in ten months, the arms race on Cyprus and the desirability of getting a settlement before the start of EU accession negotiations stimulated Holbrooke to declare that 1996 would be 'the year of the big push on Cyprus' (*International Herald Tribune*, 5 January 1996). The President's special representative, Mr Richard

Beattie, had prepared an agenda for meetings between Mr Clerides and Mr Denktaş scheduled for January 1996.

> The Turkish Cypriot side has agreed to consider support for the membership of the Cyprus Federation in the EU within the terms of a political settlement, and the Greek Cypriot side has agreed to respect, within the terms of a political settlement, the sovereignty and political equality of the Turkish Cypriot side. They are willing to discuss, without prejudice to the Treaty of Guarantee and Alliance, these issues and demilitarisation. On this basis, the two leaders will meet for direct discussions in January (*Kıbrıs*, 8 December 1995).

This diplomatic effort seems to have been scuppered by three unforeseen circumstances. The first was the dispute over Imia/Kardak, which brought Greece and Turkey to the brink of a naval battle on 29 January 1996. While this precluded direct discussions in January, Mr Holbrooke told *The Times* on 27 February 1996 that the US still hoped to bring the two leaders together. He suggested that talks would take place under similar conditions to those that had brought a compromise over Bosnia. They were confidentiality (while leaving the US with authority to talk to the press), willingness to stay indefinitely at the negotiating table, and sufficient authority of those negotiating to persuade their own communities to support a compromise. Unfortunately, a second disaster struck. On 4 March 1996, Mr Denktaş suffered a heart attack. Despite these two setbacks, in a message to Congress on 1 May, President Clinton announced that he intended to take a peace initiative on Cyprus. Mr Kornblum was sent to Athens and Ankara and in June Richard Beattie returned to Cyprus. In July Secretary Madelaine Albright was in Athens, Larnaca and Ankara to suggest *(Le Monde* 16 August 1996) the stationing of a Quick Reaction Force in Cyprus. However the American initiative was finally undermined when Mr Erbakan became Prime Minister of Turkey. He signalled his personal support for the Turkish Cypriots by visiting the island less than two weeks later, saying, 'I am here to show you that we stand with you.' In November, Holbrooke told the BBC's Radio 4 that Cyprus was 'the hottest spot on earth'.

After Clinton's re-election, the *International Herald Tribune* reported on 3 February 1997 that 'Bill Clinton's Administration is considering an all-out effort this year to break the Cyprus deadlock'. Richard Holbrooke became presidential emissary to Cyprus on 18 June 1997. A report carried by the Anatolian agency on 14 November 1997 illustrates the advantage that an American can have over a European Union diplomat. In Brussels, a Turkish TRNC journalist was denounced as an 'illegal member of an illegal state'. Holbrooke responded with the magic words that can remove most Turkish Cypriot problems with the outside world, 'I recognise the Turkish Cypriot correspondent'. This incident took place at a three-day seminar held from 13-15 November 1997 for twenty-two Cypriot businessmen, and one trade unionist, together with three Greeks and four Turks. It was a follow-up to meetings in Athens and Istanbul also organised by the University of California and Jan Egeland of Norway's Oslo Institute for Peace, famous for masterminding the Oslo process that led Israel to recognise the Palestinian right to self-determination. The *Turkish News Agency* reported Egeland as saying on 14 November (*TKRNWS*, 18 November 1997) 'Norway wants Turkey and the TRNC to be full members of the EU.... When these applications are approved by the EU, all of the problems in the island will finish'.

Holbrooke's presence in Brussels meant intense diplomacy with Commissioner van den Broek, Sir David Hannay, Mr George Papandreou and Mr Yiannos Kranidiotis. Before the seminar, *Yeni Yuzyıl* on October 30 reported Mr Holbrooke as suggesting that 'The EU might change its attitude against Turkey if the Cyprus question is solved'. In the first week of November Mr Holbrooke had four meetings with Mr Denktaş, who refused to attend the seminar lest this imply some validity in the Cypriot accession process. Mr Denktaş also offered to overlook this difficulty if the trade embargoes on Turkish Cypriots were to be lifted. Two days before the seminar, Mr Holbrooke had further meetings in Cyprus with Mr Clerides and Mr Denktaş.

After the seminar Sina Şükrü Gürel, the Turkish minister for Cyprus, suggested that Mr Holbrooke's intervention might have made things worse. Mr Pangalos expressed furious opposition to Dayton-style mediation. At a Bildenburg meeting in Atlanta the following year, Holbrooke struck a more conciliatory attitude, ruling out 'a Dayton-like controlled negotiation environment' for Cyprus. On 3 May 1998 he reassured the *Cyprus Mail*, 'We can only listen to the two sides, see if the distances are bridgeable and reducible with external assistance – not imposition, not coercion'. President Clinton similarly claimed to be only a conciliator, not a mediator, during his swing through the region in November 1998 (McDonald, 2000: 9).

3. The United Kingdom

It would be wise therefore to recognise that we are still some way short of a consensus among the key players on how to handle the two sets of negotiations, those for a settlement in Cyprus and those for Cyprus' EU accession (Sir David Hannay, 1997: 11).

The British Government has a central role in both sets of negotiations, in those for accession as much as in those for a settlement. In the EU negotiations on accession, the UK is like Greece in being a member state with special interests in Cyprus. At a conference at the London School of Economics on 30 October 1996, Mr Wright of the Foreign Office said that 200,000 Cypriots live in Britain. Some 20,000 British residents live in the South of Cyprus and some 500 in the North. The British are the biggest contingent in the 2.06 million visitors to the Republic (*World Report on Cyprus*, 1998: 7).

Among the Internationals sponsoring a settlement, the UK is a 'key player' for three reasons that are independent of its status in the European Union. Britain is a Guarantor Power, a permanent member of the UN Security Council, and the sovereign power with respect to its two bases in Akrotiri and Dhekelia. Even more than was the case with Holbrooke, the prominence accorded by successive British governments to one individual in liaising with the other Internationals has testified to the importance they attach to this role. Sir David Hannay, GCMG, has been the United Kingdom's Permanent Representative in Brussels as well as Ambassador to the United Nations.

Guarantor Power
Since 1960 Britain has interpreted its Guarantor status as a source of rights that it can choose to exercise, (James, 1998:16) rather than duties it cannot avoid. In the crisis of 1963 the British Government and its High Commissioner in Cyprus did not back the German President of the Constitutional Court, nor oppose the Makarios amendments. The

obligations to protect human rights and the state of affairs established by the Constitution are not among the five objectives of British policy over Cyprus set out for its High Commissioner in Cyprus, David Hunt, on 23 December 1964. British interests were defined in terms of its own national security: to prevent a war that might disrupt NATO, to secure a solution acceptable to Greece and Turkey, to prevent Cyprus falling under neutralist or Soviet control, to retain British facilities in Cyprus and, fifthly, to retain the ability to fly over Turkey (Sonyel, 1997: 158). The British supported NATO plans to partition the island. When Mr Ecevit flew to London with his cabinet in July 1974, Britain would only agree to a protest that Article 78 of the Constitution was being flouted. Britain refused jointly agreed action under Article 4 of the Treaty of Guarantee. As has been shown above, Mr James Callaghan refused to contemplate any action to prevent the impending Turkish landings 'other than in the context of either the UN or a general American initiative' (Polyviou 1976: 327), two eventualities not included in the Treaty of Guarantee. After the Turkish landings, military plans for unilateral counter-intervention were not approved. After 1974, the policies of all British governments have sought to avoid any involvement in war on the island that might lead to loss of life by British civilians or military personnel. Planning for the evacuation of British citizens has greater priority than planning for intervention to restore the 'state of affairs' guaranteed by treaty. The British guarantee has also been complicated in the EU context by Harold Wilson's guarantees to Gibraltarians that they need not be united with Spain.

Both communities are therefore unwilling to regard the UK Guarantor Power as either a powerful or an honest broker. Despite their isolation in international fora, Turkish Cypriot leaders have not wanted Britain to represent or defend their interests in New York and Brussels. On the other side, the Greek Foreign Secretary, Mr Pangalos, on 3 July 1996, objected to the appointment of Sir David Hannay as the EU Special Representative on Cyprus. The UK, he said, had always been indifferent to the Turkish invasion and occupation of Cyprus.

Permanent member of the UN Security Council
As a permanent member of the UN Security Council, Britain has been influential in drafting all eighty-nine UN Security Council resolutions on

Cyprus. Its veto enables the UK to tone down suggestions not to its liking. This relic of Great Power status gives Britain and France greater influence in the United Nations than other similar states. The degree to which the two European permanent members co-ordinate their positions on Cyprus with each other and with the Commission seems to vary. For example, alarmed by the rearmament of Cyprus with Russian S-300 missiles, both countries implemented a Security Council resolution regretting the arms build-up in Cyprus by imposing an embargo on supplying spare parts for armaments to the Republic of Cyprus. Yet Britain alone continued its embargo through 1999, perhaps supporting American efforts to enforce Congressional restrictions dating from December 1987 on the deployment in Cyprus of weapons supplied to Turkey and Greece.

Sovereign of two bases

As a British civil servant, it is Sir David Hannay's job to keep the issue of British sovereignty over its two 'base areas' in Cyprus from becoming an item on Alvaro de Soto's negotiating agenda. Akrotiri has a long history as the biggest base of RAF Bomber Command and Transport Command. In 1956 it was the HQ for the attack on Suez, and in 1958 for aiding King Hussein in Jordan. In 1960 Cyprus became the British HQ for the Middle East. Both bases were important to CENTO. In 1961 Kuwait was reinforced from Cyprus. The March 1974 defence review, which withdrew the Vulcan bombers, saw no role for Dhekelia. Since July 1974, Dhekelia's proximity to the Green line makes it a refuge for British and other EC nationals in a time of crisis. Akrotiri has been useful to the UK's American ally as a storage facility that can be drawn on without reference to NATO, Arab or Cypriot governments. It was a key staging post during the Arab-Israeli wars and in 1990-1 for attacks on Iraq. The US Administration is credited with preventing British departure on the occasions when this was contemplated in 1974-5 and during the 1980s. The 1998 *Strategic Defence Review* ascribed an increasing importance to Cyprus. In addition to the ninety-nine square miles under UK sovereignty, since 1960 a dozen 'retained sites' have been leased from the Republic of Cyprus in the Troodos Mountains for eavesdropping on other states' communications. The bases are useful for aerial reconnaissance, logistics, as a depot for equipment, and for reassuring UN inspectors In Iraq that they can be got out quickly. The cost to the Treasury of keeping the bases and sites exceeds £200m per annum.

When Britain joined the EEC, the bases were not treated as sovereign in the sense of being unusually large embassy grounds in a third country. Article 227 specifically excluded the sovereign base areas from the British territories in Europe to which the Treaty of Rome applied. In consequence, the two bases are not shown on maps of the European Union. In the event of accession by the Republic of Cyprus, with or without a settlement, the North of Cyprus will be included on maps as the territory of a member state while Dhekelia and Akrotiri will not. The issue raised by this anomaly cuts deeper. Just as Portugal had to accept that its historic rights in Goa established by unequal treaties in colonial times could not withstand the Indian assertion of self-determination, so the UK will have to accept the priority accorded to the principle of self-determination in modern Europe. If Cyprus were reunited on the basis of its geographical unity as an island entity, the sovereignty claimed by the British over ninety-nine square miles would become a matter of dispute. Since the European Union's identity is based on physical rather than human geography, member states are more likely to think that the island should be one than to think that the British base areas are culturally or ethnically so different as to justify their separate status. The British Government's position that the sovereign base areas are non-negotiable therefore depends on the temporary willingness of both communities to avoid raising this issue while they are looking for American and British diplomatic support against the other side. For as long therefore as the British seek to keep the bases as their sovereign territory, this particular version of the national interest is better served by a negotiating process that is never concluded by a settlement.

4. The Russian Federation

In 1953 a conservative nationalist movement in Cyprus 'began the fatal course of fighting communism at home while seeking its support internationally' (Attalides, 1979: 35). However, Moscow seems to have throughout adopted a cautious view of any 'adventurist' Cuban-style schemes to acquire an island base without a modern harbour. In 1974, and generally, Moscow's consistent policy aimed at preventing Cyprus from becoming a NATO base. However, Moscow could offer an alternative to Turkish and Greek policy-makers disaffected with Washington. Cyprus was an important factor in Ankara's rapprochement with Moscow between the withdrawal of the Jupiter missiles in 1963 and the Brezhnev interventionist doctrine of 1967 (Aydın, 2000: 124); Cyprus was less important in Andreas Papandreou's attempt to be even-handed between the USSR and the West.

After the break-up of the Soviet Union, Russia was anxious to maintain its status as an important power in Europe and as a permanent member of the Security Council. Moreover, the 'new Russians' discovered a cultural identity with Cyprus as fellow-Orthodox. Russian residents for the first time came to both sides of Cyprus, attracted partly by Cypriot money-laundering facilities. The reality of the cultural link was shown in a common sympathy with Serbia.

The Russian Federation has appointed special representatives from Victor Bioko to Vladimir Prygin. They do not have to live in Cyprus because they are not 'permanent' representatives. In May, 1998 Sergei Lavrov, Ambassador to the UN, proposed to Kofi Annan a Russian plan for peace in Cyprus. Strongly supportive of Mr Clerides' demilitarisation, he suggested a UN-supervised four-party agreement that would allow Cyprus a unified coastguard and federal police force, plus two separate community police forces (Cyprus *Mail*, 3 May 1998). This followed sales to the Republic of T-80 tanks and S-300 missiles (*Cyprus News Agency*, 4 January 1997). The EU foreign ministers protested strongly about the Russian rearmament of Cyprus, while showing understanding for Greek rearmament as a legitimate response by the Greek government to new insecurities. The European Commission used the Council's acquiescence to justify flexibility in interpreting Greek obligations in EMU.

5. The Organisation for Security and Co-operation in Europe

Since 1989, the OSCE has developed out of the 1975 Conference for Security and Co-operation in Europe to become the principal monitoring agency of conflicts between groups and across borders in East, Central and South-East Europe. As he signed the Paris Charter for a New Europe on 19 November 1990 Mr Clerides told the OSCE Council:

> Cyprus cannot remain an anachronism in Europe, the only European
> country facing occupation by a foreign army, with its citizens denied
> the exercise of their fundamental rights and freedoms, even the
> freedom of movement and the enjoyment of property and its
> demographic structure altered through the massive implantation of
> settlers.

Despite this plea, and the occasional visits to Cyprus by a few members
of the OSCE Assembly, Max von der Stoel's Secretariat and the Council
have avoided getting involved in monitoring the problems of Cyprus.

One explanation is that the Organisation's usual task of confidential
reports to governments on its treatment of minorities is hardly relevant
to a situation where the Turkish Cypriots deny that they are a minority
and do not allow the Greek Cypriot Government to enter their zone. A
second reason is that the Member States of the European Union and the
USA may not want to involve an organisation in which Russia has
influence amounting to a veto. It may also be that the Secretariat does not
want to complicate its relations with Turkey and Greece in the Balkan
imbroglio.

6. The United Nations

[The Council of Ministers] confirms that the EU intends to continue to
support with all means at its disposal the United Nations' efforts to achieve a
comprehensive settlement (Council Conclusions, 6 March 1995).

The ambassadors of all the Member States hold a weekly caucus in New
York. Three member states sit in the Security Council, two as permanent
members and another as an elected member. The Commission has
Observer status at the General Assembly and with the UNHCR, the High
Commissioner for Refugees. On Cyprus there are 'close working
contacts between the EU and the UN Secretariat' (Hannay, 1997: 10).
To avoid getting involved in the successive crises since 1963, West
European governments 'used their influence that the solution of the
Cyprus conflict should be handed over to the United Nations' (Heinze,

1986: 13).

The overlap between the EU and UN positions on the nature of the Cyprus conflict is therefore considerable. The EU has adopted the UN formula that the purpose of a settlement is to re-establish the sovereignty, independence, territorial integrity and unity of the Republic of Cyprus (See Dublin European Council Declaration of 26 June 1990, Lisbon Conclusions, 27 June 1992, 16th meeting of EC-Cyprus Association Council of 14 May 1996). The EU agrees that the means must be through voluntary negotiation between two equal sides, neither of whom recognises the legitimacy claimed by the other. As all UN members, except Turkey, recognise the wholly Greek Government as entitled to rule over all Cyprus, the status accorded to the Government by the UN is greater than that accorded to the Turkish Cypriots. The Security Council of the UN has attempted to resolve the contradiction by mandating its senior official, the Secretary-General to bring the parties together in talks on the basis of equality as communities to re-establish the unity of the Republic. The Secretary-General is also responsible for deciding every six months whether to recommend to the Security Council that the mandate for the UN peacekeeping force, UNFICYP, be renewed, with the consent of the Government and the acquiescence of the unrecognised Turkish Cypriot authorities. After four decades:

> Cyprus has become a UN metaphor for a conflict that no one can resolve, that drags on for ever, but that isn't too troublesome and can be more or less ignored *(International Herald Tribune,* 13 February, 1997).

The European governments have been heavily involved in all three aspects of the UN involvement — in drafting resolutions, in supporting the good offices of the Secretary-General, and in peacekeeping.

UN Resolutions

> The Council of Ministers... calls upon all parties to achieve a comprehensive settlement of the Cyprus question in accordance with UN Security Council resolutions, based on the concept of a bi-communal and bi-zonal Federation (Council Conclusions, 6 March 1995).

All EU statements about settling the Cyprus issue refer to UN resolutions. Not to do so would provoke strong protests from the governments of Greece and the Republic of Cyprus. The eighty-nine resolutions of the Security Council and the seventeen resolutions of the General Assembly on the Cyprus dispute have further marginalised the Turkish Cypriots in the international community.

From the perspective of the Internationals, four resolutions of the UN Security Council have been of particular importance. In 1964 the Security Council in its Resolution of 4 March (UNSC 186) recognised the wholly Greek Cypriot Government as the Government of the Republic. On 20 July 1974 the UN Security Council passed in UNSC 353 the first of a series of resolutions that call for the withdrawal of 'foreign military personnel'. While not condemning the right of Turkey to intervene under the terms of the Treaty of Guarantee, Turkey is reminded that this right is limited to upholding 'the sovereignty, independence and territorial integrity of Cyprus'. The Security Council in this resolution chose not to refer to the unusual limitations on that sovereignty written into the 1960 Constitution under which Cyprus had been accepted into the UN by the General Assembly. In Cyprus, the sovereignty of the people does not mean that the majority can give themselves a new Constitution; the sovereignty of the state is limited in that each of three external states can legally intervene to restore the balance prescribed by the founding treaties without being invited in by the Cypriot Government. The third important resolution is UNSC 541, which condemned the attempt to create a 'Turkish Republic of Northern Cyprus'. The formula of a 'bi-communal bizonal federation' contained in this as in all UNSC resolutions since 1975 rules out Turkish Cypriot proposals for a confederation because confederation presupposes the prior existence of separate states. Perhaps mention should also be made of the UN Security Council's concern over the arms build up in Cyprus and the region. In December 1998 it passed Resolution 1218, which demanded 'a staged process aimed at limiting and then substantially reducing the level of all troops and armaments in Cyprus'.

The resolutions of the General Assembly also range over many subjects, such as the fate of refugees and missing persons, the threats to cultural heritage and the environment. They too reflect the views of the Government side, giving priority to the recognised sovereignty of

Cyprus over the constitutional restrictions on the exercise of that sovereignty. For example, Resolution 2077 of 18 December 1965 stands out precisely because it notes the Government's intent to protect human rights and minority rights, at a time when the human rights of the Turkish Cypriots were under severe pressure from the Greek Cypriot Government. Yet the purpose of that resolution was less to safeguard the Turkish Cypriot community than to help the Government preserve itself from the partition plans being mooted by the USA, NATO, and both motherlands.

When the European Union, or other Internationals like the G8, call for talks without pre-conditions in accordance with UNSC or UN resolutions, they are therefore imposing conditions which the Turkish Cypriots have reason to think would leave them exposed to the domination of the majority community— the withdrawal of the Turkish army and a federal government in which Greek Cypriots would have the major say. Rightly or wrongly, these resolutions have been used in Court jurisprudence as though they were expressions of a World Government, which both European Courts have treated as law. As shown above, in the Anastasiou case, the European Court of Justice held that the European Community had a legal duty to respect the injunction in UNSC 550/1984 'not to facilitate or in any way assist the aforesaid secessionist entity'. In the Loizidou case, the European Court of Human Rights relied on the same and subsequent UN Resolutions as sufficient evidence 'that the international community does not regard the 'TRNC' as a State under international law and that the Republic of Cyprus has remained the sole legitimate Government of Cyprus'.

However, the implementation of international resolutions in the face of strong local opposition requires the mobilisation of great forces. The American and European governments that were willing to fight the large Iraqi army in defence of the Emir's right to rule Kuwait did not want to send troops against their Turkish ally on behalf of the Republic of Cyprus. As Turkey became more influential also in the General Assembly, it became increasingly difficult to secure the passage of anti-Turkish resolutions in either of the political bodies of the United Nations. As an American ally, Turkey could not be treated in the UN context as a pariah state like Iraq. The Turkish Cypriots were not treated in UN resolutions as outlaws. United Nations sponsorship of negotiations between the two communities was not intended to be about the terms of Turkish Cypriot surrender to the legally recognised authorities. The objective was political, a settlement for Cyprus that was acceptable to both communities and their motherlands.

The good offices of the UN Secretary-General

> The Council of Ministers... regrets the lack of progress in the intercommunal talks taking place under the auspices of the UN Secretary-General considers... that the developments noted in the last few months have enabled elements which could be useful for defining an agreement to be identified (Council Conclusions, 6 March 1995).

Kurt Waldheim wrote in his memoirs that Cyprus 'took up more of my time and attention...than any other confrontation' (Waldheim, 1980: 78). He had hoped to repeat his personal triumph in ending the Austrian dispute with Italy over the Alto Adige/Tyrol. Perez de Cuellar knew Cyprus well because he had been the Special Representative before he became Secretary-General. He contributed three proposals in 1985-6 and offered 'food for thought' in 1989. Boutros Boutros Ghali's 1992 'Set of Ideas' and 'non-map' are widely regarded as the basis of any settlement. His special representative, Diego Cordovez, had himself negotiated the departure of Russian troops from Afghanistan. He continued to be special adviser to the incoming Secretary-General, Kofi Annan.

At European Summits and meetings of the EEC-Cyprus Association Council, the Member States and the Commission invariably express their support for this work of the Secretary-General of the United Nations in bringing together the leaders of the two Cypriot communities for talks under his aegis. Behind the scenes, there are frequent meetings between EU, UN and US officials. Russia and the Presidents of the European Commission and Council attend the summit of the G8 leading industrial countries. It was used in June 1999 to express the view of the international community that Mr Denktaş and Mr Clerides should attend proximity talks in New York with Mr Alvaro De Soto, the deputy special representative of UN Secretary-General Kofi Annan.

At the same time, the UN side has made some informed if muted criticisms of the ill effects of European Union actions. In September

1990, UN Secretary-General Boutros Boutros Ghali gave a tepid welcome to the Cypriot application, and his successors have also let it be known that the process of Cypriot accession to the EU has impeded the task of bringing the two communities to a settlement. Echoing American diplomats, the EU is criticised for having removed any incentive for the Greek Cypriot side to seek a settlement, and for having further alienated the Turkish Cypriot leadership. Boutros Ghali's suggestion in the 'Set of Ideas' that separate referenda on accession to the EU be held in the two zones could be seen as a way of torpedoing the process through a negative vote in the North. France objected in the Security Council that the UN had no competence to determine matters internal to the EU (Axt & Brey, 1997: 180). Having brought the two community leaders face to face in 1997 at Troutbeck and Glion, the UN negotiators were frustrated by Mr Denktaş' refusal to discuss a comprehensive package unless the Greek Cypriots withdrew their unilateral application for EU membership. On 12 October 1998, Diego Cordovez as Kofi Annan's special representative gave a speech in London ascribing some blame for the impasse to the European Union. In 1999 - 2000 the UN proximity talks had such poor prospects of success that their purpose seemed rather to convince those EU member states opposed to taking on a divided island that no settlement could be negotiated.

The underlying reason for the frustration of the UN Secretariat was, however, that they had insufficient levers to persuade either side that a settlement with the other was better than the status quo. The Greek Cypriots could hope that with the backing of Greece and the UN, their promised membership of the EU would one day give them the clout to force Turkey to withdraw its troops. The Turkish Cypriots could hope that, with the backing of Turkey, they would eventually be recognised as the rulers of North Cyprus.

The 'recognition' issue bedevils the UN effort. The difficulty in setting up meetings between equal sides when the UN itself is committed not to 'in any way assist the aforesaid secessionist entity' is met by going for 'proximity' talks in which both sides talk to the UN but not to each other. The Greek Cypriots will not agree small packages of 'confidence-building measures' which imply recognition of 'the purported state of the "TRNC"'. The Turkish Cypriots will not flesh out the outline proposals of 1977, 1979 or 1992 if that implies recognition of the 'usurped title of

Government of Cyprus'. The internationals have therefore come to agree with the UN Secretariat that the negotiations must be on the basis of a comprehensive package in which nothing is agreed until everything is agreed. If that sounds difficult enough, in order to prevent the package unravelling in disputes over implementation, the legal text constructed by the Secretariat has to be so detailed that it will be self-executing in the sense of requiring no further negotiations.

The powers accorded by the UN to its Secretary-General seem insufficient for this task. Since 1968 his mandate has been limited to bringing the parties together as a conciliator. His representative's role is to shuttle between the parties to ascertain their views, bring them to accept an agenda, and invite them to negotiate. No UN official can propose a solution as a mediator, and still less impose a solution as an arbitrator. In 1965 the first and only attempt at UN mediation proved unacceptable to Turkey. Galo Plaza, the mediator and former President of Ecuador, rejected the federal bizonal solution favoured by US Secretary Dean Acheson. His report was notable for setting out the understanding of modernity held by Third World States (Attalides, 1979: 20). He recommended a unitary state with a UN resident Commissioner to monitor the rights of what he saw as the Turkish Cypriot minority.

Given the related difficulties of arranging meetings and reaching a comprehensive settlement, it remains to attempt an explanation of the European Commission's 1993 Opinion that it agreed with the United Nations that all the elements were present if there were sufficient will. The corollary is that the failure to combine these elements in a solution is due to the intransigence of the two leaders on the island. In March 1995 the Council claimed that useful elements had been identified. Two years later, on 8 July 1997, the UN Resident Representative in Cyprus, Gustave Feissel, deputy to Cordovez, told the *Voice of America* that the pieces were prepared if the two leaders would shape them to fit together. Pleased that Mr Clerides and Mr Denktaş were making their first direct contact in nearly three years, Feissel told listeners:

> Not only do we know in Cyprus what the ultimate solution is going to look like, we also have, on the table, so to speak, all the pieces that are needed to work out this settlement. So, what is needed now is for the two leaders to say, ok, let's get on with it, and then to take

all these bits and pieces that have been worked out and shape them into an overall settlement.

The ultimate solution, to adopt Feissel's unfortunate phrase, would build on the 1992 Set of Ideas. A form of words would fudge the differing views on sovereignty on the lines of the 1992 preamble:

> The Cyprus settlement is based on a State of Cyprus with a single sovereignty and international personality and a single citizenship, with its independence and territorial integrity safeguarded, and comprising two equal communities...in a bicommunal and bizonal federation, and that the settlement must exclude union in whole or in part with any other country or any form of partition or secession.

Once both leaders wanted a settlement, all they had to do was to balance their options. The more the Government side wanted strong central powers, the less the territory they could expect to be returned to the Greek Cypriot zone. The less the territory returned, the greater would be the problem of compensating Greek Cypriots unable to return to their pre-1974 homes.

This left the issue of how to reduce the numbers of Turkish troops and phase in some kind of international police force which could monitor the behaviour of the local police anywhere on the island:

> [This last] issue of security is perhaps the single most important issue for both sides. So, in many ways one of the dilemmas that we have is that what makes one side feel secure, is what makes the other side feel insecure. So we have to find an arrangement in security which will obviously respond to both concerns (Hannay, 1997: 9).

UN Peacekeeping

The UN has a 'Status of Forces' agreement with the Government of Cyprus. Every six months, when the Security Council renews the UNFICYP mandate, it notes the agreement of the Government of Cyprus. Until recently, the Turkish Cypriots have been content with the fiction that UN troops are 'honoured guests', who will not be billed for water and electricity and from whom no formal agreement is expected.

They have been prepared to give a warmer welcome to the UN than the EU for three reasons. The Turkish Cypriots regarded UN soldiers as their saviours between 1964 and 1974. Secondly, the Turkish army respects the UN flag; the local commander did not take Nicosia airport in 1974 because it was occupied by British forces flying the UN flag. Thirdly, the international presence on the Green Line requires the Greek Cypriot Government to respect the border as a cease-fire line. In the summer of 2000 the Turkish Cypriot authorities, supported by Turkey, became locked in an escalating struggle over the 'recognition' aspect of UNFICYP's mandate, which may finally provoke its non-renewal.

The British and French are also at odds in the Security Council over the usefulness of UN troops in Cyprus. Since UNFICYP was established in March 1964 168 UN peacekeepers have died. The British contribute at their own expense 750 soldiers. This is a high proportion of the total force of 1,219, plus 35 police and 234 other civilians (UNSG, 1999). The French refuse to contribute to UNFICYP, and Sweden withdrew its contingent in 1987. In 1998/9 the Cypriot Government paid only $349,151 to the regular UN budget. Yet it contributes $14.5m to the appropriation for UNFICYP of $45.3m. Greece contributes a further $6.5m. The EU-15 contributes 37.9 per cent of the separate UN budget for peacekeeping (EU Council, 1997: 2).

7. The Council of Europe

The Parliamentary Assembly

Unlike the United Nations, the Assembly of Western Europe's parliamentarians for two decades did not accept the substitution of a wholly Greek Cypriot House of Representatives for the bi-communal democracy ordained by the Constitution. When Cyprus joined in 1961, the Cypriot delegation to Strasbourg comprised two representatives and substitutes appointed by Greek Cypriot parliamentarians, and one representative and one substitute appointed by Turkish Cypriot parliamentarians. In April 1964 the Assembly of European parliamentarians refused to accept the credentials of a delegation of three Greek Cypriot substitutes. In 1966 it resolved that Cyprus is composed of two minorities (Bağcı in Axt & Brey, 1997: 163 fn). Until 1984 therefore, Cyprus was not represented in the Assembly until the Greek

Cypriot government was able to turn to its advantage the unilateral declaration of the separate statehood of the TRNC. On 23 November 1983, the Assembly rejected the 'unilateral declaration of independence of the northern part of Cyprus'. On the next day a resolution on Cyprus could not be adopted at the Committee of Ministers where six states voted against and a number abstained. In May 1984 the Assembly ratified the credentials of one Greek Cypriot representative and one substitute. It reserved one representative seat and one substitute for the Turkish Cypriot community but declared that members of the TRNC Parliament were ineligible. In 1986 the Greek Cypriot representative was allowed to take his seat. Every year Turkey voices a reservation without raising a formal objection. Turkish Cypriot parliamentarians are allowed to address the political groups. The 1995 Finsberg Report to the Assembly was frank about the hostility between the two communities, treating the Government as legitimate while reporting the views of the leaders of the Turkish minority. Lord Finsberg suggested that representatives of the communities be invited on an *ad hoc* basis to committee meetings while refraining from any action recognising the 'entity in the occupied part of Cyprus'. The Assembly has heard other reports on Cyprus, notably the Cucó report on the demographic structure of the Cypriot communities.

Human Rights
The European Convention on Human Rights allows states to complain of violations to the European Commission of Human Rights. The Commission reports on the eligibility and merits of each application. It may refer the case either to the Court of Human Rights or to the Committee of Ministers, constituted by ministers from each of forty-one member states of the Council of Europe. The Republic of Cyprus has submitted four complaints against Turkey, in 1974, 1975, 1977 and 1994. Three complaints by individual Cypriots were allowed after 1987, the year when Turkey signed up to the Additional Protocol enabling individuals also to take their complaints to Strasbourg. In 1990 Turkey further accepted that the Court could take any cases that the Commission deemed admissible.

Two Court judgements in 1995 and 1996 on the case brought by Mrs Titina Loizidou weighted the stance taken by the Commission of Human

Rights and by the pan-European Committee of Ministers even more heavily in favour of the Republic of Cyprus. On the first two governmental applications, the Committee of Ministers had decided on 21 October 1977 that 'events' in Cyprus had violated the Convention, and 'urged the parties to resume intercommunal talks'. On the third application, ministers took until 2 April 1992 to complete their consideration of the case by merely making public the Commission's report of 1983, which itself had found Turkey in breach of three articles of the Convention. On 19 October 1995 the Committee of Ministers confirmed the findings of the Commission in the joined cases brought by two individuals, Metropolitan Chrysostomos, and Archimandrite Georgios Papachrysostomou. The Commission had found no violation of the Convention, except that the Archimandrite's right to respect for his private life had been infringed. 'Part of the reasoning in the Commission's above Report was based on the consideration that Turkey could not be held responsible under the Convention for acts of the Turkish Cypriot authorities in northern Cyprus' (EComHR, 1999: Paragraph 15).

However, the Court of Human Rights in Strasbourg took a different view of the status of the parties in its preliminary and full judgements in the third case brought by an individual, that of Mrs Titina Loizidou. Like the Commission it rejected Turkey's contention that the Republic of Cyprus had no authority to act because its Government was not bi-communal. However, unlike the Commission, the Court ruled:

> As a consequence of military action - whether lawful or unlawful - Turkey exercises effective control of an area outside its national territory, whether such control is exercised directly, through its armed forces, or through a subordinate local administration (ECHR, 1996 Paragraph 52, p. 2234).

It awarded $900,000 in damages, including psychological damage, and costs against Turkey for infringing the rules governing military occupation under the relevant Geneva Convention. This judgement was not unanimous. Turkish Cypriot lawyers criticise it for over-reliance on the political resolutions of the UN Security Council without proper judicial examination of the TRNC claim to be a sovereign state and not a subordinate administration (Necatigil, 1999 and Ertekün, 1999). They also dispute the admission of a claim by individuals dating from events in 1974, thirteen years before Turkey conceded to individuals the right to complain under the Convention. Turkish Cypriot lawyers point out that the Court's view that the TRNC is a 'subordinate local administration' undermines the route to a political settlement under UN auspices through talks between equal communities, which the TRNC itself insists should now be treated as two sides represented by equal governments.

The Commission in its report of 4 June 1999 on the fourth state application against Turkey (25781/94) followed the Court's lead. In October 1999 the Committee of Ministers censured Turkey for non-compliance with the judgement. On 24 July 2000, all its members except Turkey declared that Turkey's refusal to comply with the 1996 judgement was unprecedented and in manifest disregard of its international obligations. The political effect of this pan-European support for the Court's decision puts Turkey under heavy pressure to resolve the issue. Other cases are in the pipeline. More important, Turkey's efforts to establish a respectable profile on human rights by internal reform and signing up to the two 1966 UN Conventions are undermined by being held responsible for Greek Cypriot property in northern Cyprus.

The Framework Convention
The Council of Europe's Framework Convention for the protection of National Minorities came into force in February 1998. It affirms that the protection of minorities is an integral part of human rights, and that therefore is not the exclusively domestic concern of individual states but a legitimate concern of the international community.

In reporting on the unique complexity and multiplicity of the safeguards provided for the 'principal minority' by its own Constitution, the Government of Cyprus puts the entire blame for its unworkability on the Turkish Cypriot leadership (ROC, 1999: 3). The Government is presently 'prevented by armed force from exercising authority and control and ensuring implementation and respect of human rights in the occupied area' (ROC, 1999: 7).

8. NATO and WEU

Cypriot politics have been deeply affected by the relationship between Greece and Turkey in European security organisations. As the credibility of NATO would be devastated if war between Greece and Turkey broke up its Southern flank, NATO has been the forum for reconciling their conflicts of interest. The agreement on Cypriot independence was an agreement between the Menderes government and the Karamanlis government, to which was added a six-clause bilateral agreement to co-operate against the Communist party of AKEL and to bring Cyprus within the NATO area (James, 1998: 13). NATO meetings, such as that in Lisbon in June 1971 and the Madrid meeting of Demirel and Simitis in 1996, have been the occasion for elite promises to foster harmony between governments despite the popular antagonisms over Cyprus and the Aegean. NATO even had a role in negotiations that appear to include a Greek promise in 1981 not to oppose Turkey's membership of the European Union, well before the application of 1987:

> General Rogers had obtained Turkey's withdrawal of its Notam no. 714, an air traffic regulation announcement requiring all planes crossing a median line in the Aegean during flights to the Turkish mainland to report to the Turkish authorities. This was a measure imposed during the 1974 Cyprus crisis, and it was understood to be part of the [1981] arrangement for removing it that Greece would not oppose Turkey's membership in Europe (sic); this understanding did not translate into reality (İhsanoglu in Karpat ed.,1984: 94).

For the most part, Turkey has been the more influential of the two countries in the NATO context. Its role is more important to NATO because of the size of its army and because of its geographical position. The United States has seven bases and twenty-one other sites in Turkey; its out-of-area operations in Iraq have been mounted from İncirlik. From the perspective of the American military, Turkey is crucial to any military or surveillance operations involving Israel, Iran or Central Asia. The oil routes from Central Asia, whether through the Black Sea or through Ceyhan, depend on Turkish goodwill. Turkey has an army comparable in size to that of France and Germany. Subjectively, NATO has been unpopular in Greece because of its relationship with the junta that led Karamanlis to withdraw Greek forces from its organisation, because of the anti-Americanism of the populist Papandreou government, and because of NATO's anti-Serb line in the Balkans. However Turkey has had its moments of disaffection also, over the Johnson letter of 1964, and Congressional sanctions against Turkey's troops in Cyprus. Now that NATO no longer has a collective security role, and the USA has ceased to provide military aid, Turkey has other options. It might choose to become independent of NATO constraints either as a Western power linked to Israel and the USA but not Europe, or as identified with Islamic civilisation in Central Asia as well as in the Balkans, or as linked with the Russian Federation in an alliance of dissatisfied 'outs'.

The European Security and Defence Identity

If there were to be an international force based in Cyprus as part of a settlement, Turks are likely to prefer a NATO force. For example, in November 1997 the Turkish Cypriot newspaper *Birlik* suggested that an expanded UN zone extending to Morphou might be policed by NATO troops (*Cyprus News Agency* 16 November 1997). Greeks, on the other hand, would look for a force answerable to the Western European Union. Once again, the root of the divergence lies in the fact that Greece, but not Turkey, is a full member of the European Union.

One of the compromises at the treaty of Maastricht was over the question of whether the European Union was capable of taking and implementing military decisions independently of the United States of America. The British, whose spending per capita on defence is second in the EU only to that of Greece, saw an American-led NATO as the only viable framework for both reaching decisions and mobilising resources. The French thought otherwise, and succeeded in aligning the membership of the Western European Union, a body excluding the USA, with that of the EU. Greece threatened to veto the Maastricht treaty if its status in the WEU were not raised to that of a full member like the other EU members.

This left Turkey as an Associate member, like Norway and Iceland, states which are members of NATO but not of the EU. Turkey's response, besides asserting the primacy of NATO, was to improve its status in WEU by offering to participate in planning exercises. For example, General Karadayı, after a meeting with other chiefs of staff in Bonn, on 29 October 1997 claimed that 'Turkey effectively takes its place in Western European Union's military structure at the highest level' (*TKRNWS -L*, 30 October 1997). France persuaded different member states to create the Strasbourg based Eurocorps in 1992, and the Florence-based Euroforce in 1995. After their experience of European inadequacy and American unwillingness to engage in ground operations during their joint intervention in Kosovo, the British Labour Government joined with France in the Helsinki Conclusions, promising British participation in another force of 60,000 men to be trained for intervention on the ground after 2003. The Republic of Cyprus offered 50 men as its contribution to this European peacekeeping force. At least as significant as the preparation of combat units is the progress made towards a capacity for taking decisions without relying on American leadership. The Europeanisation of NATO has been accompanied by the growth in informal, and now considerable, links between the headquarters of the EU, WEU and NATO in Brussels. The same EU foreign ministers who meet as the General Affairs Council are, together with defence ministers, members of the WEU Council and ten of them are on the NATO Council. The permanent representatives on COREPER will be briefed on any NATO angle by their home ministries. The unit of the EU Council Secretariat now responsible for preparing political co-operation in foreign and defence affairs under General Secretary Javier Solana is necessarily informed of NATO concerns. Solana's visit to Cyprus in 1999 may therefore be the precursor to greater EU willingness, with or without American troops, to maintain a joint force on the island available to back up whatever security forces are established in a settlement.

9. Organisation of the Islamic Conference (OIC)

The secular republic of Turkey has never signed the charter of this organisation set up by conservative Muslim kings outraged by the 1969 arson of the al-Aqsa mosque in Jerusalem. However, after the 1973 oil crisis OIC loans as a expression of Muslim solidarity became important to Ankara. Turkey's prominent role in the OIC has ended Turkey's diplomatic isolation at the UN to the point where it is a candidate for election to the Security Council.

Nevertheless Turkey's sponsorship of the TRNC in this forum has so far been rewarded with only limited success. Mr Denktaş addressed the OIC summit meeting in 1975. Since the 1976 meeting in Istanbul every meeting has been attended by a delegation from Northern Cyprus. Northern Cyprus has been accorded Observer status since 1979. It has received a subsidy since 1980. However, despite assurances of solidarity, the OIC has steadfastly refused to recognise the sovereignty of the TRNC. The 1983 conference in Dacca welcomed 'the Turkish Islamic community's determination not to unite with any country and to join a federal union with the Greek community in Cyprus'. The expansion of the OIC to take in the newly independent Turkic republics of Central Asia has so far made no difference.

10. The Commonwealth

The Greek Cypriot Government has represented Cyprus since 1963, actively and successfully campaigning for supportive resolutions. At the Edinburgh summit in 1997, for example, the Heads of Government called for 'the sovereignty, independence, territorial integrity and unity of the republic of Cyprus' (Paragraph 22). The fifty-four states 'expressed concern about recent threats of use of force and integration of the occupied territory by Turkey and reiterated support for President Clerides' demilitarisation proposal'. The Commonwealth leaders had agreed beforehand to appoint an envoy to Cyprus, the deputy secretary for political affairs, Krishnan Srinivasan, who had been foreign secretary of India. In 1999 the Commonwealth strongly supported the call by the G8 summit in Cologne of the richest industrialised nations for both Cypriot communities to attend the talks that the UN was being pressured to hold in New York.

11. The Non-Aligned Movement

Cyprus must also give up its membership of the Non-Aligned Movement of which it was a founder-member and in which it continues to participate actively (1993 Commission Opinion on Cyprus, Paragraph 22).

At the height of the Cold War, Makarios depicted Cyprus as central to a bloc of Non-Aligned states in the Mediterranean extending from Tito's Yugoslavia to Nasser's Egypt. Surprisingly, the TRNC committed itself in its Constitution to membership of the Non-Aligned Movement.

However, while NATO has expanded since the end of the Cold War, non-alignment like neutrality has become less salient. Since 1992 all the neutral member states have accepted Observer status in the WEU and agreed at least not to obstruct the development of a common foreign and security policy. 'It seems that Cyprus will have no problem abandoning the Non-Aligned Movement before or upon accession to the European Union' (Joseph, 1997: 119).

12. Conclusions

> Cyprus is and always has been a pawn in the great game of geopolitics (Michael Stephen, 1999: 78).

Both communities have reason to be suspicious of the Internationals. The Turkish Cypriots think that the Third World, the British, the Americans and the Russians combined against them at the United Nations to recognise the Greek Cypriots as the sole Government of Cyprus. The international embargo on contact with Northern Cyprus has increased their dependency on Turkey. The Greek Cypriots are equally convinced that the Turkish invasion was condemned in name only because the West needed Turkish support against the USSR and, since 1989, in the Balkans, Central Asia and Iraq. Hitherto most of the international organisations and the states that count have sided more with the Greek Cypriot Government, and are unlikely to admit that they themselves have been in the wrong for three decades. On the other hand, the Turks can expect their long-run greater importance to the USA, to Europe and in the Organisation of Islamic countries to redress the balance to the advantage of themselves and their Cypriot protégé.

There is no 'team' of Internationals in which the European Union plays a supporting role. However, the accession of Cyprus and the accession of Turkey to the European Union are the most powerful levers available to influence the parties to accept an externally devised settlement that, unlike the present *status quo*, can be put to both sides of the Cypriot dispute for them to accept, or not, by referendum.

| 7 |

Conclusions

Perhaps the most important task facing the European Union today is coming up with a new and genuinely clear reflection on what might be called European identity, a new and genuinely clear articulation of European responsibility, an intensified interest in the very meaning of European integration in all its wider implications for the contemporary world (Vaclav Havel to the European Parliament, March 8 1994).

The enlargement to Central and Eastern Europe is infinitely more important to the European Union than the accession of Cyprus. However, enlargement according to Vaclav Havel is less important than new answers to the questions of European identity, responsibility and integration. These three questions are just as relevant to the Cyprus problem, whether or not Cyprus is understood as important in its own right or merely as a hurdle to be surmounted if Greece is to vote for the unification of Eastern with Western Europe.

European identity
What Havel had in mind by a new European identity was the return to Europe of Central and Eastern Europeans, excluding Russians at least for the moment and Turks for the foreseeable future. His concept of Europe is close to that of a unified Europe of which the Founding Fathers had dreamed, articulated for example in the books of the Swiss writer, Denis

de Rougemont. After the unnatural division of Europe on ideological and power political lines, a shared if fragmented political culture would provide the basis of unifying European states as German culture had underpinned German unification in 1870 and reunification in 1990.

The alternative is that of a multicultural identity. Immigration from the Indian sub-continent, from North Africa and from Turkey has brought in millions of Muslims. If Muslims are not to be second-class citizens because of their religion and culture, then applications to join the European Union cannot be excluded on racial or cultural grounds, whether from Turkey, Israel, Morocco or Serbia. This argument is all the stronger with respect to Turkey because it has been a European Associate of the Community since 1960; the decision to grant Associate status to Cyprus in 1971 was not affected by the Islamic culture and religion of its Turkish Cypriot community. According to this concept, European physical geography is more important than either human geography or cultural origins. The boundaries and content of political Europe are more a product of *Bildung,* the deliberate decision of political authorities, than of a pre-existing cultural community seeking to form itself into a political society. The unanimous decision by member states whether to accept any application from a European state is largely a matter for pragmatism. No map of Europe was attached to the Treaty of Rome. Each separate existing member state has to decide whether it is in its national interest to open accession negotiations, to conclude negotiations and then to ratify the results according to its own constitutional procedures. In the case of Turkey, Greece would not be the only member state to insist that its membership is conditional on a settlement of the Cyprus conflict. The Greek decision on whether it is in their interests to include Turkey as the second most populous European state or to exclude Turkey as an enemy state has been critical to the Helsinki summit's decision to accept Turkey's candidature. The attitude taken by Greece will be crucial to the decision to open negotiations, and influential on the length of time that the negotiations will take. All member states and Turkey are likely to negotiate on the basis that there will be a long period of transition before Turkey fully adopts the *acquis*, can sell its agricultural produce without restriction, and accepts the budget balancing disciplines of Euroland.

President Havel also had a special interest in the relationship between national identity and any new concept of European identity. The return to nationalism after the Cold War had broken up his own state of Czechoslovakia into the Czech and Slovak Republics. It took place by mutual agreement, the 'velvet divorce'. In Yugoslavia, a common Serbo-Croat language had not been enough to prevent the dissolution of the state. European recognition of Croatia and Slovenia precipitated a bitter struggle on ethnic lines over Bosnia. Serbia's failure to intimidate the Kosovars led in reality to the Albanian separation from what remained of the Yugoslav Federation. A return to the pattern of power politics between nation-states had become one distinct possibility, with Germany treating Central Europe as its own sphere, eventually provoking France and Russia to combine against it. In this Europe of separate national interests, the expression of European identity would be limited to discussion groups like the Council of Europe and the OECD.

The alternative concept is of a pan-European identity less robust than national identity but sufficient firstly to pay the costs of European unification and secondly to keep the peace. There is little point to Europeans condemning Hitler's attacks on Jews and gypsies if Europe cannot collectively protect individuals and groups from being beaten up because of their religion or ethnic origins. It is at least arguable that, if West Europeans had been prepared to raise taxes to provide hard currency of Marshall Plan proportions for the countries in transition, the Serbian leaders might have found more peaceable outlets for their unemployed youth. The development of a pan-European responsibility and capacity is the only alternative to Germany playing the kind of national leadership role in Europe that America fulfils for the 'free world'.

European responsibility

In Cyprus, both before and after 1974, the consensus among statesmen and Eurocrats has been that the problem between communities was a matter to be left to them and the United Nations. The Member States of the EEC were post-imperial. They would not risk the lives of their own citizens and soldiers in intervention that went beyond the successive peacekeeping mandates of UNFICYP and the convening of meetings by the UN Secretary-General. The institutions of the European Union do not have the personnel or the will to draw up or impose the terms under which the island might be jointly ruled by two communities still engaged in mutual recrimination after their bloody divorce. No blame could be attached to European officials for the failure of the two communities to reach agreement under the auspices of the United Nations. They would be at fault if they tried to be a Superpower, imposing a settlement that would at best be difficult to implement. There was no point in attempting even-handed treatment of the two communities. An unrecognised and unhelpful Turkish Cypriot leadership would not co-operate; if it did co-operate, this would raise difficulties for EU officials of principle and timing in relation to the accession of Cyprus and therefore for other applicants in the first wave. Any serious attempt to deal with them as equals would make trouble in Nicosia for the EU Delegation and lead to vehement Greek protest in Brussels without bringing a settlement any closer. The argument for continuing with the accession and ignoring the ineffective alienation of Turkish Cypriots could be tempered by the usual invocation of Eurocrats that a lot of water would have to flow under the bridge before the accession of a divided island became a reality.

The alternative analysis is that the two Cypriot communities are too deadlocked to come to any bilateral agreement. Each is so strongly supported by its respective motherland that it has no need to reach agreement with the other community. Within each community, the domestic consensus, on which each leader relies, would be disrupted rather than consolidated by a settlement that compromised enough of each side's claims to be worth putting to separate referenda. Each community is resentful about both the actions and the inaction of the international community. The Turkish Cypriots consider that they have not been treated even-handedly, that they were not sufficiently protected by UNFICYP before 1974, and that since 1974 they have been penalised by an effective embargo for refusing to subordinate themselves to what they fear remains a hostile majority. Greek sponsorship of the Greek Cypriot application to the EU has increased the sense of alienation and consequent dependence on Turkey. The Greek Cypriot side resents the imposition of a Constitution giving undue privileges to a minority, and the failure since 1974 of the international community to remove the Turkish army by means of diplomatic, economic or military pressures.

On this analysis, the keys that could open the locked door to a solution are held by the motherlands. In 1960 the Greek and Turkish foreign ministers chose to make an agreement between themselves, giving priority to their common interests as members of NATO. The failure of the Constitution was not due to the imposition of an unworkable bicommunal arrangement by outsiders. The Constitution was accepted by the leadership of both communities, and by the Greek and Turkish electors who participated in electing their representatives on separate communal lists. What made the difference was a change of government in one of the motherlands. The Papandreou government supported, instead of restraining, President Makarios in his amendments undermining the bicommunality of the Constitution. The objective was to open the way for the Greek Cypriot majority to fulfil its desire to unite with Greece in breach of the treaties. This bold nationalism undermined those in Ankara who had restrained the Turkish Cypriot nationalists who had armed themselves to resist *enosis* and secure self-rule in a partitioned Cyprus.

Greek membership of the European Union has given Greece the power to turn both keys in whichever direction it chooses. In 1990 and 1995 it turned its own key unilaterally against any accommodation with Turkish and Turkish Cypriot views by sponsoring the membership application of the Republic of Cyprus. It may have hoped that this determination not to appease Turkey would one day lead Turkey into withdrawing its forces from Northern Cyprus under the combined pressure of the EU, the UN and the United States. The Turkish key could then rust away. Such a policy is analogous to Greek support for Greek Cypriot independence before 1959. In 1960 the British withdrew most of their conscripts from Cyprus.

The alternative Greek policy would be to recognise that Turkish military and economic power is so great, particularly given its geographical proximity to Cyprus, that it will not withdraw its identification with the Turkish Cypriots. Moreover, it is not in the interests of either the Greek Cypriots or Greece to have Turkey progress in either a fundamentalist or an independently nationalist direction. If Turkey remains in NATO and becomes either a prospective or actual member of the EU, then its foreign policy choices will be constrained, as Greek sympathy for Serbia was constrained. As a European neighbour, Turkish economic expansion is also an opportunity for Greek investment and commerce. Already much of the meat sold in Greek supermarkets is produced in Turkey. If Greece chooses this path of preferring Turkey as an EU member to Turkey as an outsider, then Turkey may be willing to prefer a well-fenced autonomy for Northern Cyprus to its present course of tit-for-tat integration of Cyprus into Turkey.

At the 1999 Helsinki Council, the Presidency from a small state proved that it could bring both Greece and Turkey to accept a compromise package at least as difficult as that negotiated by the French Presidency in March 1995. Even without an elected presidency to upgrade the common interest, the present system of six-monthly EU Presidencies can take more responsibility than the EEC could have imagined possible in 1974. As an actor, the EU can take responsibility for achieving milieu goals such as reconciling Greek-Turkish national antagonisms and precluding an anti-Islamic crusade. Nevertheless the EU cannot offer itself as a mediator even though the last attempt at mediation was two generations ago in 1965. It has identified itself too closely to the Greek and Greek Cypriot side to be acceptable to Turkey and the Turkish Cypriots. Still less can the EU be an acceptable arbiter in the sense of being able to get any proposed solution accepted by both sides. The Commission has a long way to go in understanding that Europe's irresponsibility has been shameful before it can offer a Holbrooke-style apology to both sides. The system of six-monthly 'lame duck' presidencies makes it difficult for the EU Council to use the leverage that the EU's size gives it throughout the Eastern Mediterranean. What it can contribute is money and troops towards a solution to the security, property and environmental problems of any settlement. If the EU can see itself as needing a programme of confidence-building measures that will give it a credibility with the Turkish Cypriot leadership and its voters equal to that which the EU enjoys in the South, that would itself be a huge step towards the EU taking more responsibility for the outcome of peace talks.

European integration
President Havel also raised the question of the future meaning of integration within an EU of between twenty and thirty states. Integration is an American concept that implies going beyond the unification of historic states or rule through a confederal Council. Social and economic integration in the USA has meant a degree of intermarriage and job

changes across state frontiers on a scale that is different in kind from that prevailing in Europe. In Europe over 95 per cent of the residents of every state but Luxembourg are nationals of that state, and in no state has agriculture completely disappeared. As a playwright, Havel may have had in mind giving a greater priority to cultural integration in the sense of public patronage of the arts. As a politician, he needed to know whether economic integration would mean that the richer states would redistribute to the poorer states and/or whether the richer firms of the West would take over the breweries and weapons producers of Prague. Would the poorer farmers be allowed to sell in the higher priced markets of the West and would they be found ineligible for the subsidies available to farmers from the decision-making states? As a statesman, the influence of the Czech Republic depended on how institutional reforms would rebalance the equation between the bigger states and the smaller states. German reunification had made Germany pre-eminent in terms of population and wealth over the previously equal states of West Germany, France, the UK and Italy. The enlargement to Central Europe, Cyprus and Malta would increase the numbers of small states and give them voting power in the institutions disproportionate to their combined populations.

The internal development of the EU in institutional, economic and social terms is therefore intimately bound up with its projected enlargement to Central and Eastern Europe, Cyprus and Malta. The negotiators of the Republic of Cyprus have put their expectations clearly on the table. In institutional terms they want to build on the precedent of Luxembourg to claim as of right a Cypriot Commissioner, a Cypriot Minister in each Council, a Cypriot Judge in the Court of Justice, six Members of the European Parliament, a Cypriot Governor of the European Investment Bank and, if their application to join the eurozone on accession is successful, to have their Central Bank Governor as an equal on the Board of Frankfurt Governors. If the present system continues whereby every member state holds the Presidency in rotation, then Cyprus expects to be treated like any other state; if the Presidency is redefined to be held by groups of states, then that would be acceptable. In economic terms, they optimistically ask for 'Objective One' status for the whole island, entitling Cyprus to the maximum help from the redistributive Structural Funds. In social terms, the reservations of position, and temporary derogations, are all of a technical nature designed to benefit particular sectoral interwests in agriculture or industry. Other member states are reassured that Cyprus will not be a conduit for illegal migration from outside the EU area.

However, this approach avoids the issues of integration raised by enlargement to the 'countries in transition'. The Member States in the Treaty of Amsterdam took a similar line.

If the inadequate decision-making of the European Union is to be diluted by greater numbers, then German dominance in Europe will be subject only to the considerable German sense of self-restraint. In economic terms, redistribution to the East and Cyprus will make all existing member states 'net payers', however expertly existing levels of payment from the Structural Funds are presented as a ring fenced right. Some form of direct taxation will for the first time become necessary, perhaps on individual businesses. If the European Union budget takes on the payments for peacekeeping forces, this aspect of integration will become all the more salient. This leaves the neglected social meaning of integration after Cypriot accession, neglected because it would become important in the unlikely event of a peace settlement.

It is worth recalling that the point of EU sponsorship of a settlement is twofold. The first is negative, to avoid the consequences of continued division and probable integration of Northern Cyprus into Turkey in retaliation for accession. This would not just be a matter of a change of borders without the consent of the state claiming jurisdiction. It would be a loss of territory claimed by a European member state. Economic sanctions against Turkey would be required, suspending or ending the Customs Union. Turkish nationalism might be aroused, with or without an input from anti-Western fundamentalism. Turks and Turkish Cypriots are likely to take pride in their independence in the face of international isolation and continued hostile relations with Greece. European identity would then become shaped by this conflict with Turkey as 'the non-European Other', an outcome that could have been avoided by a more responsible policy.

The positive purpose of sponsoring a settlement as the outcome to be preferred is that, as in Western Europe, a geographical basis for governance will enable former enemies to rule jointly in ways that promote prosperity and overcome historic distrust. Given the depth of distrust, to make a settlement work, the EU institutions on the one hand and the Greek Cypriots in the South of Cyprus will have to make social integration an aim in itself rather than just a by-product of economic integration. Turkish Cypriots will expect to represent what they see as their separate interests in Brussels. Structural or special funds will have to be directed to them more transparently and directly than is normally the case in allocating EU regional or social expenditure. Cyprus is not the only area in Europe where social integration through recognition of the separate identities of communities will have to be regarded as a positive good of a European framework.

The enlargement of the European Union to include the micro-state of a presently divided Cyprus therefore raises questions for the future that can only be understood by reference to the past of both entities but which go well beyond the complex confines of the Cyprus problem. A multicultural Europe including Turkey and a reunited Cyprus would be very different from the likely alternative of an anti-Islamic, anti-Orthodox, and possibly anti-American Europe defined by a continued frontier in Cyprus and between Greece and Turkey.

Select Bibliography

Documents by Institution (most recent first)

BERTELSMANN FOUNDATION
>   (1998) Research Group on European affairs 'Europe on the eve of completion', 4 July

COUNCIL OF EUROPE - www.coe.int
Committee of Ministers
>   (1995) Resolution DH 245, 19 October - on two individual applications
>   (1983) Resolution 13, 24 November - on the proclamation of the TRNC
>   (1979) Resolution DH 1, 20 January - on two joined ROC applications
>   (1977) Decision, 21 October - on two joined ROC applications
EComHR, European Commission of Human Rights
>   (1999) Commission Report on Application 25781/94, Cyprus v. Turkey, 4 June (further to 6780/74, 6950/75, 8007/77) 636 Paragraphs and 6 Appendices
>   (1976) Commission Report, 10 July
ECHR, European Court of Human Rights
>   (1996) Case of Loizidou v. Turkey (Merits) 40/1993/435/514 Judgment, 18 December
Parliamentary Assembly
>   (1994)Report on the situation in Cyprus, (Finsberg), ADOC 7206, 15 December
>   (1993) Framework Convention for the Protection of National Minorities and Parliamentary Assembly Recommendation 1201
>   (1992) 'The demographic structure of the Cypriot Communities', Report prepared by Mr Cucó, Doc 6589, 27 April

EUROPEAN UNION/ EUROPEAN COMMUNITY/ EUROPEAN
ECONOMIC COMMUNITIES
Commission www.europa.eu.int./comm/enlargement/
>(1999b) 'Regular Report from the Commission on Progress
>towards Accession...on Cyprus...on Turkey', 13 October
>(1998a), 'European Strategy for Turkey: the Commission's initial
>operational proposals', 3 March
>(1998b) 'Progress towards Accession - regular reports on...
>Cyprus...Turkey, November,
>(1998c) 'Report on developments in relations with Turkey since
>the entry into force of the Customs Union'
>(1998d) 'Proposal for a Council Decision concerning the
>conclusion of a bilateral agreement between the Community and
>the Republic of Cyprus on the Republic of Cyprus' participation
>in a Community programme within the framework of Community
>audiovisual policy', COM (98) 242
>(1997a) Agenda 2000, Communications:
>Vol 1: For a stronger and wider Europe, Doc/97/6/, 15 July
>Vol 2: Reinforcing the pre-Accession strategy, Doc/97/7, 15 July
>(1997b) Communication to the Council '...going beyond the
>customs union...with Turkey', COM (97) 394, 15 July.
>(1995a) ' Policy of the European Union: establishing a Euro-
>Mediterranean framework' *EU Bulletin*: Supplement 2/95
>(1995b) Strengthening the Mediterranean policy of the European
>Union: proposals for implementing a Euro-Mediterranean
>partnership COM (95) 72
>(1995c) White Paper: 'Preparation of the Associated countries of
>Central and Eastern Europe for integration into the Internal Market
>of the Union', May
>(1994) 'On the strengthening of the European Union's policy
>towards the Mediterranean Basin countries' COM (94) 4273, 17
>October
>(1993) Opinion on the application for membership from Cyprus:
>COM (93) 313, *EC Bulletin*: 6-1993 and *EC Bulletin*: Supplement
>4/93
>(1992a) 'Europe and the challenge of enlargement' presented to and
>endorsed by the Lisbon European Council in June 1992 *EC*

Bulletin: Supplement 3/92

(1992b) 'Report on the criteria and conditions for accession of new members to the Community' *Agence Europe*: Documents 1790, 3 July

(1992c) 'Regulation 3576/92 modifying Additional Protocol', *Official Journal:* L 364

(1991) 'Europe world partner: the external relations of the European Community'

(1990a) 'Communication ...Redirecting the Community's Mediterranean policy'

(1990b) 'Communication on strengthening relations with Turkey'

(1990c) 'The European Community and Cyprus' *European Information: external relations* 1/90, April

(1989) 'Opinion on Turkey's request for accession to the Community' SEC (89) 2290 18 December

(1982) Communication from the Commission to the Council of Ministers: 'a Mediterranean policy for the enlarged Community'

(1976) Opinion on the Greek application for membership' *EC Bulletin:* supplement 2/76

Commission miscellaneous:

(1997) Crawford, James, with Gerhard Hafner & Alain Pellet, 'Opinion: Republic of Cyprus: eligibility for EU membership', 14 October

European Union News, bi-monthly Newsletter of the Delegation to Cyprus, with a year's break to November 1999

Uniting Europe

Newsletter for Central and Eastern Europe/ European Dialogue Frontier-free Europe

Council of Ministers and European Council of Heads of State/Government

(1997) General Secretariat, press release 12401/97, 19 November

(1996) 43rd Review of the Council's work: the Secretary-general's report 4 January-31st December 1995

(1995a) 42nd Review of the Council's work: the Secretary-general's report 4 January-31st December 1994

(1995b) Council Decision on detailed procedures for the structured dialogue between the European Union and Cyprus. *EU Bulletin*: 7/8-1995, point 1.4.72

(1995c) Council Conclusions defining a general framework for the development of relations with Cyprus.
EU Bulletin: 3, point 1.4.60a

(1995d) Cannes European Council Conclusions. *EU Bulletin*: 6, point 1.1

(1995e) Draft fourth financial protocol between the European Community and Cyprus: *EU Bulletin*: 6, point 1.4.71

(1994/5a) European Observer's Reports on Cyprus to the European Union Council of Ministers 18 April 1994 & 23 January 1995

(1994b) 41st Review of the Council's work: the Secretary-General's report 1 January - 31 December 1993

(1994c) Corfu European Council Conclusions. *EU Bulletin*: 6, point 1.11

(1994d) Essen European Council Conclusions. *EU Bulletin*: 12, points 1.14 and 1.55

(1993a) Copenhagen Principles, 21-22 June. *EU Bulletin*: 6

(1993b) Council Conclusions on the Commission Opinion on Cyprus' application for accession: *EU Bulletin*: 10, point 1.3.7,

(1990) Application for membership from the Republic of Cyprus: *EC Bulletin:* 7/8,1.4.24

(1991) 'Modification of Additional Protocol' Association Council 1/91, *Official Journal*: L 372

(1987) Agreement for the second stage of the Customs Union with Cyprus, exchange of letters̲S (And protocol revising accord in light of Spanish and Portuguese membership, p. 37 seq.) *Official Journal*: L 393 of 31 December, cf *EC Bulletin:*12, point 2.2.24

(1985) 'Modification of Additional Protocol', *Official Journal:* L 288

(1981) 'Protocol consequent on the accession of the Hellenic Republic'. And Regulation EEC 1742/81 ... 'concerning the arrangements to be applied during 1981'...*Official Journal*: L 174 of 30 June

(1978) 'Protocol complementary to the Association Agreement'*Official Journal*: L 172

(1977) 'Additional Protocol [effective 1 June 1978]' *Official Journal*: L 339 (1982) European Political Cooperation Statements (on Cyprus), 4th ed., Bonn: Press and Information Service of the

Federal Government.
(1978) Declaration on Democracy of the Copenhagen European Council, 8 April
(1973) Council Regulation (EEC) no 1246/73 'Agreement establishing an Association between the European Economic Community and the Republic of Cyprus' *Official Journal*: L 133, 21 May; amended by *OJ*: L339 of 28.12.1977, *OJ*: L271 of 29.10.1979; completed by *OJ*: L 393 of 31.12.1987, p.2 and *OJ*: L 278 of 21.11.1995, p.23; further amended by *OJ*: L 278 of 21.11.1995 and *OJ*: L 100 of 15.04.1999, p.26

Court of Justice
(1994) Case C-432/92 'Anastasiou' Judgment of 5 Julyin, *Common Market Law Reports*, 72, 1995

Economic and Social Committee
CES(97) 1197 Opinion Son the enlargement of the European Union
CES(97) 1199 OpinionSon the Commission Communication Agenda 2000

European Investment Bank
(1998) 40 years activity, 1958-98
(1998) 1997 Annual Report

European Parliament
(2000) Report (J. Poos)
(1999) Report (A. Oostlander and E. Baron Crespo)
(1995) Report on Cyprus' application for membership of the EU (Jan Willem Bertens) Committee on Foreign Affairs, Security and Defence policy, Luxembourg: OOPEC a4-0156/95

European Parliament miscellaneous
(1997) Letter from Pauline Green MEP to Wilfried Martens and Jacques Santer, *Socialist Group weekly briefing* March 10

THE HELLENIC REPUBLIC
Ministry of Foreign Affairs www.gr.gov http://www.pio.gov.cy
(1994) 'Greek-Turkish relations'
http://www.mfa.gr/foreign/bilateral/relations.htm 5 February
(1999) 'Greece and the prospects of enlargement of the European Union to include the countries of Central and Eastern Europe'

Thesis: a Journal of Foreign Policy Issues

ROC, REPUBLIC OF CYPRUS www.cyprus-eu.org.cy
(1999) Report submitted to the Council of Europe by Cyprus
pursuant to Article 25, Paragraph 1, of the Framework Convention
for the protection of national minorities, ACFC/SR (99) 2, 1
March
(1998a) *The Almanac of Cyprus*
(1998b) *Cyprus-EU relations 1962-1995 www.*ucy.ac.cy website
(1998c) President Clerides' Inaugural Address, 28 February
(1982), *The Association Agreement between the Republic of
Cyprus and the EEC*, Nicosia: Press and Information office
(no date) *Cyprus: the way to full EU Membership*, 3rd edition
Koufoudakis, Van, ed , *Cyprus Yearbook* Nicosia: Cyprus
Research Centre
Cyprus News Agency (state-owned)
Cyprus Embassy (to Washington) Newsletter www.kypros.org/
Cyprus Bulletin
Cyprus Mail

CYPRUS BAR ASSOCIATION
(1989) *Turkey's violations of human rights in Cyprus* Nicosia

LOBBY FOR CYPRUS
Special European Report: the strategic benefits to the European
Union of Cypriot membership

REPUBLIC OF TURKEY http://www.mfa.gov.tr.
Mendelson, M.H.
(1997) Opinion on the application of the Republic of Cyprus to join
the European Union, 6 June, submitted to the UN by the Government
of Turkey (UN Doc A/51/951,S/1997/585, 25 July 1997) and Note
on Austria's accession to the European Union, undated, winter 1997;
reprinted as *The EU and Cyprus: an expert view*
Turkish Daily News

TRNC, TURKISH REPUBLIC OF NORTHERN CYPRUS
    Kıbrıs Turkish Cypriot daily
    (1999) *Kıbrıs* poll ofl 950 Turkish Cypriots, 6 December
    (1997) Agricultural Structure and Production 1975-1995, Nicosia:
    Ministry of Agriculture and Forestry,
    (1990) Supplementary Note to the Turkish Cypriot Memorandum
    of 12 July on The Greek Cypriot 'Application' for membership to
    the European Communities

UK, UNITED KINGDOM
    (1986-7) House of Commons papers nos 21-24. Report by the
    Foreign Affairs Committee on Cyprus
    (1979) Parliamentary debates Lords vol 401, col 2024 25 July
    (1964) FO 371/74747-C31602, 13/02/1964 George Ball in Nicosia
    to Dean Rusk and R.A.Butler
    (1959) Conference on Cyprus: documents signed and initialled at
    Lancaster House, on February 19, HMSO, Cmnd 679

UNITED NATIONS
UNGA, United Nations General Assembly
    Resolutions: (1983) 37/253; (1979) 34/30; (1978) 33/15; (1977)
    32/15; (1976) 31/12; (1975) 3395 XXX; (1974) 3212 XXIX;
    (1965) 2077 - XX
    Resolutions On Human Rights:
    (1987) 50; (1978) 17 XXXIV; (1976) 4 XXXII; (1975) 4 XXXI
    Resolutions On Missing Persons:
    (1982) 37/181; (1981) 36/164; (1978) 33/172; (1977) 32/128;
    (1975) 3450 XXX

UNSC, United Nations Security Council
    (1999) Security Council Resolution 1283(1999) extending mandate
    to UNFICYP, 15 December
    (1996) 1092, 1062
    (1995) 1032, 1000
    (1994) 969, 939, 902
    (1993) 889, 839, 831
    (1992) 789, 774, 750

(1991) 716
(1990) 649
(1989) 646, 634
(1988) 625, 614
(1987) 604, 597
(1986) 593, 585 and ANNEXE II, S/18102/Add1 of 11 June
(1985) 578, 565
(1984) 559, 553, 550
(1983) 544, 541, 534
(1982) 526, 510
(1981) 495, 488
(1980) 482, 472
(1979) 458, 451
(1978) 443, 440, 430
(1977) 422, 414, 410
(1976) 401, 391
(1975) 383, 370, 367
(1974) 365, 361, 360, 359, 358, 357, 355, 354, 353, 349
(1973) 343, 334
(1972) 324,315
(1971) 305, 293
(1970) 291, 281
(1969) 274, 266
(1968) 266, 261, 254
(1967) 244, 238
(1966) 231, 222, 220
(1965) 219,207, 206, 201
(1964) 198, 194, 193, 192, 187, 164

United Nations Secretary-General UNSG

(1999) Report of the Secretary-General (Kofi Annan) to the UNSC on the UN Operations in Cyprus S/1999/

(1997a) Report of the Secretary-General (Kofi Annan) to the UNSC on the UN Operations in Cyprus S/1997/437

(1997b) Secretary-General's letter to the President of the Security Council concerning his mission of good offices in Cyprus S/997/40

(1996) Report of the Secretary-General on the United Nations

operation in Cyprus, S/1996/1016, 10 December
(1995) Report of the Secretary-General (Kofi Annan) to the UNSC
on the UN Operations in Cyprus S/1995
(1994) Report of the Secretary-General on his mission of Good
Offices in Cyprus (confidence-building) S/1994/629, 30 May1994
(1993) Report confidence-building measures S/26026 of 1 July
(1992) 'Set of Ideas' S/24472 attached to Report of the Secretary-
General of 21 August.
(1977) Report of the Secretary-General pursuant to Paragraph 6 of
SC Resolution 401 (1976), 30 April [1977 guidelines]

UNITED STATES *http://infoweb.newsbank.com/bin/gate.exe*
(1997) Department of State Background notes, September
(1995) *US policy towards Cyprus:* hearing 104th Congress 1st
session, House of Representatives Committee on international ..
· ·

WORLD TRADE ORGANISATION
(1997) *Trade Policy Review: Cyprus*

Books

Alexandrakis, Menelaos, Lagakos, E., and Theodoropoulos, V.
(1987) *The Cyprus problem 1950-1974, an introspection* [in Greek].
Alford, Jonathan ed.
(1984) *Greece and Turkey: Adversity in alliance.* Aldershot: Gower
Attalides, Michael
(1979) *Cyprus: nationalism and international politics.* Edinburgh: Q Press
Avery, Graham and Fraser, Cameron
(1998) *Enlargement of the European Union.* Sheffield: Sheffield Academic
Press
Axt, Heinz-Jürgen and Brey, Hansjörg, eds
(1997) *Cyprus and the European Union: new chances for solving an old
conflict.* München: Südosteuropa-Gesellschaft
Axt, Heinz-Jürgen ed.
(1997) *Greece and the European Union: stranger among partners.* Baden-Baden:
Nomos-Verlag

(1996) *Cyprus and the EU - accession of a divided island?* München: Friedrich-
    Ebert-Stiftung
Baç Müftüler Meltem
(1997) *Turkey's relations with a changing Europe.* Manchester: M U P
Bahcheli, Tozun
(1990) *Greek-Turkish relations since 1955.* Boulder: Westview
Baier-Allen, S. ed.
(1998) *Looking into the future of Cyprus-EU relations.* Baden-Baden: Nomos-
    Verlag
Balkır, C. and Williams A.
(1993) *Turkey and Europe.* London: Pinter
Ball, George
(1982) *The past has another pattern: memoirs.* New York: WW Norton
Bölükbaşı, Suha
(1988) *Turkish-American relations and Cyprus.* London: University Press of
    America
Brey, H., ed.
(2000) *Cyprus and its accession to the European Union: positions and
    expectations of the Cypriots and of the International Community.*
    Munich: Südosteuropa-Gesellschaft
Carver, Michael
(1986) *Cyprus in transition, 1965-1985.* London: Trigraph Ltd.
Church Clive
(1990) *Widening the Community circle.* London: UACES occasional paper,
    6
Clerides, Glafcos
(1979, 1991) *Cyprus: my deposition.* 3 vols. Nicosia: Alithia Publishing
    Company
Constas, Dmitri ed.
(1991) *The Greek-Turkish conflict in the 1990s.* NY: St Martin's Press;
    London: Macmillan
Couloumbis, T. and Yannas, P.
(1995) *Greek security challenges in the 1990s Balkans: a mirror of the new
    international* order. Istanbul: Eren Yay
Crawford, James
(1979) *The creation of States in International Law.* Oxford: Clarendon Press

Crawshaw, Nancy
(1978) *The Cyprus revolt: an account of the struggle for Union with Greece.*
London: George Allen and Unwin
Denktaş, Rauf
(1988) *The Cyprus Triangle.* London: K Rüstem and Bro.
Dodd, Clement H. ed.
(1999) *Cyprus: the need for new perspectives.* Huntingdon: The Eothen Press
(1993) *The political, social and economic development of Northern Cyprus.*
Huntingdon: The Eothen Press
Dodd, Clement H.
(1998) *The Cyprus imbroglio.* Huntingdon: The Eothen Press
(1995) *The Cyprus issue: a current perspective.* 2nd edition, Huntingdon: The
Eothen Press
Emel Doğramacı *et al.*, eds
(1997) *Proceedings of the First International Congress of Cypriot Studies.*
Gazımağusa: Eastern Mediterranean University Press
Drevet, J. F.
(1991) *Chypre, île extrême: chronique d'une Europe oubliée.* Syros:
Alternatives
Durrell, Lawrence
(1957) *Bitter lemons.* London: Faber and Faber
ECMI, European Centre for Minority Issues
(1999) *Insular regions and European Integration: Corsica and the Åland islands
compared,* November, no. 5
Ertekün, Necati Münir ed.
(1996) *Le statut des deux peuples à Chypre.* Lefkoşa: TRNC Public
Information Office
Ertekün, Necati Münir
(1981) *In search of a negotiated Cyprus settlement.* Nicosia
Featherstone, Kevin and Ifantis, C. eds
(1996) *Greece in a changing Europe: between European integration and Balkan
disintegration.* Manchester and NY: Manchester University Press
Fuller, Graham E. and Lesser, Ian
(1993) *Turkey s new geopolitics.* Boulder: Westview
Garton Ash, Timothy
(1994) *In Europe s Name.* 1993 Jonathan Cape, republished London: Vintage

Heinze, C.

(1986) *Cyprus conflict 1964-1985*. London: K. Rüstem & Bro.

Herzog, Roman

(1999) *Preventing the Clash of Civilisations - a peace strategy for the 21st Century*. New York: St Martin's Press

Hitchens, Christopher

(1984) *Cyprus* London: Quartet books, republished as

(1997) *Hostage to History: Cyprus from the Ottomans to Kissinger*. London: Verso

Holbrooke, Richard

(1998) *To end a war*. NY: Random House

Huntington, Jr., Samuel P.

(1997) *The clash of civilizations and the remaking of world order*. New York: Simon & Schuster

Ifestos, Panayiotis and Tsardanidis, H.

(1993) *The relationship of Cyprus with the European Communities, 1972-1990*. Athens: Papazis Publications

Ifestos, Panayiotis

(1987) *European Political Cooperation*. Aldershot: Avebury

Ioannides, Christos

(1992)*Cyprus: domestic dynamics, external constraints* NY: New Rochelle Ltd

Iokamidis, P.

(1993) *European Political Union*. Athens: Themeloi

(1992) *Greece in the search for a new architecture*. Athens: Themeloi

(1979) *The relations between Greece, the EEC and the United States*. Athens: Papazis Publications

James, Alan

(1986) *Sovereign statehood: the basis of international society*. London: Allen & Unwin

Joseph, Joseph P.

(1997) *Cyprus: ethnic conflict and international politics: from independence to the threshold of the European Union* London: Macmillan

Karpat, Kemal ed.

(1984) *The Cyprus dispute and the birth of the Turkish Republic of Northern Cyprus*. Nicosia: Rüstem & Bro.

Kazakos, Panos and Ioakimidis, P.

(1994) *Greece and EC membership* evaluated. London: Pinter

Kissinger, Henry
(1979) *The White House years*. London: Weidenfeld and Nicolson
Körner, Heiko and Shams, Rasul, eds
(1990) *Institutional aspects of economic integration of Turkey into the
European Community*. Hamburg:Verlag Weltarchiv, GMBH
Koumoulides J.
(1986) *Cyprus in transition*. London: Trigraph
Kyle, Keith
(1997) *Cyprus: in search of peace*. London: Minority Rights Group
International
Kymlicka, W.
(1995) *Multicultural Citizenship: a liberal theory of minority rights*. Oxford:
Clarendon Press
Kyrris, Costas
(1996) *History of Cyprus*. Nicosia: Lampousa Publications
Lapidoth, Ruth
(1997) *Autonomy: flexible solutions to ethnic conflicts*. Washington DC:
United States Institute of Peace Press
Ludlow, P.
(1994) *Europe and the Mediterranean*. London: CEPS for Brassey's.
McDonald, Robert
(1988/9) 'The problem of Cyprus' *Adelphi* Paper 234
Mango, Andrew
(1999) *Atatürk*. London: John Murray
Markides, Kyriacos
(1977) *The rise and fall of the Cyprus Republic*. New Haven and London: Yale
University Press
Mayes, Stanley
(1981) *Makarios: a biography*. London:Macmillan
Mehmet, Özay
(1990) *The Cyprus problem: from the UN to the EEC*. Istanbul: Bosphorus
University
Melakopides, Costas
(1996) *Making peace in Cyprus: time for a comprehensive initiative*.
Kingston, Ontario: Queen's University

Middlemas, Keith

(1995) *Orchestrating Europe: the informal politics of the European Union, 1973-1995*. London: Fontana

Mirbagheri, Farid

(1997) *Cyprus and international peacemaking, 1964-1986*. London: Hurst

Moran, Michael ed.

(1997) *Rauf Denktash at the United Nations*. Huntingdon: The Eothen Press

Necatigil, Zaim

(1996) *The Cyprus question and the Turkish position in international law*. 2nd Edition London: Oxford University Press

(1985) *Our republic in perspective*. Lefkoşa: the author

Oberling, Pierre

(1982) *The road to Bellapais: the Turkish Cypriot exodus to Northern Cyprus*. New York: Columbia University Press

Panteli, Stavros

(1984) *A new history of Cyprus* London: Eastwest Publications,

Panteli, Stavros

(1990) *The making of modern Cyprus - from obscurity to statehood*. Cyprus: Interworld publications

Parsons, Sir Antony

(1995) *From Cold War to Hot Peace: UN interventions 1947ș1995*. London: Penguin

Peterson, John and Bomberg, Elizabeth

(1999) *Decision-making in the European Union*. London: Macmillan

Pettifer, James

(1998) *The Turkish labyrinth*. London: Penguin

(1994) *The Greeks*. London: Penguin (first published by Viking in 1993)

Pijpers, Alfred

(1990) *The vicissitudes of European Political Cooperation*. Leiden: CIP-Gegevens Koninkluke Bibliotheek

Polyviou, Polyvios

(1980) *Cyprus: conflict and negotiations 1960-1980*. London: Duckworth

(1976) *Cyprus: in search of a Constitution: negotiations and proposals, 1960 -75*. Nicosia: Nicolaou and Sons

(1975) *Cyprus: the tragedy and the challenge*. printed in England by John Swain and Son

Reddaway, John
(1986) *Burdened with Cyprus, the British connection.* London: Weidenfeld and
    Nicholson
Redmond, John
(1993) *The next Mediterranean enlargement of the European Community:
    Turkey, Cyprus and Malta?* Aldershot: Dartmouth
Regelsberger, E., de Schoutheete de Tervarent, P., and Wessels, W.
(1997) *Foreign Policy of the EU: from EPC to CFSP and beyond.* Boulder:
    Lynne Rienner
Richmond, Oliver P.
(1998) *Mediating in Cyprus.* London: Frank Cass
Robins, Philip
(1991) *Turkey and the Middle East.* London: Pinter for RIIA
Said, Edward
(1994) *The politics of dispossession.* London: Chatto and Windus
Salih, İbrahim
(1978) *Cyprus: the impact of diverse nationalisms on a state.* NSA:
    University of Alabama Press
Shlaim Avi and Yannopoulos, G.N., eds
(1976) *The EEC and the Mediterranean countries.* Cambridge: Cambridge U.P.
Sjöstedt, Gunnar
(1977) *The external role of the European Community.* Farnborough: Saxon
    House
Sonyel, Salahi
(1997) *The destruction of a Republic.* Huntingdon: The Eothen Press
Stavridis, Stelios
(1999) *Foreign policies of the EU s Mediterranean states and applicant
    countries in the 1990s.* London: Macmillan
Stavrinides, Zenon
(1975) *The Cyprus conflict - national identity and statehood.* Wakefield,
    England: The author. Reprinted with an introduction by Michael
    Moran (1999) Lefkosa: CYREP
Steffani,W. ed.
(1998) *Zypern.* Göttingen: Südosteuropa Handbuch: Band 7
Stephen, Michael
(2000,1997) *The Cyprus question.* London: the British - Northern Cyprus
    Parliamentary Group

Talmon, Stafan,

(1998) *Recognition of States in International Law* Oxford: Clarendon Press

Tamkoc, Metin

(1988) *The Turkish Cypriot state: the embodiment of the right of self-determination*. London: Rüstem

Theodhoropoulos, V., Laghakos, E., Papoulias, G., and Tzounis, I.

(1995) *Reflections and Considerations about our Foreign Policy*. Athens [in Greek]

Theophanous, Andreas

(1996) *The political economy of a federal Cyprus*. Nicosia: Intercollege Press

Tocci, Nathalie

(2000) *The 'Cyprus question': reshaping community identities and elite interests within a wider European framework*. Brussels: Centre for European Policy Studies

Toynbee, Arnold J

(1922) *The Western question in Greece and Turkey: a study in the contact of civilizations*. London: Constable

Tsardanidis, Charalambos

(1988) *The politics of the EEC-Cyprus Association Agreement 1972-1982*. Nicosia: Cyprus Research Centre

Tsoukalis, Loukas

(1981) *The European Community and its Mediterranean enlargement*. London: Allen and Unwin

Valinakis, G.

(1991) *European Policy and Defense Co-operation*. Athens: Papazisis publications

Waldheim, K

(1985) *The challenge of Peace: in the eye of the storm*. London: Weidenfeld and Nicolson

Wilson, Rodney

(1992) *Cyprus and the international economy*. New York: St Martin's Press

Woodhouse, C. Montague

(1982) *Something ventured*. London: Granada

Xydis, Stephan

(1973) *Cyprus: Reluctant Republic* The Hague: Mouton

Zürcher, Erik

(1993) *Turkey: a modern history*. London: Tauris

Articles

Anayiotis, George

(1991) 'The application of Cyprus for European Community membership: a negotiating framework between Greek Cypriots and Turkish Cypriots' *Cyprus Journal of Economics* 4:2, December

Aydın, Mustafa

(2000) 'Determinants of Turkish foreign policy during the Cold War' *Middle Eastern Studies* 36:1

Badinter Commission

(1992) Opinions no. 1 (29 November 1991) and no. 9 (4 July 1992) in *International legal materials* 31 pp 1497 and 1524

Bahcheli, Tozun and Rizopoulos, N.

(1996/7) 'The Cyprus impasse: what next?' *World Policy Journal* XIII: 4, Winter

Bahcheli Tozun

(1997) 'Domestic political developments' in Klaus-Detlev Grothusen, Winfried Steffani and Peter Zervakis, eds, *Zypern Südosteuropa-Handbuch* band VIII. Göttingen: Vandenhoeck and Ruprecht

Bartmann, Barry

(2000) 'Facing new realities: The TRNC and unrecognized states in the International System' *Perceptions* IV: 3

Bıçak, Hasan Ali

(1997) 'Recent developments in Cyprus - EU relations' in Emel Doğramacı *et al.*, *Proceedings of the First International Congress on Cypriot Studies*. Gazımağusa: Eastern Mediterranean University Press

Booss and Forman,

(1995) 'Enlargement: legal and procedural aspects' *Common Market Law Review* 32

Brewin, C.

(2000a) 'The image of the Turk in Europe' in Nedret Kuran Burçoğlu, ed. *The image of the Turk in Europe from the Declaration of the Republic in 1923 to the 1990s*. Istanbul: The Isis Press

(2000b) 'European Union perspectives on Cyprus Accession' in *Middle Eastern Studies* 36: 1, January

(1996) 'Turkey and the European Union' *Cambridge Review of International Affairs* X: 1

(1982-1992) 'Annual Review of the activities of the European Communities' *Journal of Common Market Studies*

Caplan, R.

(1998) 'Crisis in Kosovo' *International Affairs* 74: 4, October

Catsiapis, Jean

(1996) 'L'Union européenne et la crise gréco-turque d'Imia' in *Etudes Helleniques/Hellenic Studies* 4: 2, Autumn

Cem, İsmail

(2000) 'How Turkey can contribute to Europe's brighter future' in G. Merritt, ed. *Has the EU enlargement process lost its way?* Brussels: Philip Morris Institute

Çiller, Tansu

(1999) 'Turkish foreign policy in its dynamic tradition' Turkish Ministry of Foreign Affairs, February 7

Constantinides, S and Arnopoulos, P.

(1996) 'The Aegean dispute' in *Etudes Helleniques/Hellenic Studies* 4: 2, Autumn

Constantinou, Costas M and Papadakis, Yiannis

(2001) 'The Cypriot states *in situ*: cross-ethnic contact and the discourse of recognition' *Global Society,* January

Constantinou, D

(1980) 'Chypre-CEE: l'amère expérience d'une Association' *Nouvelle Revue Internationale* 11

Crawshaw, Nancy

(1994) 'Cyprus: a crisis of confidence' *The World Today* 50: 4, April

de Ballaigue, C.

(1999) 'Conciliation in Cyprus' *Washington Quarterly* 22: 2, October

Demetriades, Lellos

(1998) 'The Nicosia Master Plan' *Journal of Mediterranean Studies* 8: 2

Dunér, Bertil

(1999) 'Cyprus: North is North and South is South' *Security Dialogue* 30: 4, December

The Economist Intelligence Unit

(1996) 'Country report: Cyprus/Malta 1995/6'

Eralp, A.

(1988) 'The second enlargement process of the EC and its possible effects on Turkey's external relations' *Yapı Kredi Economic Review* 2/3, Jan/April

Ertekün, Necati Münir

(1995) 'The Greek Cypriot eagerness and agitation for EU membership- why?' *Kıbrıs* 31 January

(1984) 'The historical background of the Cypriot Turkish Declaration of Independence, 15 November 1983' in K. Karpat ed. (1984) *The Cyprus dispute and the birth of the Turkish Republic of Northern Cyprus.* Nicosia: Rüstem

Fagerlund, N.

(1997) 'The special status of the Åland islands in the European Union' in L. Hannikainen and F. Horn, eds *Autonomy and demilitarisation in a changing Europe.* Dordrecht: Kluwer Law International

Gobbi, H.

(no date) 'Rethinking Cyprus' Tel Aviv

Gordon, P.

(1998) 'Storms in the Med blow towards Europe' *The World Today* 54: 2

Groom, A.J.R.

(1986) 'Cyprus: back to the doldrums' *Round Table* 300

Gsänger Hans

(1980) 'The EEC and Cyprus and Turkey' in Seers, D. and Vaitsos, C. eds, *Integration and uneven development.* London: Macmillan

Gündüz, Aslan

(1996) 'Discord between Greece and Turkey' *Etudes Helleniques/Hellenic Studies* 4: 2 Autumn

Hahn, B. and Wellenreuther, R.

(1992) 'Demographische Strukturen in der Turkischen Republik Nordzypern' *Orient* 33: 2

Hannay, Sir David

(1997) 'Cyprus at the crossroads' 9 October, Brussels: Royal Institute, published in *Studia diplomatica* 50: 3

Heinze, Christian

(1985) 'The attitude of the Western countries and the action taken by the United Nations' *New Cyprus*, November

Holbrooke, Richard

(1995) 'America: a European power' *Foreign Affairs* 38

James, Alan

(1998) 'The Making of the Cyprus Settlement 1958-60' *The Cyprus Review* 10: 2, Fall

Jansson, Roger

(1997) 'The Åland islands' *Eipascope* 1997/2

Joffé, George

(1998) 'The Euro-Mediterranean partnership: two years after Barcelona', *The Royal Institute of International Affairs*, Briefing Paper no. 44, May

Joseph, Joseph S.

(1997) 'Theorising about ethnopolitics and international politics: some conclusions from Cyprus' *The European Journal of Social Sciences* 10: 1, March

(1996) 'Cyprus at the threshold of the European Union' *Mediterranean Quarterly*, Spring,

(1990) 'International dimensions of the Cyprus problem' *Cyprus Review* 2: 2, Fall

Kabaalioğlu, Haluk

(2000) 'EU membership and constitutional requirement' *Perceptions* IV: 3

Kamusella, Tomasz

(1999) 'Ethnic cleansing in Silesia 1950-89 and the Ennationalising policies of Poland and Germany' *Patterns of prejudice* 33: 2

Kamusella, Tomasz and Sullivan Terry

(1999) 'The Germans of Upper Silesia: the struggle for recognition' in Karl Cordell ed. *Ethnicity and democratisation in the New Europe*. London and New York: Routledge

Keene, A.

(1997) 'Enlargement: Cyprus' *European Dialogue* 4, July-August

Kourvetaris, G.

(1988) 'Greek and Turkish interethnic conflict and polarisation in Cyprus' *Journal of Political and Military Sociology* 16: 2, Fall

Kramer, Heinz

(1997a) 'Cyprus - Briefing Paper' *Conflict Prevention Network of the European Commission*

(1997b) 'The Cyprus problem and European Security', *Survival* 39: 3 Autumn

Krebs, R.
(1999) 'Perverse Institutionalism: NATO and the Graeco-Turkish conflict'
    International Organisation 53: 2, Spring
Krenzler, H. and Schomaker, A
(1996) 'A new transatlantic agenda' *European Foreign Affairs Review* 1: 1
Kycourgos, C.
(no date) 'L'association de Chypre à la CEE (Paris: PUF, Travaux et recherches
    de l'Université de Droit)
Kyle, Keith
(1997) 'Squall hits "Year of Cyprus"' *The World Today* 53: 2
Lindley, Dan
(1997) 'UNFICYP and a Cyprus solution: a strategic assessment', Cambridge,
    Mass: MIT Defence and arms control studies program working paper
    no. 4, May
McDonald, Robert
(2000) 'The prospects for relations between Greece, Turkey and Cyprus'. Paper
    for Association for Cypriot, Greek and Turkish Affairs, 28 January
Mearsheimer, John
(1990) 'Back to the future: instability in Europe after the Cold War',
    International Security 15, Summer
Michaelides, Alecos
(1996) 'Cyprus accession to the European Union: a vision and a challenge
    for today'. London School of Economics, 30 October
Nas, Çiğdem
(1997) 'The enlargement policy of the EU and its link with the external
    dimension of Human Rights policy: Turkish case' *Marmara Journal
    of European Studies*, 5: 1-2
Necatigil, Zaim
(1999) 'The Loizidou case: a critical examination', Ankara: Centre for Strategic
    Research, SAM papers 8/99 and *Perceptions*, IV: 3, November
(1995) 'The Cyprus question and the role of international organisations'
    Journal for Cypriot Studies, Autumn
(1993) 'The Cyprus conflict in international law' in C.H. Dodd ed. (1993) op.
    cit.
Nicolaides, Phedon
(2000) with Bollen, F. 'Summary of Proceedings of the 3rd European
    Conference on Enlargement of the European Union, *Eipascope,* 1

(1998) 'Negotiating effectively for accession to the European Union'
    Eipascope, 1
(1996) 'Enlargement' *Eipascope*, 3
(1990)'Cyprus and the European Community: looking beyond 1992' *Cyprus
    Review,* 1, Spring
Nugent, Neill
(1997) 'Cyprus and the European Union: a particularly difficult membership
    application' *Mediterranean Politics* 2: 1
Olgun, Ergün
(2000) 'Turkish Cypriot view: a Confederation for the "Island of Cyprus"' in
    G. Delcoigne et al, *The need for new perspectives on Cyprus*,
    Brussels: Université Libre - CERIS
(1993)'Economic overview' in Dodd, Clement H. *The political, social and
    economic development of Northern Cyprus*. Huntingdon: The Eothen
    Press
Pace, Roderick
(1997) 'Enlargement and the Mediterranean dimension of the European Union:
    the role of Cyprus' paper at Intercollege Conference on *Cyprus and
    the EU*, 7-9 May
(1995) 'Assessing Malta's bid to join the EU' University of Reading GSEIS
    Discussion paper no. 54
Poulton, Hugh
(1999) 'The struggle for hegemony in Turkey: Turkish nationalism as a
    contemporary force' *Journal of Southern Europe and the Balkans* 1:
    1, May
Preece, Jennifer Jackson
(1998) 'Ethnic cleansing as an instrument of Nation-State creation: changing
    state practices and evolving legal norms' *Human Rights Quarterly*
    20: 4
Redmond, John
(1997) 'From Association towards the Application for Full Membership:
    Cyprus' relations with the European Union' in Axt and Brey, op. cit.
Rhein, Eberhard
(1996) 'Europe and the Mediterranean: a newly emerging Geopolitical area?'
    European Foreign Affairs Review 1: 1, July
Rocard, Michel
(1997) 'A new EU framework for tackling crises' in *How can Europe prevent*

conflicts? Brussels: Philip Morris Institute, November

Schäuble, Wolfgang and Lamers, Karl

(1994) 'Reflections on European Policy' reprinted in Nelsen and Stubb, *The European Union: readings on the theory and practice of European integration*. Lynne Rienner, 1998

Smith, Julie

(2000) 'An ever larger Europe?' *RIIA Briefing Paper New Series*, no. 14, May

Sönmezoğlu, Faruk

(1996) 'The Cyprus question and the United nations 1950-1987' in K. Karpat ed, *The Cyprus dispute and the birth of the Turkish Republic of Northern Cyprus*. Nicosia: Rüstem

Soveroski, M.

(1999) 'EU enlargement: prospects and potential pitfalls along the way' *Eipascope* 2

Soysal Mümtaz

(1999) 'A solution for Cyprus through statehood' *Perceptions* IV:3, November

Stavridis, Stelios and Hutchence, Justin

(2000) 'Mediterranean challenges to the EU's foreign policy' *European Foreign Affairs Review* 5

Stavridis, Stelios

(1999) 'Double standards, ethics and democratic principles in foreign policy: the EU and the Cyprus problem' *Mediterranean Politics* 4: 1

Stavrinides, Zenon

(1999a) 'Greek Cypriot perceptions on the Cyprus problem' in C.H. Dodd, ed., *New perspectives*. Huntingdon: The Eothen Press

(1999b) 'Is a compromise settlement still possible? Revisiting the Ghali "Set of Ideas"' *The Cyprus Review*, 11: 1, Spring

Stephanou, C. and Tsardanides, Charalambos

(1991) 'The EC factor in the Greece-Turkey-Cyprus triangle' in Dmitri Constas, ed. *The Greek-Turkish conflict in the 1990s*. London: Macmillan

Stone, Leonard

(1997) 'Interpreting the interpretation: contemporary Turkish foreign policy' *Perceptions,* March/May

Theophanous, Andreas,
(1998) 'The European Union and Cyprus: accession negotiations and prospects for a solution of the Cyprus problem`, paper at Rheinische Frederik-Wilhelm-Universität, Bonn, 20 January
Tovias Alfred
(1997) 'The EU and Mediterranean countries' *Marmara Journal of European Studies* 5: 1-2
Trojan, Carlo
(1996) 'Beyond the Intergovernmental Conference: the tasks ahead for EIPA', *Eipascope*, special issue.
Tsakolyannis, Panos
(1997) 'The EU and the common interests of the South' in Edwards, G. and Pijpers, A. *The politics of European treaty reform*. London and Washington: Pinter
(1980) 'The European Community and the Greek-Turkish dispute' *Journal of Common Market Studies* XIX:1 35-53
Tsardanidis C. and Nicolau, Y.
(1999) 'Cyprus foreign and security policy: options and challenges'in S. Stavridis *et al.*, eds, *The foreign policies of the European Union`s Mediterranean States and Applicant Countries in the 1990s* Basingstoke: Macmillan
Tsardanidis, Charalambos
(1988) 'The European Community and the Cyprus problem since 1974' *Journal of Political and Military Sociology* 16, Fall
(1984) 'The EC-Cyprus Agreement: ten years of a troubled relationship 1973-1983' *Journal of Common Market Studies* XXII: 4, June
Tsoukalas, C.
(1999) 'European modernity and Greek national identity' *Journal of Southern Europe and the Balkans* 1: 1, May
Uğur, Mehmet
(1996) 'CustomsUnion as a substitute for Turkey'smembership?'*Cambridge Review of International Affairs* X: 1
UN Association of Northern Cyprus
(no date) 'Cyprus and the European Union: the Turkish Cypriot view'
van den Broek, H
(1997a)'Cyprus and the European Union' speech to the North Cyprus Young Businessmen's Association, 27 February

(1997b) 'Bi-communal cooperation: the path to mutual trust and
reconciliation' Speech 97/272, Nicosia, 2 December
Vaner, Semih
(1996) 'Chypre et l'Union Européenne' *Politique Etrangère*, 61: 3
Vassiliou, G.
(1999) 'Towardsa larger, yet more effective European Union' in Meritt, G. ed.,
Should the EU be redesigned? Brussels: Philip Morris Institute
Vernant, J.
(1974) 'Chypre et la coopération des Neuf' *Défense Nationale*, December
Warner, Jonathan
(1990) 'Importing voters. Does it work?' *New Cyprus*, September/October
Wilson, Rodney
(1994) 'The external economic relations of the Republic of Cyprus' *Round
Table*, 83: 329
Yeşilada, Birol
(1996) 'Turkey's Membership in the EU' in Kemal Karpat ed., *Turkish foreign
policy: recent developments*. Madison: Wisconsin

Abbreviations

AP	Accession Partnership between EU and each candidate country
AKEL	Greek Cypriot Progressive Party of the Working people (Communist)
Balladur Pacts	Central and East Europe mostly bilateral 'good neighbour' pacts
CAP	The Common Agricultural Policy
CEEC	Central and East European Countries
CFSP	Common Foreign and Security Policy, 2nd Pillar of EU
CLP	Turkish Cypriot Communal Liberation Party - Mustafa Akıncı
COREPER	Committee of Permanent Representatives of member states in Brussels
COREU	Confidential network for telegrams between EU foreign offices
CTP	Turkish Cypriot Republican Turkish Party - Mehmet Ali Talat
Dead zone	UN buffer zone, also called the Green Line
DEKO	Greek Cypriot Democratic Party - Spyros Kyprianou, President
DESY	Greek Cypriot Democratic Rally - party of Glafcos Clerides
DG	Directorate-General -Commission unit akin to a Ministry
DPT or SPO	Turkish State Planning Organisation, Ankara
EC	European Community
EcommHR	European Commission of Human Rights, Strasbourg
ECHR	European Court of Human Rights, Strasbourg

ECU	European Currency Unit, 1979 seq.
EDEK	Greek Cypriot Socialist Party - Vassos Lyssarides, President
E.DE	Greek Cypriot United Democrats - George Vassiliou, President
EEC	European Economic Community or Communities,(also including Atomic and Coal and Steel Communities) 1st pillar of EU
EFTA	European Free Trade Association
EIB	European Investment Bank
EOKA (-B)	National Organisation of Cypriot fighters (-B is post-independence)
EP	European Parliament
EPC	European inter-governmental Political Co-operation in foreign policy
ESDI	European Security and Defence Identity
EU	European Union
EUA	European units of account - equivalent to dollars
EURATOM	European Atomic Energy Authority
EURO	European Currency
EUROSTAT	Office for collating European statistics
G7	Group of the 7 richest industrial nations, plus EU and Russia.
GATT	General Agreement on Tariffs and Trade
GCA	Greek Cypriot Administration
GISELA	*Groupe InterService Elargissement*
IGC	Inter-Governmental Conference, for revisions of the Rome Treaty
JHA	Co-operation in Justice and Home Affairs, 3rd Pillar of EU
KEA	Greek Cypriot Euro-Democratic Renewal Party - Alexis Galanos
KISOS	Greek Cypriot Social Democratic Movement
Maghreb	Algeria, Morocco, Tunisia
LOME	African, Caribbean and Pacific Associates of the EEC

NATO	North Atlantic Treaty Organisation
NE.O	Greek Cypriot New Horizons-- founded by Archbishop Chrysostomos
OJ	*Official Journal,* (L for Legislation; C for Notices)
OPEC	Organisation of Petroleum Exporting Countries
OSCE	Organisation for Security and Co-operation in Europe
PHARE	Poland and Hungary: Aid for Reconstructing Economies (extended to include other CEECs and expanded in scope)
ROC	Republic of Cyprus
Schengen	Most EU and all Nordic countries in frontier-free co-operation
Single Market	Commission programme to complete EC internal market
TAIEX	Technical Assistance initially for Single Market harmonisation
TKP	Turkish Cypriot Communal Liberation Party - Mustafa Akıncı
TMT	Turkish Resistance Organisation
TRNC	Turkish Republic of Northern Cyprus
UBP	Turkish Cypriot National Unity Party - Derviş Eroğlu
UNFICYP	United Nations Peacekeeping Force in Cyprus
UNGA	United Nations General Assembly
UNHCR	United Nations High Commissioner for Refugees
UNSC	United Nations Security Council
VAT	Value Added Tax
WEU	Western European Union
Working Group Officials	Mostly from member states for *ad hoc* discussions
YHB	Turkish Cypriot Patriotic Unity Movement - Özker Özgür

Index